4 DAYS, 40 HOURS

Reporting a Revolution
in Work and Leisure

The original edition of *4 Days, 40 Hours* was remarkable not only for the urgency with which it was researched, written and rushed into print, but for the wide-ranging influence it has had ever since. In calling it "the definitive book on the matter", the *Wall Street Journal* was being conservative. For most businessmen and business journals in the U.S., the book has become the "bible" of the rearranged working week. Much of this success is due to the energy and enthusiasm of Riva Poor, editor and co-author of the book. Called a "high priestess of the movement" by *Newsweek*, she remains the most vitally concerned authority on the 4-day week, having written many articles about it. She also publishes a newsletter on the subject and lectures widely.

For the Pan edition, Mrs. Poor has completely reorganized the original text, beginning with case histories and ending with theoretical material. Although the tone and the specific references in the original chapters are necessarily American, their subject matter is rapidly becoming relevant for other countries throughout the world.

This point is examined in the second section of the book, containing three new articles. In two specially commissioned chapters (14 and 15), Mr. Theo Richmond discusses recent experiments with 4-day in Britain and Australia. In the long final chapter (16), Riva Poor presents her two-year follow-up report, answering all the questions she has repeatedly been asked about this important business innovation.

CONDITIONS OF SALE

4 Days, 40 Hours

Reporting a Revolution in Work and Leisure

Edited by Riva Poor

Foreword by Paul A. Samuelson

Specially revised for the British edition
with a follow-up report by Riva Poor
and new material prepared by Theo Richmond

PAN BOOKS LTD : LONDON

First published in the United States of America
1970 by Bursk and Poor Publishing, Inc.

First British edition published 1972 by
Pan Books Ltd.,
33 Tothill Street, London, S.W.1.

ISBN 0 330 23389 0

Printed in Great Britain by
Cox & Wyman Ltd.,
London, Reading and Fakenham

ACKNOWLEDGEMENTS

I am grateful to the many contributors to this book. As with most books, so many people contributed that there are just too many to thank each one, one by one. Still, special recognition does belong to my partner Edward C. Bursk, Editor of *The Harvard Business Review*, for faith and enthusiasm, to my co-authors for researching and writing their articles in record time, and to the pioneering 4-day managers and employees for extensive cooperation and insight.

I would also like to express special thanks to my parents Irving and Thelma Magaril, who reared me to be a businessman, and to my dear husband Ward, partly just for being himself and partly for being a true helpmeet.

Riva Poor
Cambridge, Massachusetts
October, 1970

TABLE OF CONTENTS

Part II

FOREWORD
by Paul A. Samuelson

Paul A. Samuelson, Institute Professor, Massachusetts Institute of Technology, was an adviser to President Kennedy, and was awarded the Nobel Prize in economics, in 1970. A past president of the leading economics societies, he is the author of the bestselling textbook Economics *(8 editions, and a couple of dozen foreign languages). Aside from being a research economist, he also writes a column for* Newsweek.

Progress comes from technical invention, and we shall be ever grateful to the discoverer of fire, the inventor of the electric dynamo, and the perfector of hollandaise sauce. But there are also momentous *social inventions*. Indeed, as society becomes more affluent, these may become increasingly vital. Without language we should still live in the cave, and all honour to that unknown genius who discovered that disputes of precedence could be settled by the toss of a coin.

The 4-day week is precisely such a social invention. Just as double entry bookkeeping may have done as much for the standard of modern life as the development of smelting, so will new ideas that enable mankind to find the good life be needed in our present age of anxiety. As an economist, I find most interesting about the 4-day week pattern the fact that it offers new variety of choice in an area where modern man has had the fewest personal options. If other people work nine to five, then you must conform at the peril of being denied your daily bread.

Yet the dollars we earn, we may spend on literally thousands of different items of our own choosing: he who looks into the modern department store and complains of not finding his heart's desire should be condemned to live in an earlier century where you ate what grew outside your door, and were condemned to do so all the days of your life. In contrast with this freedom in the spending of the money we earn, the modern industrial régime denies us a similar freedom in choosing the work routine by which we earn those dollars, denying us even that variety of choice which prevailed in a pastoral and hunting environment.

Of course this opportunity to do one's own thing is not the only important aspect of the 4-day week. To the historian of long trends in economic development, it is merely one facet in the steady sweep towards greater leisure and less lifetime toil in a society growing more affluent. With it must be lumped the already shorter 5-day week, the longer period of retirement, the prolongation of years of formal education, and the trend towards more holidays and longer vacations both summer and winter.

To the militant trade unionist, the move towards a 4-day week, whether a 40-hour week or 32-hour week, is one more skirmish in the continuing battle for higher standard wage rates, improved work conditions on the job, and improved fringe benefits for retirement and health needs. Particularly in declining industries, such as railroads, coal, and steel, unions have long been concerned to share out and maximize the dwindling supply of employment opportunities – through reduced workweeks and other devices, of which some variant of the 4-day week is one possibility.

To some canny employers, the 4-day week is a gimmick for getting the jump on the opposition: it is a way of being different, of doing what others are not doing, in the hope of attracting workers away from other employers in tight labour markets.

There is no need for me to stress these many economic aspects of the 4-day week. The experts who have contributed to this book have dealt informatively with these and other matters. So let me emphasize the overall economic significance of introducing greater flexibility of choice in that important part of our life during which we earn our living and do our jobs. First, there is no need to reduce the work-week merely in order to avoid mass unemployment. The time when there was only a certain amount of work to do is past. Modern knowledge of fiscal and monetary policy can end for all time the ancient scourge of depression and chronic unemployment. Second, there are a great variety of patterns whereby people can choose to take out the fruits of economic progress in enhanced leisure and reduced work.

People do differ. The mother who wishes to work outside the home has different needs and rhythms than the childless bachelor or semi-retired executive. All tend to benefit when each is permitted to do his thing. If some workers, perhaps newly married and in the part of the life cycle when needs for cash to buy durable goods are at a maximum, wish to use the new-found leisure for moonlighting in second jobs, Godspeed them. So long as you are not taking the bread out of my mouth – and with proper macro-economic, fiscal and monetary policies we can now make sure that this is the case – why should I care?

It is fashionable today to decry the Gross National Product, as a materialistic indicator of frantic living and a source of pollution to the environment. Heaven knows it is high time that the quality of life should begin to receive its just due. Yet we must render up to material progress the recognition that it does offer us the possibility of the good life. In days of old, when men really did work from dawn to dark, fathers never had a chance to know their children. Perhaps the future will reveal that one of the most profound effects of shorter workweeks will be a change in the structure of the family itself, as the division of labour between husband and wife in the home is changed to redress the ancient curse of female drudgery.

But at this point the economist must step aside and defer to the historical sage and social prophet.

INTRODUCTION
TO THE ORIGINAL EDITION

We see the 4-day, 40-hour workweek as spreading in our society – and spreading rapidly. The key purpose of our study is to provide useful information about this innovation while the information is *still* useful.

Most authoritative studies take years to develop; and while they are of interest to the public when they are finally published, they lose usefulness for the decisions that have to be made during the years when the public is awaiting the information. We, however, have tried to chart this new development in society *now* while it is first happening; and we take particular satisfaction in knowing that we are the first to recognize that the 4-day movement is sufficiently important to document, and the first to analyse it for the public.

Because the 4-day, 40-hour workweek is new and there-fore largely an unknown, 4-day will raise many questions in people's minds: What is it for? How does it work? Is it beneficial? What are the drawbacks? How should *I* handle a 4-day conversion? Where will it lead us? and so on.

We set out to provide working answers to these and other questions raised by the 4-day week, and to provide these answers in a way that would be useful to our readers. We are providing answers quickly for people who need the information right now; providing them from different points of view, so the picture will be well-rounded; and providing the data along with the analyses, so readers can form their own conclusions for their own purposes. The methods we have stressed in order to provide the reader with quick, thorough, and objective information have necessitated a certain amount of repetition among the articles in order to permit each author to develop his theme from his own point of view. We hope the reader finds the repetitions useful, rather than annoying.

This book started with my reaction of fascination upon coming across just one 4-day firm in May, 1970. Since then, we have located three dozen 4-day firms and over 7,000 4-day employees – and a few 3-day firms as well. We feel certain that there are both many more 4-day firms than we were able to discover in the four months spent on this study and also that more and more firms are converting to 4-day every day.

Where is 4-day leading us? As with all other moves in the workweek, it is undoubtedly a benchmark along the route to fewer and fewer working hours – to a 4-day, 32-hour week, to a 3-day week, and so on. But the key question is always: *when?* For the last generation, 4-32 has been raised as a possible goal for labour, and it will become widespread eventually, we feel sure; but, meanwhile, 4-40 provides the leisure that workers crave, *without* harming firms – in fact with positive benefits to them, as this book will describe.

Riva Poor
Bursk and Poor Publishing, Inc.
Cambridge, Massachusetts
October, 1970

INTRODUCTION
TO THE PAN EDITION

One of the special tortures of being an author is the fear that after a time you may look back on what you have written and heartily regret, oh, perhaps every other word.

It was very gratifying in preparing this book for the Pan edition to find that I did not need to change a word of it, although we wrote the original version almost 2 years ago. My continuing research of 4-day companies confirms the findings we initially reported. Also, independent researchers, responding to the large reaction created by our book, have corroborated our original findings by obtaining very similar results in their own research.

It is also very nice to have your predictions vindicated by time. The growth of 4-day has indeed been rapid, as I predicted. It has swept across the U.S.A. and into other countries as well. An Australian professor reported to me a year ago that there were then about 100 4-day firms in Australia. Several German firms are using 4-day today. And there have been some British firms on it for quite a few years.

Reviewers, managers, workers, and others have hailed this book as "the bible" of the rearranged workweek. The *National Observer* said that businessmen rely on this book as new mothers rely on Dr. Spock. And the business editor of the *Washington Post* Hobart Rowen said the book "fired America's imagination". *Library Journal* selected the book as "one of the best business books of 1970", and the American College Library Association publication, *Choice*, just recently put the book on its list of "outstanding academic books for 1972".

Over 4,000 articles have been written about 4-day in the past 2 years – about half of them based on our book. Many of these articles have gone out around the world, helping to spread the news of this innovation. Translations of *4 Days, 40 Hours* have already been published in Japan and in the Netherlands, and now, with this edition, the book will be available in over 50 countries.

All this is extremely gratifying. It is a wonderful feeling, knowing that you have contributed, and I am grateful to have had the opportunity – all the authors are.

For the Pan edition, we have added a second section to the book containing 3 new articles. Mr. Theo Richmond adds Chapter 14, discussing recent British experience with 4-day; and Chapter 15, commenting on similar experiments in Australia. I have added Chapter 16, which is my own 2-year follow-up report, answering all the major questions that people have repeatedly asked me about the subject.

I hope we have made it clear to readers that the basic concept of 4-day is applicable anywhere, because *4-day is the concept of optimizing work scheduling* – of making the work-week work *for* the firm instead of against it. Firms are breaking out of the traditional mould of scheduling work. They are individualizing their scheduling, in order to meet the needs of their individual work tasks and at the same time the needs of their individual set of workers.

Just one final note: I would like to explain to the reader why this book puts so much emphasis on management considerations, while so de-emphasizing employees' concerns. This is hardly due to lack of interest in workers; this emphasis is necessary because the employee's decision is so much *simpler* than the manager's decision. It is one thing for a worker to decide he wants a 3-day or 4-day weekend. It is quite another thing for business to provide it. The employee has only to decide if he *likes* the idea of trading longer work-days for longer weekends, while the manager must wrestle with a host of decisions in order to determine the feasibility of a scheduling change. Since management's decision is more complex and since management must make the ultimate go or no-go decision, it is quiet appropriate to give more attention in a guide book such as this to management's concerns.

Another reason for focusing on management is that 4-day is an innovation that increases productivity, and declining productivity is a problem of crisis proportions in the U.S.A., in Britain, and elsewhere at this time.

Since rising productivity has been key to the emergence of our civilization with its many benefits (disputed and otherwise), it is critical that we locate, explore, and utilize innovations like 4-day that can bolster the productivity necessary for improving the quality of life we have so far achieved and that we all hope further to improve.

Riva Poor
Cambridge, Massachusetts
June, 1972

Part One

1

REPORTING A REVOLUTION IN WORK AND LEISURE: 27 4-DAY FIRMS
by Riva Poor

Riva Poor, co-founder of Bursk and Poor Publishing with Edward C. Bursk, Editor of The Harvard Business Review, *is a management consultant who started one of the first and most successful minority business programmes in the country. She has owned and operated several small businesses, has edited several business reports and newsletters, and has two Masters degrees from Massachusetts Institute of Technology (one from the Sloan School of Management and the other from the Department of City and Regional Planning).*

[This chapter contains the original research on the 4-day workweek innovation. The interview results were copied and made available to the other contributors to this book for their use in preparing their chapters.*]

WHAT 4-DAY IS

This book is an objective report about an innovation in work scheduling that affects firm's profits and employees' lives.

The 4-day, 40-hour workweek is a fairly simple reallocation of work hours from 5 days to 4 days begun at over 3 dozen American firms. The original number of work hours is maintained for the most

*Although this study encompasses only the 27 4-day pioneers that could be located during the period of June–August, 1970, its validity has been demonstrated in subsequent research studies by Mrs. Poor, using hundreds of additional 4-day companies. It is also backed up by the work of numerous independent researchers who initiated 4-day studies in response to the enormous public interest generated by the initial publication of this book.

part; but because they are grouped differently, there is a change in the impact of the hours on the performance of the firm and on the usability of the employees' leisure.

Four-day provides advantages for both the firm and its employees. By lengthening the workday, the employee gets a 3-day weekend with no pay loss. The firm gets a wide number of benefits including improvements in output, customer relations, flexibility for overtime, recruitment, absenteeism, turnover, tardiness – and employee relations!

Note that 4 days, 40 hours is not the 4 days, 32 hours that unions are beginning to talk about again, although it is possible that 4-40 could lead to 4-32, and will probably do so *in the long run*.

Variety of Arrangements: Although the book is about 4 days, 40 hours – a rescheduling of total work hours on a 4-day basis – not all 4-day employees work 10 hours a day during the 4 days. Some firms receive such large production boosts from converting to 4-day that they can afford to reduce their total workweek to 36 hours, and still come out ahead. Others do not have a 40-hour week to begin with, so dividing their total workweek by 4 leaves 9 or 9½ hours per day. In several cases, it could be said that the workweek is actually reduced somewhat – but usually not by much, because, generally, such things as forgone coffee breaks and fewer start-up times compensate for the reduction. The fewest total work hours among the firms is 35 hours – at a new division of a company that opened its doors with the 4-day week as part of its plan. Take-home pay is not cut, but in a few cases there is a pay raise incident to normal labour negotiations.

Several of the 4-day firms are open for business only 4 days a week; two have a 4½-day week; and others are open as many as 7. There are many variations, too, on which days the firms are open, on their numbers of shifts, their purposes for being on 4-day, and their results. Sometimes, certain types of employees are not included in 4-day – particularly, in sales and shipping-and-receiving departments.

New Precedents Set: Aside from scheduling workers on a 4-day basis in industries where it had not been tried before, a third of the 4-day firms set the new precedent of being open for business just 4 days a week. Kyanize Paints, Inc., does this in 2 of its 3 branches – in Everett, Massachusetts, and in Springfield, Illinois – and plans to institute 4-day eventually at its newly acquired Houston plant.

The 4day Tire Stores chain of 8 stores in California is on 4-day at all of the stores. Each is open only Thursday through Sunday, when tyre sales are the best.

For Auto City, only the night shift is on 4-day; and it is Monday through Thursday. The manager reports it is difficult to set up a night shift on a 5-day basis, because the men don't like to work Fridays. But he was able to recruit 18 skilled engine rebuilders in 2 weeks by advertising the 4-day, or rather 4-night, shift.

Some firms intend to be open a 4-day week, but wind up doing so much overtime on the fifth day that it is hard to say they are really open just four days a week. Maybe later on they will be.

Number of 4-Day Firms: This book reports the experiences of all the 4-day firms we could locate in the United States between June and September, 1970,* including 5 firms that tried it and abandoned it. We located the firms through Kenneth Wheeler (see Chapter 12), through other 4-day firms, through newspaper and magazine mentions, through trade associations, and so on. We report both the pros and cons, so readers can apply their own judgements to meet their individual needs.

There are undoubtedly many more 4-day firms than we located. (Lately, we hear of a new 4-day firm every day or so.)

This chapter reports on the first 27 firms that I located, during the period of June–August, 1970. I interviewed the management of each of these firms personally, mostly by telephone. Seven of the other authors also interviewed many of the firms; and hundreds of employees gave their opinions in several dozen personal interviews and in scores of written questionnaires.

The facts, therefore, have been analysed by several professionals; and the book presents their several viewpoints.

WHAT'S SIGNIFICANT ABOUT 4-DAY?

Whatever our current workweek is today, or on any day, it was not handed down to us on Mount Sinai by the Lord Himself. If we find ourselves thinking of the 5-day workweek – or any other kind of workweek – as an immutable fact of life, it can only be because we are simply accustomed to it that way. For about half of the United States population, those people under 35 years old, the workweek is

*Except one large firm that we heard of through a third party, which did not want to be cited.

in a sense an immutable thing, because they have always known it
one way, 5 days long, all their lives. (In many countries, the workweek is still 6 days long; and in these countries 6-day probably seems
an immutable fact of life.) Anyway, I know that I, just short of my
34th birthday, found it amazing to come across a page one article in
the May 8, 1970, *Boston Globe*, headed: "A Happy Revolution: The
4-Day Week," by Ken O. Botwright. It seemed so simple an idea,
so obviously appropriate to so many problems; yet simple and obvious as it is, so revolutionary to me. (That was the day this book
began.)

The other half of the U.S. can remember when the 5-day week was
not standard, when there was a 5½-day week, and even a 6-day week.
This wasn't so long ago, either. The first known 5-day week appeared
in the United States as recently as 1908, and was unique for several
years. A decade later, in 1918, there were only a handful of 5-day
firms. And in 1929 only 5% of the American labour force was on
5-day.

What was there before these days? Simply this: for centuries the
workweek proceeded from sunrise to sunset 6 days a week. And I
wouldn't be surprised if some of the religious intensity of pre-
twentieth century came from the relief from work provided by a
Sabbath Sunday. The cavemen probably hunted 7 days a week.

The point is, the workweek really was immutable for centuries, and
probably eons. It is only recently (since the Industrial Revolution)
that the workweek has begun to change. The change appears to be an
ever more rapidly accelerating one, in part because the technology
that makes the changes possible is ever more rapidly improving.

The 4-day workweek is *very* new – whether we're talking about
4 days, 32 hours or 4 days, 40 hours. But new things, if they work
well, have a way of catching on very rapidly in today's world. So they
are worth looking at when they arrive.

The 4-day, 40-hour workweek has recently arrived. I'm not about
to tell you: everyone is going to 4-40 this year, so watch out. And
I'm not trying to *sell* you the idea of converting to 4-40. But I am
saying this: 4-40 is new; it works fairly well; and the country has a
recent history of moving ever more rapidly to shorter and shorter
workweeks. The 4-40, 4-32, and even the 3-day workweek will probably be here eventually. So let's look at 4-40 now, to see what we can
learn from it. And let's see if there is anything we can use from it
today, for today's problems and goals.

DÉJÀ VU

We worked very quickly (but thoroughly) in preparing this book, because we wanted to bring the information to you while it is still timely and useful. Had we worked at the usual pace for research and publication, it seemed conceivable that the whole country could convert to 4-day – or even to 3-day (see Chapter 13) – before you could read it.

Still, a funny thing happened on the way to the printers, so to speak. With all the rush and the remarkable cooperation of the 4-day firms and authors, just 5 days before type-setting, Professor Linda Sprague (see Chapters 8 and 10) brought over a book that says word for word many of the things we had written for you!

Were we scooped? Well, sort of. It was a National Industrial Conference Board book, *The Five-Day Week in Manufacturing Industries*, published in 1929.* Reading it was a *déjà vu* experience. Apparently, the same controversy raged then about 5-day as will very probably rage about 4-day. People worried about: Would it work? Is it representative? Who's doing it? How do they work? Is it too fatiguing? What happens to production? And wages? And morale?

In 1929, the NICB reported that the number of employees on 5-day was "insignificant," "only" about 5% of the work force at the time (500,000 on 5-day). This is far more than the number we know of on 4-day at present. Other contrasts are that there were few continuous process firms going to 5-day, and many of the conversions had been forced by unions. In contrast to early 4-day history, large numbers of the workers were in printing, the garment industry, and the building trades. Also, in 80% of the cases the hours of labour were reduced, because so many firms had been working 54-hours-a-week schedules. Thus, numerous employees suffered income loss.

These factors are the few dissimilarities between the 27 firms we report on here and those in the NICB study. Ours include several continuous process firms; all initiated 4-day through management, not through labour; and none are in printing or the building trades (although one is in garment making). Ours involve metals, textile manufacture, service, retail trade, etc.

Otherwise, the *déjà vu* experience is almost complete. Both then and now the firms were predominantly in manufacturing, and with the exception of Ford Motor Company then, the firms were small. NICB reports an average of 155 workers. Our average is 185, ex-

*This is the source of the 5-day statistics reported in this chapter.

cluding Reader's Digest (3,500). (Percentage of female workers is dissimilar, though: 25% for 5-day, and 60% for 4-day.) In both cases many began the new schedule as a summer or temporary experiment. Some firms started and then abandoned 5-day when 5-day was new, just as some firms have started and abandoned 4-day.

Results were also remarkably similar: 70% of the 5-day firms had no loss of production, despite being on reduced hours. But most of the 4-day, 40-hour firms have *increased* productivity considerably!

4-DAY HISTORY IN THE OIL INDUSTRY

The 4-day week for employees is not so new as it may seem at first glance. Although I, for one, didn't know about this until I started to study 4-day, drivers of fuel oil and gasoline delivery trucks at most of the major oil companies have been on 4-day scheduling for the past 30 years. So, the idea is only new and revolutionary for other industries that are only now beginning to utilize 4-day, or to contemplate it.

At the oil companies, many other variations in scheduling drivers were tried before settling on 4-day. Five 8-hour days left Saturdays hanging. Three $13\frac{1}{2}$-hour days made the men too tired to handle the trucks safely. Alternating the 3 days of work was not efficient for the drivers either. Four-day was settled on as providing the best utilization of equipment on a round-the-clock basis, without undue hazard to the drivers.

Between the 10-hour shifts are 2-hour periods to service the trucks; so the men are not held up by repairs when their shifts arrive. If a seventh day is needed, as it sometimes is in winter, the men go on overtime. A Gulf Oil Corporation dispatcher said: "The men think it's terrific – they love the 4-day week. It gives them 3 days off. And it's great for vacations, because they can take a whole week, when they want to, by switching their schedule with another driver."

Still, the 4-day week is not universal for the drivers in this industry. As a representative of Mobil Oil Corporation said, 4-day "has met with employee resistance in some geographical locations. Whether drivers work on this schedule, or on the more normal 5-day week, is governed strictly by local conditions." Gulf adds that it is a matter of different traditions in different parts of the country. For example, as to Sunday work, "You won't find the drivers working Sundays below the Mason-Dixon line, east of the Mississippi. But in the north, you've got the bad northern weather which makes Sunday deliveries important."

The major oil companies are also examples of firms that provide *different* schedules in the *same* firm to meet differing needs of production and/or working conditions. According to Gulf, refineries operate three 8-hour shifts a day, 7 days a week; and the men alternate weekend days. For drilling sites, outside contractors may be hired; and these, in turn, hire workers on varied schedules. Some of the drilling sites are in remote places where the men are away from home, and there is nothing to do but work, eat, and sleep. The workers work 12 hours on and 12 hours off, 7 days a week, for 4 to 6 weeks; and then take 2 to 3 weeks off.

There are other industries too, not only those where the men are away from home and travelling, where the schedules may vary with the work situation. As Professor Sprague points out in her article, we ought to think more often of how to use a break in the mould to suit our needs better. Why be tied to a schedule that is not optimum for your firm – or for a *division* of your firm?

WHAT'S IN THIS BOOK?

What's in this book? The answers to the following questions: Who's doing it? Why? How? With what advantages? What disadvantages? And where might it lead us?

The first half of the book contains thirteen chapters taken from the original U.S. edition. (With the exception of this section, the original chapters have been left virtually intact, with my up-dated comments appearing as footnotes.)

In a later section in this opening chapter you'll find the summary statistics on the 27 firms; and in the following chapter, there are profiles of 26 of these firms, plus 13 others – in order to give you details on what's going on where.

In the third chapter, L. Eric Kanter gives us a profile of employee reactions at several firms in his "Thank God It's Thursday!" The reactions are, by and large, very positive; but some typical negatives are given. One secretary says: "I am not really involved in the 4-day workweek and I hope it remains that way . . . Isn't the 10-hour day a step backwards?" Another woman, whose office is on 4-day, writes: "I can spend more time with the children and do more sewing, which is my hobby. The disadvantage is getting up on Monday morning, but that has always been a problem with me." Another woman, a factory worker who is very pleased with 4-day, says: "It's less expensive to travel to work 4 days instead of 5; and there is also less money to pay out to babysitters." Many add that commuting is now easier.

Chapter 4 covers a survey that Jim Steele, a Ph.D. Candidate at the University of Montana, and I did of 168 employees at 13 of the 4-day firms, in "Work and Leisure: The Reactions of People at 4-Day Firms." We find 92% of the employees are pleased about 4-day. Of the *new* employees, 34 out of 44 stated that 4-day was an important reason for their joining the firm; and none said it was a disadvantage. We also tell you how they spend their leisure. Moonlighting is way up (a fact a number of firms don't mind; some actively encourage it). Such things as camping, travel, movies, shows, and sports are much bigger. Nine out of 168 have purchased vacation homes. Only 6 people say they are bored. About 33% report increased spending; and several of these say they've finally had to cut back. Anyway, whether more or the same amount of spending, the *patterns* of spending are different now.

Chapters 5, 6 and 7 sketch three very different organizations in detail, with particular attention to the factors considered most important in making the decision to convert to 4-day. In Chapter 5, "An Industrial Pioneer Rescued by the 4-day Week," Mr. Kanter describes one of the oldest continuing firms in New England, Lawrence Manufacturing, a textile mill that had to do something vigorous about recruitment, or face moving out or closing down.

Chapter 6, "The 4-Day Week at a 7-Day Hospital", by Ray Richard, shows a service organization trying to cut labour costs without cutting service – or pay. Then John L. Schohl explains why he chose the unusual schedule "4 Days On, 4 Days Off" in a situation where he had to be very mindful of expenditures for capital equipment.

In Chapter 8, "Fewer Days or Fewer Hours," Professor Linda Sprague points out where the shorter workweek fits into the continuous history of labour-management battles over fewer hours and more pay. Until now, she says, management has always fought a rearguard action.

D. Quinn Mills, Professor of Labour Relations at the Sloan School of Management, Massachusetts Institute of Technology, predicts 4 days, 40 hours, will not catch on. In the ninth chapter, "Does Organized Labour Want the 4-Day Week?" Professor Mills points out that although the employees at the current 4-day firms are enthusiastic about 4-day, organized labour takes a dim view of the 9-hour or 10-hour day. Unions are pushing for 4-32, and are likely to resist 4-40 with vigour; but, he says, the reactions of the unions at the 4-day firms are positive.

"Breaking the 5-Day Mould" is Chapter 10. Here Professor Sprague spells out a number of methods to use in analysing your scheduling loads, to determine whether 4-day, or some *other* schedule, would work out better for you. Break the mould, by all means, she advises, if you've got the kind of customer demand that requires it. What have you got to lose?

In "Interface with the Outside World," Chapter 11, Grant Doherty, Sales Promotion Manager for Kyanize Paints, tells what some of the pitfalls can be when you change your schedule; and tells how to deal with them so you can "cry all the way to the bank".

Ken Wheeler, a management consultant who specializes in 4-day conversions, tells us: "How to handle a 4-day Conversion" in the twelfth chapter. The key phrase, he and his associate Dr. Philip Bogdonoff say, is *prior planning.**

One of the differences between the NICB's book on 5-day and ours on 4-day, is that theirs was written 11 years after there were a handful of 5-day firms, and ours is only a year after the first handful of 4-day firms. Presumably, the first book on 3-day will come one month after the first 3-day firms! But, no; the first 3-day book, *More Timewealth For You*, has been written *before the fact* by economist Dr. Millard C. Faught. In Chapter 13, "The 3-Day Revolution to Come", Dr. Faught explains why he is convinced that 3-day will be here, and be here soon. He sees 4-day as an early sign, but no more than that.

*The 4-day schedules have raised legal problems for some American firms, particularly where women employees' hours of labour exceed state regulations requiring fewer hours for women than for men. In the original U.S. edition of this book, the Assistant Attorney General of Oklahoma, Tim Leonard, gives a clearly thought-out ruling which has the effect of law in Oklahoma. We omit the chapter in the British edition, because it is primarily a discussion of American law; but we will mention his points here, because his ruling has been important in the spread of the 4-day week in the U.S.A., and therefore has historical significance that may interest the British reader.

His argument goes like this: (1) if women are being denied the opportunity to have a 3-day weekend, because the state law doesn't permit them to work the same number of hours as men, then women are being discriminated against; (2) discrimination against women is against the U.S. Constitution; (3) United States law has precedent over state law; (4) therefore, the state law regulating women's hours is null and void; (5) therefore, women can work as long a day in Oklahoma as men can. He cites rulings in other states too.

11

The second half of the book consists of new material researched and written during the spring and summer of 1972.

Chapters 14 and 15 were specially commissioned for the Pan edition from Theo Richmond, an independent journalist who had already made some preliminary investigations into the 4-day week. In Chapter 14, "Britain and the 4-day Week", Mr. Richmond examines the reception which 4-40 has met in Great Britain. This analysis is followed by profiles (some of them very detailed) of several British 4-day pioneers. Chapter 15 provides profiles of a number of firms making similar experiments in Australia.

In the long final chapter, "Two Years Later: A Follow-up Report", I answer the questions which I have been asked most frequently about the 4-day week.

WHAT IS THIS BOOK USEFUL FOR?

It should be useful for:
 • **company decision makers**
 If you've decided to convert, where do you go to learn from someone else, before you plunge ahead?
 If you're just musing about it, where do you go to find out whether to consider it seriously?
 If you have some unsolved problems, and you are *not* thinking of 4-day, is there something here that may turn the trick for you?
 • **union men**
 What's behind this move?
 How do the workers feel about it?
 • **business analysts, management consultants, staff advisers, production schedules, personnel men**
 If this is what's happening, do you want to know about it?
 • **business suppliers, services, recreation industries, land developers, urban planners, government men**
 You, too, right?
 • **students of history and observers of today's world**
 Interesting, isn't it?

WHAT KIND OF FIRMS ARE ON 4-DAY?

I had expected to find great similarity among the 4-day firms. Instead, the diversity of 4-day firms is amazing. Types of business, for example, include manufacture, service, retail, and wholesale. And the sizes of the firms, the production processes (of manufacturers), the seasonality of demand, the length of time in business, the locations, and the characteristics of the labour forces are strikingly dissimilar.

The major threads tying the firms together are their purposes for trying 4-day: concern for employees' welfare and incentive, which will be discussed below. There may be a slight tendency for some of the 4-day firms either to be more labour-intensive or more capital-intensive than other firms (in other words, somewhere away from the norm for firms); and also to have a larger proportion of female employees than other firms. The accompanying List of 4-Day Firms (on page 14) shows the basic statistics for each of the 27 firms studied.

Types of Firms: Two thirds are manufacturers. Their fields are: abrasives products, electronic balancing devices, foods (both frozen and delicatessen), loudspeakers, metal castings, missile heads, paint rollers, paints and coatings (2 firms), paper boxes, petroleum products (2), pneumatic accessories, sheet metal fabrication (3), textiles, and underwear. (The oil companies are on 4-day for deliveries only.)

The 4 retail firms include clothing, fast foods, and 2 tyre store chains that also have commercial and wholesale components. One of the retail firms is on a 4½-day week, at its offices only. The one strictly wholesale firm is a used-car auctioneer. The 4 service firms include: architecture, automatic data processing, a hospital, and a major publisher that is on a 4-day week in May only.

Seasonality: Ten have seasonal fluctuations in demand; eleven do not.

Batch Process or Continuous Flow: Three manufacturers labelled their processes as continuous; 4 said they were somewhere between continuous and batch process; and 9 were batch process or job shops.

Single Firms or Multi-branches: Twelve of the 27 are single firms; that is, one firm, one location. Fifteen are multi-branched; ranging from two divisions in different states, to over a thousand divisions or franchises across the nation (1 firm) or around the world (2). Eight firms have 2–7 branches; 3 firms, 8–10; and 1 has 1 local office, but divisions and other arrangements around the world.

LIST OF 4-DAY FIRMS

Note: Chapter 2 contains profiles of 26 of these 27 firms plus 13 other firms located too late for entry here.

Name	Location	Number of Employees	Type	Notes
American Lacquer and Solvents Co. of Florida	Tampa Florida	54	mfg. paints, lacquers, etc.	
Auto City, Inc.	East Boston Massachusetts	130	wholesale auto auction	night shift only
Bridgeford Foods and Packing Co.	Anaheim California	240*	mfg. frozen foods and delicatessen	discontinued 4-day
Geo. H. Bullard Co., Inc.	Westboro Massachusetts	120	mfg. abrasives	
Carbonneau Industries	Grand Rapids Michigan	250*	mfg. loudspeakers	discontinued 4-day
Crocker Co., Inc.	Burlington Massachusetts	44	sheet metal fabricators	
Dalton Precision Division	Cushing Oklahoma	97**	precision metal casting	multiple locations
4day Tire Stores	Newport Beach California	34	retail and wholesale, tires	multiple locations
Jules Gillette	North Miami Florida	10*	retail, mens' clothing	multiple locations; discontinued 4-day
Gulf Oil Corporation (one of many terminals)	Chelsea Massachusetts	132**	mfg. and sale of petroleum products	multiple locations; drivers only
Haines, Lundberg and Wachler, Architects	New York City New York	400*	service, architects-engineers	multiple locations; discontinued 4-day
R.C. Hollow Metal Co.	Denver Colorado	29	metal fabrication	4½ days, summer only
Interstate, Inc.	Braintree Massachusetts	50	mfg. paint rollers	
Kyanize Paints, Inc.	Everett Massachusetts	115**	mfg. paints, polish, coatings	multiple locations
Lawrence Manufacturing Co.	Lowell Massachusetts	215**	mfg. knit fabrics	multiple locations
McDonald's Corporation	Chicago Illinois	741**	retail, fast food industry	multiple locations; 4½ days, summer only; offices only
Merrill Engineering Laboratories	Denver Colorado	25-30**	mfg. balancing and aligning equipment	multiple locations
Milton Machine Co.	East Weymouth Massachusetts	5	mfg. electronic components	
Mobil Oil Corporation (one of many terminals)	Dearborn Michigan	100**	mfg. and sale of petroleum products	multiple locations; drivers only
Mother's Tire Company	Atlanta Georgia	18*	retail and wholesale tires	multiple locations; discontinued 4-day
New England Metal Spinning Co., Inc.	Malden Massachusetts	26	metal fabrication	
C.A. Norgren Co.	Littleton Colorado	500**	mfg. pneumatic accessories	multiple locations
Reader's Digest	Pleasantville New York	3,500	service, publisher	multiple locations; May only
Rex Paper Box Co., Inc.	Braintree Massachusetts	65	mfg. folding paper boxes	
Roger Williams General Hospital	Providence Rhode Island	1,200	service, hospital	nursing services only
Nathan Solomon and Co., Inc.	Lowell Massachusetts	140	mfg. ladies' sleepwear	
Name withheld by request	Massachusetts	100**	service, data processing	multiple locations

*When they were on 4-day.
**Does not include those at branches.

Geographic Location: The firms are located throughout the country, and in some cases, throughout the world, but home offices and single firms are more heavily concentrated on the east coast. The Boston area has 11 of the 27 home offices. Three home offices are in New York, and 1 each in Rhode Island and Pennsylvania. Three firms are in the south; 2 in Florida, and 1 in Georgia. A total of 19 on the east coast. Two firms are in California; 3 in Denver; and 1 each in Chicago, Oklahoma, and Michigan. Branches are just about all over the country.

The concentration of firms in some areas (Massachusetts, Colorado, Florida, and California) appears to be more a function of how innovation spreads than of how geography affects business. The word is spread by local news media and by trade associations. Also, some of the principals are acquainted with each other; for example, several of the principals at Jules Gillette, 4day Tire, and Mother's Tire have worked together in the past.

Years in Business: Two of the firms started business in the 19th century; one in 1826, and one in 1899. The newest firm is about $1\frac{1}{2}$ years old, and opened its business on 4-day – 4day Tire Stores, with 8 branches. Only a few other firms have been in business for less than 5 years.

Size of the Firms: Judging by their numbers of employees, there is a large distribution of sizes. About one third of the firms have 215 or more employees (the largest is 3,500); about one third have 100-140 employees; and only a little over a third have fewer than 65 employees.

MORE THAN HALF OF 4-DAY FIRMS HAVE 100 OR MORE EMPLOYEES.

Number of Employees	Number of Firms
5-18	3
26-65	8
100-140	8
215-250	3
400-700	3
1,200-3,500	2
Total=27	

The figures actually *under*represent the number of employees at 4-day firms, (1) because at the oil companies we could count only the 2 terminals we interviewed, excluding those we did not interview (since it was difficult to get correct information); and (2) because for most of the firms we did not count employees at branch offices and franchises. McDonald's, for instance, has 1,400 restaurants which are not included. In a sense, the added information is not strictly necessary: we have established the minimum figures, which are more interesting than the outsizes.

While 4-day is not (so far) a very-big-business phenomenon, it is not a tiny-business phenomenon, either. The median number of employees is 115, which is well above the median size of businesses in the United States. (And the mean average is 300; or 185 if we exclude the largest firm.)

Proportion of Males and Females: The proportion of female workers at 4-day firms is about 60:40 which is greater than the proportion of females at firms around the country (40:60). The range in per cent of females is from zero at one firm to 95% at several. (The 25% females on 5-day, when 5-day first began, reflected the average number of women working then.)

Average Age: Average age of 4-day workers is about 35 years. The range of averages at the firms is 25 to 42 years.

Average Seniority: Average seniority is about 5 years. The range of average seniority is from $\frac{1}{2}$ year to 15 years.

Forward-Looking Firms: Several of the firms are pioneers with other new personnel practices. Reader's Digest has had the 35-hour week for many years. C.A. Norgren was one of the first firms to have employee profit-sharing and wage continuation for factory workers at times of sickness or accident.

IMPLEMENTATION

When? The dates on which the firms we know of converted to 4-day range from 1940 through today.

Several of the early 4-day experiments were discontinued (1960–1962). Thus, aside from the oil firms, there is only one other firm with extensive 4-day experience – Merrill Engineering Laboratories, with

MOST FIRMS STARTED 4-DAY IN 1969 OR LATER.

Dates	Number of Firms
1940	2
1960	1
1962	2
1965	1
1969	15
1970, so far	6
Total=27	

$5\frac{1}{2}$ years on 4-day. The others have 6 months to $1\frac{1}{2}$ years' experience.

Many of the firms approached 4-day on an experimental basis. Fourteen said they had trial periods for 4-day ranging from 1 month to 1 year. Only 6 said they simply planned 4-day, and then plunged ahead. Almost all firms consulted with employees, beforehand, in one way or another.

Proportion of labour force on 4-day: The 27 firms and branches interviewed for this report had 6,800 employees on 4-day out of 8,300 (a *minimum* of 1,500 are not on 4-day, since in many cases there are other uncounted workers at uncounted branches – most of which are not on 4-day). The proportions of 4-day workers at the firms range from a high of 100% on 4-day at several firms to a low of 8% at one firm and 28% at another. The mean average on 4-day at these firms is a maximum of 80%.

Who is excluded from 4-day? The salesmen at manufacturing firms are always excluded from 4-day, since the people they sell to are working on 5-day. The next most frequently excluded are the managers. Shipping and receiving are next, and, finally, office workers.

Half of the women at 4-day firms are on 4-day, and half are not, excluding the largest firm. If the largest firm is included, 75% of the women are on 4-day. But there are 9 firms that have none of their women on 4-day. In most cases, the women are excluded because there is a need for production to be on 4-day, and for the office to be open 5 days.

In a few cases, the women are excluded because the firm was unaware that it could obtain a waiver of the restrictions against long hours for women. (In these cases, we were able to assist the firms by informing them that waivers *are* obtainable in most states; that many firms have received them.)

17

Generally, the firms with women on the types of 4-day schedules that violate their state's regulations first *try* the schedule, and then, after trying it, obtain a waiver.

In several of the firms, employees are given a choice of 4-day or 5-day; so that there are 4-day and 5-day workers working side by side on their different schedules. Firms that handle the 4-day adoption process in this fashion (by individual choice) tend to report that more and more workers elect 4-day as time goes by. The 39 profiles in Chapter 2 provide a few examples of firms starting with 50% electing 4-day, and getting 80% after a month, and 100% after a year.

WHY DO THEY DO IT?

In every case that we know of, the 4-day idea was initiated by management, and not by labour. Also, it was a *top* management innovation. Why?

The firms choose 4-day to gain a variety of advantages. The most prevalent purposes involve labour. The 27 firms cited 49 labour reasons and 22 non-labour reasons for 4-day.

The labour reasons, in order of greatest frequency, are: more incentive, better morale, or better living conditions for employees; reduction of labour costs as a percentage of sales; recruitment of *more* labour; recruitment of *better* labour; reduction of absenteeism; and/or reduction of tardiness or turnover.

The non-labour reasons, in order of frequency, are: increased output; decreased production costs; reduction of other non-labour costs (for example, better utilization of capital equipment); improved throughput, better sales promotion; and/or better profits on sales.

Several firms have been innovators in personnel policies in the past, and are simply continuing their precedents. The Reader's Digest, for instance, has been on a 35-hour week for years; and DeWitt Wallace, Co-Chairman, says their 4-day week puts the Digest once again in the forefront of what he is convinced will be a major trend.

The 4-day idea has spread in a variety of ways, as mentioned elsewhere, but one aspect of 4-day is common to all the 4-day decisions: 4-day is seen as providing advantages simultaneously to the firm and to labour. The advantages to the firm are varied; but for labour, it is the 3-day weekend.

HOW DOES THE WORKWEEK CHANGE?

Most firms had been working hours above the average for the U.S.A. So, although the firms in many cases reduced the number of hours in their workweeks, the total hours they now have in the workweeks are by and large *not* far below the national average. The median number of hours in the workweeks at the 4-day firms (excluding overtime) is 36, and the mean average is 36.7. In comparison, the mean average for the United States in 1969 is 37.0 hours – a difference of only 0.3.

The current hours in the 4-day firms' workweeks are given in the Chart of Hours, Days, and Shifts, below. All rest breaks and lunch breaks are omitted from the count; and the totals are rounded off to the nearest hour.

CHART OF 4-DAY FIRMS' HOURS, DAYS, AND SHIFTS

Hours Per Week		Days Open Per Week		Shifts	
Hours	Number of Firms	Days	Number of Firms	Shifts	Number of Firms
40	4[1]				
39	2	7	4[1]		
38	1	6	3		
37	5[1]	5½	1	1	17[4]
36	8[2]	5	7[1]	1½	2
35	4[1]	4½	3	2	4[1]
34	3	4	9[3]	2½	4
Median = 36	Total = 27	Median = 5	Total = 27	Median = 1	Total = 27

Note: Numbers in parentheses indicate the number of firms in that category that discontinued 4-day — a total of 5 firms. There appears to be no particular significance to the pattern for these firms; except possibly, that 3 of them were open for business only 4 days, and 3 are at or below the median number of work hours for the group.

Of the firms for which there is both *before* and *after* information, 4 firms increased their total hours, and 13 decreased their hours. Both the mean and the median average decreases for all 17 firms were 1 hour and 10 minutes. The increases ranged from 15 minutes to 1 hour. The decreases ranged from 30 minutes to 4 hours. The median reduction for the 13 firms was about 1 hour and 45 minutes, and the mean average was very close. For 10 firms, no comparison could be made, either because we collected no *before* information (4 firms), or because there was no basis for comparison (4 new firms *opened* on 4-day, and 2 other firms converted to 4-day 30 years ago).

Sixteen of the firms have $\frac{1}{2}$-hour lunches; two have $\frac{3}{4}$-hour lunches; and none reports a 1-hour lunch. But only 3 firms reduced their lunch periods.

As mentioned before, the firms are open for business varying numbers of days per week, hours per day, and shifts per day. Nine firms are open only 4 days a week; 2 are open $4\frac{1}{2}$ days, summer only, or May only; and 8 are open $5\frac{1}{2}$ days or more. The median is 5 days. Seventeen firms have 1 shift only. Eight have 2 or $2\frac{1}{2}$ shifts. (The $2\frac{1}{2}$ shifts usually run two 10-hour shifts, sometimes with two 2-hour shifts, sometimes with one 4-hour shift.)

I think it is important to note that the reduction of one day's work hours naturally brings an accompanying reduction in the week's total number of rest, coffee, wash-up, and lunch breaks. The firm also gets less start-up and stoppage (in effect, gets more work hours in the new week when the same number of work hours is compressed into the 4 days). Even where the new week has *fewer* total work hours, there can also be overall gains from having fewer start-ups and breaks to pay for. In addition, in some cases, firms that reduced the workweek also eliminated or reduced some breaks, gaining still more production hours. (Also, most firms had been working hours above the average for the U.S.A.)

WHAT HAPPENS TO THE WAGE BILL?

Most of the firms pay for a standard 40 hours a week, regardless of the actual number of hours in their new standard workweek. There was no change in weekly paycheck for 17 of the 22 firms for which a before and after comparison is practicable (those firms that have recent prior experience on non-4-day schedules). The firms usually have held the paycheck constant by juggling their interpretation of straight hours and overtime hours, counting some prior straight time hours as overtime hours. Some simply gave a rate increase while reducing the total hours paid for.

Of the 5 firms that changed their paychecks, only 1 reduced it (by reducing the number of hours the paycheck is calculated on). One of the 4 that increased their paychecks increased both their workweek and their paycheck by 1 hour (workweek, actually by 50 minutes). One increased its workweek by 50 minutes and its paycheck by a full 10%. The 2 other firms increased their pay rates to compensate for inflation although they decreased work hours.

The paychecks being as high or higher than before 4-day means that most workers received an increase in *rate* of pay, because most are working fewer hours for the same total paycheck. Even if we allow for fewer paid breaks and for greater amounts of productive worktime, there is still an effective increase in rate of pay. Of course, for those at the 4 firms with absolute increases in paycheck, the increase in rate of pay is still higher. For the one firm with a reduced paycheck, the generally frequent opportunity for overtime may make the workers come out ahead anyway; they get to overtime sooner in the week.

Attendance Bonus Systems: A bonus system was instituted by 3 of the firms that reduced their workweek and by 1 that increased it. Their workweeks are approximately 36 hours excluding breaks. Employees are paid for 40 provided that they work the full 36 hours. If they work less than 36 because of lateness or absence, they lose some of their standard pay for that time and also some or all of their weekly attendance bonus. (Only 1 of the 4 firms still has attendance problems; and that firm reports the severity of its problem is reduced.) Fines are not levied when there are bona fide reasons for lateness or absence.

The bonus system gives a higher pay rate to those workers who choose to work the amount of time the firm requires, and a lower rate to those workers who choose to work what the firm regards as a less desirable amount. This pay difference can be viewed as a differential rate for more and less desirable workers or as a form of overtime.

Overtime: Almost all the firms have, and pay, overtime for hours beyond their new standard workweek. Many are job shops or have seasonal variations in demand. But some firms have no occasion for overtime, or have all employees on salary or at piecework pay rates with a guarantee against piecework. In each of the firms that does have overtime, it is handled differently. The method seems to be tied to the way in which the firm solved the dilemma of maintaining the same weekly paycheck for a new work schedule with fewer hours in it. Some pay overtime each day for hours above their new daily schedule (above 8, 9, $9\frac{1}{2}$, etc.). Others pay overtime only for those hours at the end of the week that exceed whatever the new standard total is (ranging from 34 to 40). A few pay overtime only when the hours exceed their *old* standard workweek.

WHAT RESULTS?

The greatest number of improvements sought were in labour factors, and it is in labour factors that the greatest number of improvements are obtained. (See Table of Purposes and Results.) The 27 firms cited 77 improvements in labour factors. The most frequent benefit is incentive, morale, or better living conditions for employees; and the second most frequent is reduction of absenteeism (15 of 22 firms). The other improvements, in order of frequency of mention, are: increased number of job applications; easier recruitment; reduction in labour costs as a percentage of sales; reduced labour turnover; reduced tardiness; and reduced overtime.

A striking result is that the firms generally obtained more improvements than they had looked for. This was especially prevalent among non-labour factors, where they cited 48 improvements.

TABLE OF PURPOSES AND RESULTS
The Firms Generally Obtained More Than They Had Sought.
(Note: Not all firms answered all questions.)

Performance Categories	Purpose for 4-Day	Results on 4-Day			
		Better	Same	Worse	Total
LABOR FACTORS					
Absenteeism	4	15	2	0	17
Benefit or Incentive[1]	19	17	4	1[5.]	22
Costs	7	9	4	3[4.]	16
Overtime	2	4	1	1	6
Recruitment: more[2]	8	12	2	0	14
Recruitment: better[3]	5	9	4	0	13
Tardiness	2	5	7	1	13
Turnover	2	6	3	0	9
Total	49	77	27	6	110
NON-LABOR FACTORS					
Costs	4	3	0	0	3
Customer Service	1	7	6	3[5.]	16
Ease of Scheduling	0	0	4	12	16
Flexible Scheduling	0	4	0	0	4
Production Costs	4	10	3	1[6.]	14
Profits on Sales	2	8	3	0	11
Output	5	12	6	0	18
Throughput	3	3	0	0	3
Sales Promotion	3	1	0	2[5.]	3
Total	22	48	22	18	88

1. Change in morale was used as a measure.
2. Number of applications was used as a measure.
3. Ease of recruitment was used as a measure.
4. All said added costs are compensated for by increased production and sales.
5. All discontinued 4-day.
6. Compensated for by sales; so profits are the same.

Output was up for 12 firms. Production costs were down for 10 firms. Profits were up for 8 firms; and customer service was better for 7. (Note: not all firms answered in all categories. The questions of purposes and results were unstructured, and categories were set up after the firms' answers were collected.)

Increases in total output and in throughput were obtained in many cases at firms where the number of hours of labour had been reduced. It is sometimes said that most firms operate at less than peak efficiency. The question is why? The results of 4-day firms indicate that total number of hours on the job is less critical to output than other factors, such as distribution of hours and employees' willingness to produce.

Some of the firms found *some* disadvantages. Twelve firms found scheduling more complex on 4-day, but none discontinued 4-day for this reason. (In fact, none of the firms discontinuing 4-day even mentioned having more complex scheduling.) Other disadvantages cited by some of the firms that are *pleased* with 4-day are fatigue for employees, increased workload for supervisors or management, and shipping and receiving problems for firms open only 4 days. The firms claim that these disadvantages are more than compensated for by the advantages.

The 5 firms that discontinued 4-day cited disadvantages that none of the other firms mentioned: complaints by employees, poor customer service, and worsened ability to promote sales. The firms that discontinued 4-day cited the *same* types of advantages that the other firms did. It appears that the types of factors that they alone had difficulty with are therefore critical factors. None of the other 22 found problems in critical areas.

On the whole, advantages far outweigh disadvantages, and more advantages were obtained than had been anticipated. Some of the advantages, though, particularly easier recruitment, will be temporary if 4-day becomes widespread.

WHY SOME FIRMS DISCONTINUE 4-DAY

The 5 firms that discontinued 4-day after trying it for several months to a year's time or so have a variety of different reasons, and have very few things in common with each other, except that they report disadvantages that none of the other firms report. There are 2 manufacturers, 2 retailers, and 1 service firm.

Three have customer-related reasons for discontinuing 4-day. The architecture-engineering firm found some major clients were dissatisfied with the unavailability of *key* personnel. Their purpose for trying 4-day for the summer was to encourage vacations at other times in the year, to keep the work force more even throughout the year. But, although the employees liked it, and though the firm found it had more flexibility for dealing with a suddenly increased workload, and so on, they had to discontinue it. The firm reports it would like to go on 4-day again in the future when there is a new set of clients.

Two retail firms – one, a discount men's clothing store; the other, a discount tyre store chain – were both new firms when they tried 4-day. (Only 4 out of the 27 studied are new firms.) Not enough customers showed up. The owner of the clothing store says he could not afford to risk further experiment after a few months' trial. One of the owners of the tyre store said his stores could not afford to spend enough on promotion to make 4-day work out. He, too, says he would like to try 4-day again, with a bigger promotional budget. The purpose behind these retailers' moves to 4-day was to keep labour costs down and also have the firms be different enough to attract customers easily.

The manufacturers' reasons are unrelated. One, in frozen and delicatessen foods, tried 4-day when the workload was high and a key consideration was utilization of equipment – a 7-day, 20-hours-a-day week. When the workload dropped, the greater difficulties for management became key; so 4-day was dropped. The owner comments that they were pleased with 4-day when they needed it.

Another manufacturer, of loudspeakers, says he went on 4-day for his employees' sake, and also because the firm would get better productivity with fewer start-ups. After a year, 60-65% of the girls were disgruntled; so it was discontinued. He says he feels he was at fault for not presenting 4-day thoroughly. He calls it, "a failure of leadership."

As to characteristics that the firms have in common, or have in *contrast* to the firms remaining on 4-day, there is little to report aside from the fact that 2 of them are *new, very small* retailers; that 3 have customer problems; that 3 of them were among the earliest 4-day starts (2, in 1962; 1, in 1960); and that none are located in New England. The other characteristics fit the pattern of the continuing 4-day firms, except that none of these firms had better recruitment as a primary purpose for 4-day, which is an important reason for many other firms.

A NOTE ON RETAILERS

The 4 retailers are McDonald's Fast Foods, 4day Tire Stores, Mother's Tire Stores, and Jules Gillette's discount men's clothing. McDonald's is on 4-day in its offices only; and, there, only in the summer. Mother's and Jules Gillette discontinued 4-day.

So, basically, there is only one set of retail stores on 4-day, the 4day Tire chain. The owners say 4-day is good for keeping their costs and prices under those of the competition, and that 4-day has had advertising value. Unlike the other 2 retail stores, they promoted 4-day very heavily – $100,000 in their first year of operation. Secondly, they are open Thursday through Sunday; the other 2 were closed Sundays. Thirdly, they have a 40-hour week, while the others had 36 and 35 respectively.

I think that each of these factors – promotion budget for the new stores (all 3 were new), Sunday opening, and 4-hour to 5-hour difference in hours opened – played a part in the results. The California tyre stores also have the advantage of being in a district where Sunday sales are both legally permitted and socially accepted.

These 3 retailers provide an example of retail stores being open for 4 days only; but not an example of retail stores using 4-day manpower scheduling on 5-day, 6-day, or 7-day openings, which is another alternative to consider. Could 4-day be useful to a retailer open 5 or more days? It has not been tried, to our knowledge, yet it may be worth exploring. (See Chapters 10 and 16 for scheduling ideas.)

HOW DO THE FIRMS EVALUATE 4-DAY?

After giving specifics, most of the firms were asked to give their overall reactions, impressions, and judgements of what 4-day is doing for the firm. Here are their evaluations.

HOW DO YOU FEEL ABOUT THE 4-DAY WEEK, FROM THE POINT OF VIEW OF WHAT IT IS DOING FOR YOUR COMPANY?

Feelings	Firms
Very satisfied	12
Satisfied	2
Indifferent	3
Too soon to tell	5
Discontinued	5
Total=27	

WOULD YOU RECOMMEND IT TO OTHERS?

Recommendations	Firms
Yes	11
Depends on type	5
No, they don't know how to use it	1
Total=17	

Would You Do It Again? Yes=20; No=1 (total=21). Two of the affirmative firms are firms that discontinued 4-day. Both say they plan to try 4-day again. The 1 negative firm is also a firm that discontinued 4-day. Even the firms that said they felt indifferent to 4-day say they are pleased they tried 4-day, and would do it again.

Would You Do it in the Same Way? Yes=12; No=8 (total=20).

Here are the things they would do differently (the last two comments are from firms that discontinued 4-day):

1. Would pay overtime after the 8th hour in a day, to provide more incentive.
2. Would settle vacation days and their rate of pay before converting, to avoid disputes afterwards.
3. Would allow old employees an extra day off each month without deducting from the bonus, but not new recruits; to discourage abuse and to reward employees who work more years at the firm.
4. Would advertise itself more heavily, to make the firm better known and to bring more customers.
5. Would change other plant rules at the time of introducing 4-day, to get improved work rules at a more favourable time. An exchange of favours.
6. Would spend more time explaining and pursuading employees to choose the 4-day option, rather than the 5-day option; so fewer new workers would need to be hired and trained for the 4-day shift.
7. Would spend more on advertising, because feels 4-day could have worked for the new firm had they spent more.
8. Would spend more time explaining and introducing 4-day to the employees, so they would accept it.

Do You Expect Any Erosion of Gains You've Made on 4-Day, or Any Problems in the Long Run? Yes=2; No=13; Don't know=1 (total= 16). Those saying *yes* felt they would lose their current advantage in recruiting as 4-day spreads.

ARE SOME FIRMS PAYING HIGHER WAGES THAN THEY NEED TO?

Since many 4-day firms report long waiting lines for jobs where once there were few or no applicants, it raises the question: are they over-paying by paying the same wages they used to?

As discussed above, although there were very few pay increases, the reduction of hours means an increased *rate* of pay. There is also less money being spent on transportation to and from work and, in some cases, on babysitters. These are effective pay increases for employees, though small ones.

But there is an additional effect of the 4-day week. The reallocation of work hours also means, of course, a reallocation of leisure hours. The same number of leisure hours appears to be much more valuable bunched together on 4-day than when spread out, as on 5-day. Several chapters report the workers saying they are able to do things on the 3-day weekend that they could not do on a 2-day weekend, and so forth. This means an increase in the marginal utility of the leisure hours; and, therefore, a boost to a higher level of satisfaction for the consumer of the total package of leisure and wage income. Also, because transportation to and from work is now generally less time-consuming, there is an absolute increase in the number of leisure hours available, which are now more valuable hours.

In short, 4-day provides increased pay rate, decreased expenses, more leisure hours, and a distribution of leisure hours that makes them more useful and more valuable whether they are used for leisure or for gaining additional income at a second job. Any one of these alone is a benefit to the workers. Together, they make a vastly improved "pay" package for the same job.

Most of this vast improvement in "pay" is not taxable, either, which makes it even better. Considering that monetary pay increases are generally very quickly eaten away by both a rising tax rate and also spiralling inflation, a 4-day is one of the very few types of pay increases a worker can collect which he can also retain intact over time!

The change is not a total advantage, of course. There is a trade-off against some additional fatigue on the job from the longer hours; and also some inconvenience in meshing the 4-day schedule with family, friends, and institutions still on 5-day. Still, the workers seem to come out ahead.

The answer to whether pay is too high must include the improvements the firms obtain. If profits are improved on the same or a lesser wage bill, as many firms report, some of this improvement may justify the higher "pay" package for the workers. The question is probably *un*answerable in terms of logic or ethics, and only answerable in terms of action. (One firm reported paying lower wages to new 4-day employees.) The answer is: to experiment.

WILL IT CATCH ON?

Any effort to predict whether 4-day will spread has the advantage of looking back on the advent and spread of the 5-day week in the U.S.A. There are many similarities in the two phenomena. Both started with relatively small businesses; both with predominantly manufacturing firms; both with some firms abandoning it along the way; and both in order to give a benefit to labour at little or no cost to the firm. In both cases, output did not suffer, although the 4-day results are much better than 5-day since there is less reduction in total hours with 4-day.

One of the more interesting parallels, to me, is the innovations emerging in New England. New England, particularly Massachusetts, has been a continual hotbed of innovation, in a country that has done a lot of innovating. Massachusetts was the first state to have laws restricting females' hours of labour to protect them from abuse (1879); the first state to offer free public education; the home of the Suffragette movement; and now the home of the women's liberation movement, and so forth. The first 5-day firm started here in 1908; and the first 4-day firms as well. Why this happens I cannot say, but it is fascinating that beneficial innovations repeatedly occur at and spread from the long-established northeast coast, the heart of the so-called Establishment.

Unlike 5-day, 4-day is taking place at managements' initiative while unions in other industries are still on 5-day, but are pushing for 4-32. Four-day is taking place during a recession, when profits are being squeezed, and also when many moulds are being broken.

Four-day is a reallocation of work hours, and occasionally, a small reduction as well, by firms that had had workweeks longer than the average for the U.S. It is usually a year-round occurrence, but sometimes a summer thing. It usually begins as an experiment, or on a trial basis; and usually is a conversion from 5-day, but sometimes new firms open with 4-day.

This book was written primarily to be useful to people who have decisions to make. It is based on a careful study of 4-day firms by professional business analysts and practitioners. And all the facts are reported along with their opinions, both pro and con. The reader can, therefore, draw his own conclusions.

A number of us see 4-day as part of today's mould-breaking, and see today's mould-breaking as a thing of ever-increasing pace.

In my opinion, 4-day will spread, and spread rapidly, because it works well. Firms, by and large, are more efficient on 4-day; and employees, by and large, are better off with a 3-day weekend. It may also be better for the nation: if firms are more productive on 4-day, then 4-day has potential for increasing the GNP.

Whether or not 4-day spreads,* it is significant that 4-day experiments are happening at a moment in history when many other nations (Russia, for one example) have only just recently reduced their workweek from 6 days to 5, and much of Europe, for instance, is still on 6-day. Conservative Americans may rejoice in this example of the benefits of our brand of capitalism. But there is still more to it.

We note a startling reverse in who actually constitutes the leisure class in America. Over the past decades, managers and professionals have come to work increasingly longer hours and more days per week. Meanwhile, labour has tended to work increasingly fewer hours and fewer days. This is not a complaint – merely a comment on American life today.

Whether 4-day spreads or not, now that it's here, let's see what we can do with it. How can we use it to meet our goals today? Particularly, what if anything can it do for *you*?

---

*The 4-day week has indeed spread, as predicted. At this writing, less than two years later, there are 1,500 4-day firms in my files. And, based on time lags in receiving information in the past, one can estimate that these 1,500 in our catalogues indicate approximately 3,000 firms actually experimenting with 4-day today.

2

PROFILES OF 39 4-DAY PIONEERS
by Riva Poor

These profiles of firms pioneering the use of rearranged workweeks were developed mostly from telephone interviews conducted during June–September, 1970. The first 26 profiles are those of the firms that were interviewed in depth for report and analysis in Chapter 1. The remaining firms were discovered too late or turned to 4-day too late for inclusion in Chapter 1.

While one cannot keep figures in date for a movement that is in a state of rapid flux, readers can nonetheless get a feel for some of the advantages, disadvantages, and opportunities of 4-day, by reviewing the profiles.*

On 4-Day
American Laquer & Solvents Company of Florida
Tampa, Florida
(MANUFACTURE)

Union: Chemical Workers Union.
Description: Manufactures paints, lacquers, enamels, flexographic inks, and reducing compounds. One of several affiliated corporations.

---

*Although the data has changed in the almost 2 years since these profiles were originally recorded, they are still useful. They illustrate diverse situations in which 4-day applies, and also show diverse levels of satisfaction with its use.

A few of the firms reported here as still being on 4-day have since discontinued using it – and some of the firms that I reported here as having discontinued 4-day have now readopted it, having changed their schedules to overcome the problems they experienced. Also, some of the 4-day companies have changed to a 3-day week.

Batch process. Not seasonal. Fifty-four employees (19 in union). Average age, 36.5 years; average seniority, 5.5 years.

Purpose: General welfare of the employees . . .

Implementation: Started 4-day in May, 1970. Open Monday through Thursday, 17 hours a day. Fridays, if needed. Two shifts. Forty-eight workers on 4-day (10 females). Not included are sales and management. Workweek was decreased by 2 hours and 20 minutes, to 36 hours.

Results: Morale and production – better.

Company Comment: Plan to keep it.

On 4-Day
Auto City, Inc.
East Boston, Massachusetts
(WHOLESALE)

Union: None.

Description: Rebuilds used cars for Chrysler, for wholesale auction. Not seasonal. One hundred thirty employees. Average age, 32; average seniority, 1.5 years.

Purpose: To recruit a night crew, to increase inventory to auction.

Implementation: Started 4-day in July, 1970. Night crew only. Monday through Thursday; but firm is open Monday through Saturday. No females on 4-day (no female mechanics). Workweek – 34 hours for night shift.

Results: Too early to tell final results, but they recruited 18 skilled workers after advertising just 2 weeks. Will be able to bring inventory level to 1,000 cars. (Several employees work 2 shifts. Pay is $200/week guarantee against piecework, per shift.)

Company Comment: Men don't like to work Friday nights. This way they can do all their work Monday through Thursday. The day crew doesn't need 4-day; they can take a day off whenever they need to.

Discontinued 4-Day
Bridgefords Foods and Packing Company
Anaheim, California
(MANUFACTURE)

Union: None.

Description: Manufactures frozen foods; also has a delicatessen line. Not seasonal. About 240 employees (20% female). Average age when 4-day was started, about 25; now, about 30.

4 Days, 40 Hours

Purpose: To utilize plant and equipment maximum hours.
Implementation: Started 4-day in 1962. Seven days a week; two 10-hour shifts a day. People worked 4 days on, 4 days off (first week, Monday through Thursday; second week, Tuesday through Friday; third week, Wednesday through Saturday, etc.). Used 4-day for about 1½ years. No women on 4-day. Production only.
Results: Gave maximum utilization of resources commensurate with orders, although the schedule was hard on management. Discontinued 4-day when sales declined to a point where maximum utilization was not an important factor, and management discomfiture was.
Company Comment: At the time we were very pleased with it, but we don't need it now.

On 4-Day
Geo H. Bullard Company, Inc.
Westboro, Massachusetts
(MANUFACTURE)

Union: None.
Description: Manufactures abrasives products for industry and for do-it-yourselfers. Continuous process; and not seasonal. One hundred-twenty employees (20 females). Average age, 29; average seniority, 7.5 years.
Purpose: More labour, better labour. Higher proficiency, and, therefore, reduced costs.
Implementation: Started 4-day in September, 1969. Open Monday through Thursday. Had had 1½ shifts; now has 1 shift. The 112 people on 4-day (20 females) include all employees except sales representatives and top management. Reduced workweek by 1 hour and 10 minutes, to 34 hours, 40 minutes.
Results: Better morale; recruitment greatly facilitated (applications up 200%); virtual elimination of absenteeism (down 50%); substantial productivity increase (10.2% above 5-day level, despite 20% new trainees in work force); and resulting in unit cost reductions.
Company Comment: Profits are up 5%. Our business has picked up, because we give better service now. We're very satisfied.

Discontinued 4-Day
Carbonneau Industries
Grand Rapids, Michigan
(MANUFACTURE)

Union: None.
Description: Manufactures loudspeakers for radio and TV. Closer to batch process than continuous flow. Had 250 employees at the time; now, about 100 (85-90% women). Average age then, about 30; now, about 22.
Purpose: Better for employees; also, greater output on fewer start-ups.
Implementation: Started 4-day in 1960, Monday through Thursday; for about 1 year. Thirty-six hours work; 40 hours pay. After a year, took a vote, by voting machine ("probably the only firm in the country to have one"); about 60-65% were against it.
Results: Discontinued 4-day, because the girls did not like the extra pressure of turning out the same amount of work in less time.
Company Comment: Feel it was a failure of leadership on my [the President's] part.

On 4-Day
The Crocker Company
Burlington, Massachusetts
(MANUFACTURE)

Union: None.
Description: Steel fabrication, both thin and thick. Batch process. Seasonal for the first time this year (swimming pool wall panels and rubbish containers). Founded in 1919. Forty-four employees (2 women). Average age, 40, but large range; average seniority, 5 years.
Purpose: More labour, better labour, and to cut down on overtime.
Implementation: Started 4-day in June, 1969. Open 4½ days a week, Monday through Friday, 1 shift. Nine people are not on 4-day – top management and office workers (2 females). Increased workweek by 20 minutes, to 38 hours, 40 minutes.
Results: More labour, but not enough better labour. Have not cut down on overtime.
Company Comment: Profits are the same. We're moderately satisfied, but not turning cartwheels over it. It hasn't done what we'd hoped it would do. We need the skilled workers to overcome the overtime

33

problem. We don't have the skilled people we need; they just aren't available.

Planned 4-Day for Plant Opening
Dalton Precision Division
Cushing, Oklahoma
(MANUFACTURE)

Union: Industrial Workers Union.
Description: Division of Dalton Foundries, Warsaw, Indiana. Precision casting of industrial products – hydraulic valves, compressors, etc. Process is between continuous and batch process. Semi-seasonal; dips in third quarter. Plant opened in May, 1969. Currently, 97 employees (45 females). Median age, 30.
Purpose: To operate equipment close to 160 hours a week, without disadvantages of a swing shift for employees; and to attract small farmers to the work force.
Implementation: Opened plant with 4-day in the plan. Started 4-day in August, 1969, when work got up to speed. Open 7 days a week, 2 shifts. Each is 4 days on, 4 days off. Expanding rapidly and plan, eventually, 2 turns on each of the 2 shifts. Of the 90 workers on 4-day, 50% are female; this will rise to 60%. Top management takes turns getting a full weekend off. Four others, shipping and office, are not on 4-day. Workweek averages 35 hours. [*More about 4 on, 4 off in Chapter* 7.]
Results: Real advantage to operate equipment 140 hours a week. Also, can ship castings on Saturdays and Sundays. But there is no make-up day available if you get behind.
Company Comment: In this rural community, 4-day fits well with farming. Because of the 4 full days of daylight off, people can operate their farms and still work here: 2 incomes.

Always on 4-Day
4day Tire Stores Company
Newport Beach, California
(RETAIL & WHOLESALE)

Union: None.
Description: Eight retail tyre branches, 3 of which are franchised. Some wholesale. All opened since August, 1969. Sales are somewhat higher in summer. Thirty-five employees (2 females). Average age,

25. The 2 owners own and operate an advertising agency which provides the promotional service for the chain.

Purpose: To avoid the conventional, and to compete better; to lower labour costs by operating only the optimum sales hours.

Implementation: Open Thursday through Sunday, when tyre sales are best. First year's promotion budget – $100,000. All employees on 4-day except the 2 owners and 2 office workers. Open: 40 hours.

Results: Did $1.5 million in sales, first year. Lose a little in the wholesale end Monday through Wednesday, but make it up on the weekends.

Company Comment: Four-day helps us undersell our competitors. Sales are increasing by leaps and bounds. Can't keep up with sales. If we had it to do again, we'd plunge ahead even more heavily on advertising.

Discontinued 4-Day
Jules Gillette
North Miami, Florida
(RETAIL)

Union: None.

Description: Discount store, men's clothing (82 sizes). No pedestrian traffic. Three stores, all told; 2 with pedestrian traffic.

Purpose: To be different. Concept was leisurely shopping and convenience, for drivers.

Implementation: Started 4-day at the discount store only, in November, 1962, with the opening of the store. Ten employees at the time. (One other store in existence at the time.) Open Thursday through Sunday, 35 hours.

Results: Discontinued after 3–4 months. Not enough sales. Felt they were chasing people away by being closed.

Company Comment: You have to be open at the consumer's convenience: late morning through late night. Maybe it would have worked out if we had stuck to it. But if it didn't work, a year later we'd have had a big loss. You can win the battle and lose the war. We were a new store, and we couldn't afford to experiment.

4 Days, 40 Hours

30 Years on 4-Day
Gulf Oil Terminal*
Jamaica Plain, Massachusetts
(TRUCKING)

Union: Gulf Employees of New England. (Other terminals are represented by the Oil, Chemical, and Atomic Workers, etc.)
Description: Deliveries of fuel oil, gasoline, motor oil, and diesel fuel. One of many terminals on 4-day across the nation. Seasonal. Terminal employs 125–140 workers. Ages 22–63 years old. Seniority: half employed over 20–25 years.
Purpose: Efficient 6-day, round-the-clock schedule; and to cut overtime.
Implementation: Drivers only, about 65 men on 4-day. Six days a week, 24 hours a day. Two 10-hour shifts, with two 2-hour repair periods, between shifts. Workweek – 40 hours.
Results: Fewer men per truck, better utilization of equipment. No holdup for truck repairs; therefore cuts overtime. Reduces costs.
Company Comment: We tried many other schedules. This is best, and the men feel the 3-day weekend is terrific.

Discontinued 4-Day
Haines, Lundberg and Waehler
New York, New York
(ARCHITECTS/ENGINEERS)

Union: None.
Description: Architectural and engineering firm with branch in Newark. Not seasonal. Four hundred employees. Average age, 38 years; average seniority, 13 years.
Purpose: To encourage employees to defer summer vacations, to have employees available during summer months.
Implementation: Summer only, Memorial Day through Labour Day, 1969. Open Monday through Friday. One shift; all employees, except field workers. Increased workweek by 15 minutes, to 39 hours.
Results: Discontinued. Even dispersion of vacation times; flexibility for overtime; and employees liked it. But availability of supervisors was poor, and work scheduling was more difficult; therefore some major clients didn't like it.

*An interview with **Mobil's Dearborn, Michigan, Terminal** yielded nearly identical results; it is therefore omitted.

Company Comment: We were disappointed not to renew it, and we may do it again in the future.

4½ Days, in Summer
R.C. Hollow Metal Company
Denver, Colorado
(MANUFACTURE)

Union: None.
Description: Sheet metal fabrication; door frames, window frames, and doors. Job shop. Division of W. Ray Crabb, Inc., Sales and Engineers. Twenty-nine employees, 100% male. Average age, 28; average seniority, 3.5 years. (About 20% attend school in the evenings.) Generally, a lot of overtime (4 hours).
Purpose: For employees. Heard others were doing it; wanted to experiment.
Implementation: Started 4½ days in summer, 1969. Monday through Thursday, 36 hours. In winter work four 9-hour days, and one 8-hour day (44 hours). Because of workload, had 4½-day for only 2 months in 1970 (3 months in 1969).
Results: Advantages are for the employees; also better for machine maintenance. There's a problem shipping on Fridays (no problem receiving).
Company Comment: An experiment. Don't feel strongly about it either way. It's a toss-up as far as getting the job done. Employees wanted to do it again; but efficiency suffers on long, hot summer days. Especially with so many employees in school at nights, we would really lose out if we had 4-day instead of 4½.

On 4-Day
Interstate, Inc.
Braintree, Massachusetts
(MANUFACTURE)

Union: None
Description: Manufactures paint rollers. Continuous process. Higher sales in spring and autumn. Fifty employees (32 females). Average age, 50; but influx of college girls in the summer. Average seniority, 2½–3 years.
Purpose: Provide more incentive; recruit better labour.
Implementation: Started 4-day in June, 1969. Open Monday through

4 Days, 40 Hours

Thursday, and a half day on Friday for overtime and for process workers. One and a half shifts (added "mothers" shift); open longer hours. Except for management and sales representatives, all 46 on 4-day. Reduced workweek by 2 hours and 15 minutes, to 35 hours, 40 minutes.

Results: Easier recruitment; and almost all systems improved. But extra hour is fatiguing for the workers.

Company Comment: Very satisfied. We reduced labour costs from 16% to 14% of sales; saving – $30,000.

On 4-Day
Kyanize Paints, Inc.
Everett, Massachusetts
(MANUFACTURE)

Union: Kyanize Shop Association.

Description: Manufactures paints, furniture polish, chemical resistant coatings (urethanes, silicones, etc.). Branches in Springfield, Illinois, and Houston, Texas, which is the aero pact division. Batch process. Seasonal. One hundred fifteen employees in Everett, 30 in Springfield, and 25 in Houston (21 females in Everett). Average age, 40; average seniority, 15 years.

Purpose: Felt it was nice for employees and that they could do as well in 4 days as in 5.

Implementation: Started in March, 1969. Open Monday through Thursday. One shift. All on 4-day, except the salesmen and the Texas plant (a new acquisition, not yet converted to 4-day). Reduced workweek by 1 hour and 20 minutes, to 35 hours and 20 minutes. Increased paycheck to compensate for inflation.

Results: All systems improved, excepting union relations and turnover which were already good.

Company Comment: We received a lot of benefits that we had not anticipated. It's the greatest thing since sliced bread, and we look forward to reducing the workday still further. [*See Chapter 11.*]

On 4-Day
Lawrence Manufacturing Company
Lowell, Massachusetts
(MANUFACTURE)

Union: None.
Description: Founded in 1826. Division of Ames Textile Corp.

Manufactures industrial knit fabrics. Seasonal. Closer to continuous process than to batch process. Employs 215 (100 females). Sixty percent of the workers are about 40 years old, and have about 14 years seniority. New group, about 23 years old, has been there less than a year.

Purpose: Recruit more labour; reduce absenteeism and turnover.

Implementation: Started in December, 1969. Open Monday through Thursday, and use Fridays for extra production. Two and a half shifts. Factory on 4-day; office, professionals, and management, not. Increased workweek by 50 minutes to 36 hours, 40 minutes – actual minutes of work; increased take home pay 10%.

Results: Improvements in all systems, but absenteeism has not improved as much as hoped for.

Company Comment: We probably could not have continued unless we did something like this. We achieved, in part, all that we expected; but some objectives are longer in coming. [*See Chapter 5 for in-depth profile.*]

4½ Days, in Summer
McDonald's Corporation
Chicago, Illinois
(RETAIL)

Union: None.

Description: Fast food chain of 1,400 branches, started in 1955. Six regional offices. Employs 310 in main office and 431 in regional offices. Average age, 29. Average seniority, 4 years.

Purpose: To enable employees to take better advantage of daylight savings time and to spend more time with families.

Implementation: Started spring, 1969. Half day off on Fridays, summers only, during daylight savings. Office personnel only; not restaurants. Reduced workweek by half an hour (summer only), to 37 hours.

Results: Gains in morale, attitude towards firm, absenteeism, and efficiency. There is a small increase in tardiness, because the earlier arrival hour creates some transportation problems.

Company Comment: We feel the programme has been exceptionally successful. But we could not do it in the restaurants (we have many part-timers for peak loads, there).

4 Days, 40 Hours

5¼ Years on 4-Day
Merrill Engineering Laboratories
Denver, Colorado
(MANUFACTURE)

Union: None.
Description: Manufactures electronic balancing devices, and aligning equipment. Associated with other, related business firms. About 25-30 employees (3 women).
Purpose: For employees.
Implementation: Started in April, 1965. One shift, Monday through Thursday. Office is open on Friday; and no women are on 4-day. Workweek is 40 hours, with overtime after 36. "At first the older employees thought it was a crazy idea; so we just had volunteers on 4-day (50%). At the end of the year, though, 100% [of men] were on it."
Results: Production, absenteeism, and profits improved. Recruitment and retention improved. A disadvantage for employees is that some have wives who work 5 days; and some others' wives make them work Fridays at home.
Company Comment: No deterioration of 4-day's benefits over the 5½ years.

On 4-Day
Milton Machine Corporation
East Weymouth, Massachusetts
(MANUFACTURE)

Union: None.
Description: Manufactures missile components for Government. Not seasonal. Due to cutbacks in contracts, reduced labour force from 45 to 5 people, from 3 shifts to 1 shift. Average age, 42; average seniority, 2.5 years.
Purpose: To get more and better labour, to give employees a long weekend, and to permit moonlighting.
Implementation: Started in June, 1969. Open Monday through Thursday. One shift of 36 hours, 40 minutes.
Results: Better productivity.
Company Comment: Although we no longer need to recruit, 4-day works well; so we're still doing it.

40

Discontinued 4-Day
Mother's Tire Company
Atlanta, Georgia
(RETAIL, SOME WHOLESALE)

Union: None.
Description: Three retail tyre stores; some commercial and wholesale sales. Higher sales in summer months. Opened first store in January, 1969. Now employ 18 people.
Purpose: Lower labour costs. Hoped lower costs, and consequent lower prices, would bring more customers.
Implementation: Tried 4-day July through October, 1969. Open Wednesday through Saturday. (Had 2 stores at that time.) Everyone on 4-day, but some managers worked longer hours. Then open 36 hours; now open 6 days, more hours.
Results: Discontinued 4-day. While labour costs were lower, sales were not good enough.
Company Comment: It was too weird for the South, but we could have overcome this. I still feel it's a sound and workable concept. But it needed a sound promotional budget, over a longer period than we could do it. Thinking of trying it again later on.

On 4-Day
New England Metal Spinning Company, Inc.
Malden, Massachusetts
(MANUFACTURE)

Union: None.
Description: Metal fabrication; machine shop. Not seasonal. Employs 26 people (3 females). Average age, 40; average seniority, 5 years.
Purpose: Incentive for employees.
Implementation: Started 4-day in March, 1970. Open Monday through Thursday; but Friday and Saturday, too, if needed. One shift. Twenty-one on 4-day (1 female); all except office, foremen, and management. Decreased workweek by 1 hour and 45 minutes, to 37 hours.
Results: Too early to tell, but it looks like all systems are the same. Labour costs may be higher.
Company Comment: There seems to be no advantage for the firm: the advantage is for the help. I try these things. I came up from the ranks myself, so I have empathy for the worker.

41

4 Days, 40 Hours

Just Starting 4-Day
C.A. Norgren Company
Littleton, Colorado
(MANUFACTURE)

Union: None.
Description: Manufactures air processing systems – filters, regulators, lubricators, valves, dryers and fluidic devices designed to protect air driven tools and equipment and control the air that powers them. Products are distributed throughout the free world; manufactured in 7 countries outside the U.S.A. Appears to be the world's largest in its field. Employs 500 in Littleton (64 women). Average age, 38; average seniority, 7 years. One of the first firms to have profit-sharing, and salary and wage continuation for sickness and accident.
Purpose: For employees, and as a surrogate for a wage increase. Also expect that absenteeism for personal business reasons will decline.
Implementation: Had a task force investigate 4-day at other firms before deciding its move. Starting 4-day, September, 1970, Monday through Thursday, for all Colorado staff, except sales. Thirty-seven hours (a shorter day on Thursday).
Results: Not yet on 4-day as we go to press.
Company Comment: In a world that has so many non-work activities to enjoy, and in Colorado especially, our people will get to take advantage of life to its fullest.

4-Day in May
Reader's Digest
Pleasantville, New York
(SERVICE)

Union: None.
Description: Publishes magazines and books; circulation, 17.5 million. Seasonal. Employs about 3,500 people (about 80% female), at offices in Pleasantville, New York City, etc. Average age, about 35. The firm has been a leader in personnel practices; it pioneered the 35-hour week, and has a 4-week vacation for employees after one year's employment.
Purpose: For employees' benefit.
Implementation: Started in May, 1969. Monday through Thursday, in May only. Almost all personnel are on 4-day; but a skeleton crew

is maintained by staggering the off day for some employees. The workweek is reduced to 28 hours, in May, which averages out to a 35 minute reduction per week throughout the year.

Results: Good for morale. They cannot determine whether costs are higher, but think that their employees work harder to make up for the day off.

Company Comment: DeWitt Wallace, Co-Chairman, says 4-day puts them "once again in the forefront of what I am convinced will eventually be a major trend."

On 4-Day
Rex Paper Box Company, Inc.
Braintree, Massachusetts
(MANUFACTURE)

Union: None.

Description: Manufactures folding paper boxes; varied sizes, materials, printing, and construction. Not seasonal. Batch process. Sixty-five employees (16 female). Average age, 37; average seniority, 5.5 years.

Purpose: To get more labour; and to reduce labour turnover, tardiness, and absenteeism. To create better atmosphere.

Implementation: Started 4-day in June, 1969. Open $5\frac{1}{2}$ days a week. Converted from 2 shifts to 1. All but 6 people are on 4-day (15 females). Reduced workweek by 4 hours, to 36 hours.

Results: Profits are up, but this may not be due to 4-day. "We had a staggering backlog of business; so we changed several things simultaneously with introducing 4-day."

Company Comment: Our industry has been depressed for several years; we don't have the profits in this industry to pay high wages for unskilled labour. This was our only alternative for competing for labour.

On 4-Day
Roger Williams General Hospital
Providence, Rhode Island
(SERVICE)

Union: None.

Description: General hospital, open 7 days a week. About 1,200 employees (mostly women). University-affiliated.

4 Days, 40 Hours

Purpose: To meet the needs of employees; to compete better in the labour market; to provide better continuity of care, and better transfer of information from shift to shift; and to reduce the use of temporary substitutes in nursing teams. An experiment. [*More, in Chapter 6*.]

Implementation: Started experiment with 4-day in December, 1969, in Coronary Care Unit. Nursing Services, only; and only at those stations that elect to go on 4-day. About 300 people, so far. Two and a half shifts; work 3 days one week, and 4 days the next. Workweek averages 35 hours, reduced from 40 hours. Also put in new wage and salary programme.

Results: Seem to be meeting their goals; but is as yet unresolved whether 4-day costs more or actually saves money for the Hospital.

Comments: All signals are "go," so far; but it will require thorough evaluation, after a year's time, before a definitive judgement can be made.

On 4-Day
Nathan Solomon and Company, Inc.
Lowell, Massachusetts
(MANUFACTURE)

Union: None.

Description: Manufactures ladies' sleepwear. One hundred forty employees (20 females). Average age, 34; average seniority, 5 years (25%, 10 years; 25%, 1 year or less).

Purpose: To get more and better labour.

Implementation: Started July 15, 1970, with 50% on 4-day, leaving the choice up to the workers. By mid-August, 80% had chosen to convert. The office and the cutting room are not on 4-day (the latter, by its own option). Five-day workers are now working a 37½ hour week (getting paid for 40); and 4-day workers are working 36 hours (paid for 38), Monday through Thursday. Workweek used to be 38¾ hours (paid for 40), usually with 4 hours overtime.

Results: Attendance is excellent during the week, and more people are willing to work overtime. So far, there are no new employees, but firm has not yet advertised for help.

Company Comment: It's too early to tell. Employees are worried that they may eventually lose some overtime hours; we'll have to work this out for them.

On 4-Day
Name Withheld by Request*
Massachusetts
(SERVICE)

Union: None.
Description: Data processing firm specializing in payrolls. Subsidiary of national corporation with branches around the country. Partly seasonal (W2 forms, etc.). One hundred employees (64 women). Average age, 28; average seniority, 2 years (staff expanded 100% in last 2 years).
Purpose: To meet peak loads. Payrolls must be done by Thursday. "Four-day is a big necessity; 3 days, 12 hours each, would be even better."
Implementation: Started 4-day in January, 1969. Firm is open 24 hours a day, 7 days a week, with 3 shifts. Four-day is used for bottleneck operations only: for 20 keypunchers (out of 55) and a few each of computer operators, control clerks, and delivery men. Total on 4-day: 28 (21 women). Employees were given a choice of 4-day or 5-day. Four-day workweek is 34 hours.
Results: Throughput is improved, but supervision and scheduling are more complex.
Company Comment: Four-day is a great thing to try, and to use where the workload dictates it. There is a problem of fatigue for the workers; but it is offset, from the company's viewpoint, by the flexibility in scheduling we get. I wish it were legal at the moment. [Did not know waiver from regulation limiting females' working hours was available. Is now applying for it.]

LATE ENTRIES
The data from these firms was received too late to work into Chapter 1. All but one of these companies are still on 4-day or 3-day weeks, and none have unions.

On 4-Day
Abbey Etched Products, Inc.
Boston, Massachusetts
(MANUFACTURE)

*Pending waiver of legal restriction on hours of labour permitted for females.

4 Days, 40 Hours

Description: Acid metal etching; 6 employees (no females).
Purpose: For employees.
Implementation: Started September, 1969. Four 10-hour days; business open 5 days; manager works 3 days (!).
Comment: Enormously pleased with it.

Discontinued 3-*Day*
Anacomp, Inc.
Indianapolis, Indiana
(SERVICE)

This very small data processing firm moved to a 6-days-a-week schedule when it experienced increased sales demand. The firm put 10 people on $12\frac{1}{2}$-hour shifts, 3 days a week, in order to get 6 days of 24-hour-a-day coverage without incurring overtime. When sales demand later decreased below the former original level, the firm abandoned the 3-day schedule along with its 6th day of operation in the course of making general personnel cutbacks. The manager says 3-day was fine, the problem was the recession.

On 4-Day
Bank of New York
New York, New York
(SERVICE)

Description: Commercial bank; 3,700 employees.
Purpose: To get better throughput for Fiduciary Data Control Department (115 employees – 80% female); to get work onto computer without delay or constant overtime.
Implementation: Started 4-day around March, 1969; FDC Department only; for about 40% of the staff. Four-day and 5-day shifts work side by side; 4-day shift is noon to 9.45 PM (rotating day off); 5-day is 9.00 AM to 5.00 PM; both, 35 hours a week. Girls are permitted to leave work early if finish quota early; otherwise, are paid overtime. Special circumstance: large proportion of so-called "hardcore" employees.
Results: Throughput, better; overtime, $600 every 2 weeks (down from $2,000); turnover, 0-18% (industry average, 50%); morale, high. But because 4-day is scheduled late in the day, 5-day is preferred shift; 4-day is used for new employees. Note: Department

46

Head cautions that 4-day is not solely responsible for all results – see below.

Company Comment: In 1½ years on 4-day, there is no diminution of benefits. The work gets out faster, the atmosphere is more productive, and the department gets on the computer earlier. But, 4-day is not a panacea: things like 4-day are minimal things – like hygiene. It's how you treat people that counts: they want mobility, and excitement, and to feel that they are being treated well.

On 4-Day
Booksmith Distributing Corp.
Boston, Massachusetts
(WHOLESALE)

Description: Warehouses and distributes for parent firm – Paperback Booksmith – and other book stores in several nearby states; seasonal; 21 employees.
Purpose: For employees.
Implementation: Started 1969, for summers only (fifth day, needed in busier season); four 10-hour days for 16 people; office, open 5 days.
Results: "Hippie employees love it . . . *mental* fatigue is a problem . . . but it's groovy for the summer!"

On 4-Day
Cromwell Corporation
South Bend, Indiana
(MANUFACTURE)

Description: Job machining shop; 22 men.
Purpose: Maximum utilization of machinery.
Implementation: Started April, 1965, by John Schohl (author of Chapter 7) with 2 employees; 4 days on, 4 days off, except for supervisor; open 7 days in calendar week.
Results: Four machines can produce as much as 10 machines would on a regular schedule; employees like it; no problems.
Comment: Wouldn't want to change. So many sales depend on your being able to do the work right away – this way, we can.

4 Days, 40 Hours

On 4-Day
Home Savings Bank
Boston, Massachusetts
(SERVICE)

Description: Thrift institution; deposits, $280 million; 100 employees.
More than half of business is conducted by mail; no branches.
Implementation: Started 4-day, September, 1970, for entire bank
except top officers. Formerly open 9.00–3.00 most days; now open
8.30–5.30 all 5 days. Rotating day off. Also added $240/year attend-
ance bonus – $20/day, deducted for unauthorized absence.
Results: Aside from providing longer hours for customers' business,
the firm received large increase in applications for employment.
Company Comment: Until now, it's been a labour market; and labour
has been dictating the terms. With increased applications for employment and attendance bonus (if abused, it will provide reason for
replacing some employees), we hope to upgrade the staff over time –
all leading to better customer service. Four-day cements the relationship between management and employees. In the long run, I feel
employees everywhere will agitate to get their firms on 4-day, and
4-day will spread.

On 4-Day
Label Art, Inc.
Milford, New Hampshire
(MANUFACTURE)

Description: Manufactures pressure sensitive labels; 20 employees (8
female).
Purpose: To improve work rules – coffee breaks, sick leave.
Implementation: Started March, 1970; four 9½-hour days, 15 pro-
duction people – no coffee breaks; open 4½ days.
Results: Better work flow, output, loyalty base; and happier people.

On the 3-Day Week
Mutual Life Insurance of New York
Syracuse, New York
(SERVICE)

This very large insurance company, whose famous acronym is
48

MONY, has had 33 of 40 computer console operators in its upstate New York computer facility on three 12½-hour days for about 2 years now. The extra ½ hour is for continuity between shifts. The computer facility is open 24 hours a day, 5 days a week – making a schedule much more complex (though still workable) than on a 6-day opening. They say it works well.

On 4-Day
Police Department
Huntington Beach, California
(GOVERNMENT)

Description: Police Department for city of 130,000; employs 200 (85% attend school); understaffed for population size since there is a twofold increase on weekends to use 9½-mile beach; has police officers association.
Purpose: More staff for weekend and daily peaks (9.00 PM to 3.00 AM), less staff for slow hours (3.00 to 7.00 AM).
Implementation: Started May, 1969; 90-day test period; four 10-hour days for 160 people (10 female) – not for administration and services. No rotation of off days creates desired overlaps and cutbacks.
Results: Morale up; arrest rate up (80%); overtime costs down (40% – saving $62,000); men do better in school; no fatigue problem.
Comment: Works very well. Now about 600 police departments are on it.

On 4-Day
Radio New York Worldwide, Inc.
Scituate, Massachusetts
(SERVICE)

International short wave transmitting facility; divison of Bonneville International Corp.; started 4-day in June, 1968. The 5 employees, all engineers and members of the International Brotherhood of Electrical Workers, Local No. 1228, work a 5-week schedule that mixes 8-hour and 10-hour days. Purpose was to cover noon to 10.45 PM, 7-day operation; and it works well.

4 Days, 40 Hours

On 4-Day
Royal Label Co., Inc.
Boston, Massachusetts
(MANUFACTURE)

Description: Manufactures labels; 32 employees (6 female).
Purpose: Morale, and savings from longer production runs.
Implementation: Started September, 1969; four 10-hour days for all production employees (18); office and sales, open fifth day.
Results: Better employee relations, savings on production, plus easier recruitment.

On 4-Day
Sullair Corporation
Michigan City, Indiana
(MANUFACTURE)

Manufactures rotary screw air compressors. Has about 60 of 150 employees on 4-day, since January, 1970. Factory is open 4 days, office 5 days, resulting in exceptional morale, the same or better productivity, and no problems.

On the 3-Day Week
Name Withheld by Request
Massachusetts
(MANUFACTURE)

The owner of this tiny harpsichord manufacturing firm and his 2 employees lead a bucolic existence 4 days a week, and come into town to work on their backlog of orders only 3 days a week. Unlike all the other examples cited in this book, this company's 3-day week involves the owner's choosing to limit workdays at his firm, in order to maximize leisure days, rather than involving an attempt to maximize the firm's profits. The owner asked us to withhold his name, because he says he already has more orders than he wants to fill. The firm's name and telephone are, for the same reason, not listed in the telephone book.

3

THANK GOD IT'S THURSDAY!
by L. Erick Kanter

L. Erick Kanter is Staff Correspondent for Newsweek's *Boston Bureau, covering New England. He previously covered manned space flights in Houston, and President Lyndon B. Johnson at his ranch.*

"When I go out in my neighbourhood on Fridays now – to the shopping centre or down to the service station – people are always asking me: 'Hey how come you're not working today?' And I just laugh and laugh." That's how life is these days for a packer in the shipping department of a Boston-area company.

"I have more time to be at home with my family now," says a young housewife who works for Dalton Precision. "It's like getting full-time wages for working a part-time job."

Such sentiments* are common among this tiny – but rapidly expanding – segment of the American work force: the employees of organizations that have lopped one day off the traditional 5-day week. As might be expected, not every worker claims to enjoy the 4-day week, but such grumbling generally is a consequence of the human tendency never to be satisfied, rather than any sincere desire to go back to working 5 days. An overwhelming percentage of workers at companies that have made the switch indicate a definite preference for the 4-day week, even if it causes minor inconveniences.

*The reactions of the pioneering 4-day workers reported in this chapter have turned out to be typical of reactions of workers across the U.S.A., judging by newspaper and magazine interviews in the past year or so by hundreds of reporters across the country. To the extent that workers in all countries share the same hopes and dreams, one may expect these reactions to be shared by workers around the world.

51

LEISURE AND FAMILY

Among the many reasons that workers claim for liking the 4-day week, by far the most prevalent is the increased time available, especially to spend with the family.

"I own a pickup truck and camper, and I have more time to spend with my family camping in the summer," says a truck driver with Gulf Oil. "During bad weather," he adds, "I've got extra time for doing interior work in my house. To sum it up, there's more leisure time. And as far as disadvantages go, I find none."

"As a working mother and wife, it gives me an extra day to enjoy life and get caught up on my housework," says a woman who works in the front offices of the Geo. H. Bullard Co.

In some cases, such as the packer who keeps being asked why he's not working on Fridays, there appears to be some subtle form of prestige attached to working only 4 days. "I really catch hell from my neighbours for having so much time off," says one worker with a big grin, "and I love every minute of it."

The general enthusiasm for having more time for leisure and being with the family takes many specific forms: housewives getting their house cleaned on Friday so that they can engage in recreational activities with their husbands on Saturdays and Sundays; a man who now has enough time on weekends to drive to his married son's house in another state, whereas he could only visit him on vacations or holiday weekends previously; the man who moved to Los Angeles and got his first chance to fulfil an old dream – a visit to Santa Barbara – when his company switched to the 4-day week.

OTHER BENEFITS

In addition to the enjoyment aspect of extra leisure, there are practical benefits for the workingman with a weekday off.

"A big problem for the workingman has always been that so many of the basic services he needs are only available during the hours he has to work," says Ken Andonian, manager of one of the 4day Tire Stores in Los Angeles. "Banks, government agencies, doctors, dentists, all sorts of important places like that are mostly closed on weekends and in the late afternoon. That means that the poor workingman either doesn't get his business taken care of when he needs to, or he takes time off from work, and that hurts his paycheck, and maybe even his standing with his boss. The only other alternative is to let his wife handle a lot of his business. Those of us who are now on the 4-day week just don't have that kind of problem anymore."

Since 4day Tire Stores are open on Thursdays, Fridays, Saturdays, and Sundays, several employees have voiced the complaint: "Yes, it's nice to have all that time off, but I don't get to see my friends much anymore, since they still have regular weekends off."

"It's true," admits Mr. Andonian, "that it was hard to give up weekends when we first worked out this plan. But after a while you really come to realize that you're better off with the extra spare time. I've worked at other tyre stores before this one, and I've never seen such high morale."

HOW ABOUT THE LONG WORK SHIFTS?

The most common complaint from workers who do not profess to be totally satisfied with the 4-day week is that the new work shifts (generally expanded from 8 hours to 9 or 10) are too long and tiring. None of these people (with the exception of one grouchy old lady in her 60's) would admit, however, that they would actually prefer returning to the 5-day week.

The complaints are predictable:

"I get home too late to have a good supper with the family."

"Now I get into the heavy commuter traffic, and it takes me longer to get to and from work."

"Ten hours is too long a day for a working wife. When will I get my housework done?"

"Nine hours is just too long to stand up in one day."

Undoubtedly, the best explanation for this kind of dissatisfaction is the one given by Mr. Doggett of Lawrence Manufacturing that it is just natural for anyone to want to work a shorter shift under almost any circumstances.

One of the most negative remarks came from a secretary at a 4-day company who is not herself on 4-day: "I am not really involved in the 4-day workweek and I hope that it remains that way. If the 4-day week were extended to office workers, I would be forced to take a part-time job instead of a full-time one. How can I cook the meals and keep our home straightened when I had worked all my spare time away? Also, I'm not so sure that I would like my husband to work those hours. He is completely exhausted when he continually has to put in extra hours during the week. The 8-hour workday was originally instituted by men and women who were tired of working every minute of the day. Isn't a 10-hour workday a step backward?"

Obviously, it is harder physically to work 10 hours in a day, but many other workers recently interviewed refuted the argument against longer shifts on the grounds that the extra day off more than makes up for them by providing so much extra rest time in addition to the other benefits.

"I actually feel more rested now," claims one middle-aged man, whose company recently switched to 4-day. "You get involved in so many activities during that 2-day weekend, that you just never got your proper rest like you do now."

"A lot of our people were calling in sick when they were just plain tired," says Miss Lorraine Fraser, Director of Nursing Services at the Roger Williams Hospital in Providence, Rhode Island. The hospital has been experimenting with a modified version of the 4-day week (see Chapter 6), and the fatigue problem was an important reason for changing. "Now we don't have much absenteeism because of fatigue," says Miss Fraser. "Our people don't get so tired anymore because the days off come more frequently now."

The traffic problem is minor by comparison, and was mentioned by only 2 workers – one who complained and another who said that under the new work plan he *misses* the worst traffic.

"And don't forget," adds an executive, "that as far as traffic is concerned, under the 4-day system you have one entire day that becomes freed of any commuting time at all."

The complaint about not having time every day to do housework simply does not stand up against all the raves about having an entire weekday free to do housework, instead of only weekends, as in the past. "The 4-day week is the best thing that's ever come down the pike as far as housewives are concerned," declares one enthusiastic woman.

THE SPENDING FACTOR

One obvious consequence of working fewer days is the extra opportunity for spending money during the additional leisure time. While several persons who were interviewed mentioned spending extra money for beer, betting at the racetrack, and keeping the family entertained, no one seemed upset.

In fact, one executive seems to like the opportunity. "I take my wife out to lunch every Friday," he says. "And that's a lot more interesting than a lot of the business lunches I go to, and it's certainly more enjoyable than having a sandwich at my desk on a busy day. Besides, she deserves it after all these years."

UNION ENTHUSIASM

Only a few of the organizations now on the 4-day workweek have unions in their shops, but the union leaders in those shops definitely like the 4-day week.

For instance, Mrs. Dolores Guinn, the women's union steward for Local No. 8 of the Industrial Workers Union at Dalton Precision, says: "I can't think of one of our people who would want to go back on the 5-day week. If you have a family and work a 5-day week, that 2-day weekend just doesn't give you the time to do much of anything. But the way we have it now [4 days off and 4 on] is great. You can get your housework done and still have some time left over for recreation, or visiting, or whatever you feel like doing."

"The 4-day week is the best thing that's ever happened to us," states Mr. Anthony "Tony" Noce, president of the union at Kyanize Paints, Inc. "With that extra day off the guys seem to work harder on the days that we are here. Even losing our coffee break was all right. We are allowed to take the coffee right to our work stations now, and we wind up drinking more of it than ever before – we just don't lose our momentum."

WORK IS MORE ENJOYABLE FOR SOME

The morale factor has frequently been cited by workers as well as executives as an important product of the 4-day week. "People just seem to enjoy their work more, knowing that they're going to be off a day sooner," says one worker.

"When you walk around and talk to the people on Wednesdays you can sense a definite feeling of excitement," says one supervisor. "It's as if the whole thrust had changed from the idea of 'Thank God it's Friday' to 'Thank God it's Thursday'."

"You somehow seem to work steadier – more efficiently – when you know you're doing the same amount of work in 4 days that you used to do in 5," says another worker. "You just seem to feel better about having all that extra time off."

"The work somehow seems to go faster when you know that you're only working 4 days," says one employee of the 4day Tire Stores. "It's like being able to look forward to a 3-day vacation every week," agrees another.

IMPLICATIONS FOR THE FUTURE

Beyond all the specific testimonials that the 4-day week is better for one reason or another – and despite the small minority who grumble about it – there stands the obvious truth that the 4-day, 40-hour week fulfils a basic desire that is common to most human beings: more free time without a corresponding loss of pay.

The plain fact is that vast numbers of workers currently on 5-day weeks frequently skip a day on the pretence of ill health, and many of the days they do spend on the job are marginally productive.

"In the old days," says an executive of a company on the 4-day week, "when we still worked 5 days, if a guy felt a little lousy or wanted to play golf or go fishing – or just take his wife somewhere – he'd call in sick and then probably feel a little guilty about it. That isn't necessary anymore. Now, the extra day off means that the guy can do that kind of thing on the up and up."

Of course, much of the value that the 4-day week has in producing such attitudes is that it is still unique. Any worker on the 4-day plan is an exception among his peers, and thus his extra day off is truly something special. If every company suddenly switched to 4-day, much of the novelty would quickly wear off.

As one worker put in a recent interview: "The only disadvantage of this here 4-day week that I can think of is that it's got me spoiled; I'll never be able to go back to working 5 days."

4

WORK AND LEISURE: THE REACTIONS OF PEOPLE AT 4-DAY FIRMS
by Riva Poor and James L. Steele

James Steele is a Ph.D. Candidate at the University of Montana where he teaches both statistics and introductory sociology courses. Riva Poor, co-author and editor of this book, majored in social sciences at Bennington College and in Organizational Development at the Sloan School of Management, Massachusetts Institute of Technology.

[This chapter reports the impact of 4-day on working people's lives – both at home and at work. It is based on interviews with employees at the first thirteen firms that the Editor was able to locate.*]

In 1899 Thorstein Veblen published his classic work, *The Theory of the Leisure Class,* in which he examined the life style of the upper class. At that time only the wealthy could afford leisure, but this is no longer so! The shorter workweek that has developed over the past 100 years has had the important social and economic consequence of transforming the working class into a new leisure class. The 4-day workweek further enhances the leisure available to the new leisure class by regrouping many of the hours into a 3-day weekend.

One objective of this study was to find out how employees react to this new leisure and to the companies that provide it. Other purposes included an examination of the effects of the 4-day workweek upon managers, upon employee spending patterns, and upon patterns of use of leisure. In short, what difference does the 4-day week make to people's lives, and how do they feel about it?

*The results obtained here have been duplicated by independent researchers who have since interviewed 4-day workers at some of these firms and at additional 4-day firms.

4 Days, 40 Hours

This study of people at thirteen 4-day firms was conducted in July and August, 1970, through the use of personal interviews (tape recorded, in some cases) and a survey questionnaire (included at the end of this article). The findings confirm and add detail to many of the observations made in previous chapters. Also, the fact that it was an intensive study lends increased credibility to the general proposition reported throughout this book that the 4-day workweek is working well at most places.

The responses of 168 people (including 20 managers) show that the 4-day week has been well received by both labour and management. As noted in previous chapters, managers report that it aids recruitment, cuts down absenteeism and tardiness, practically eliminates labour turnover, and, in general, results in improved company morale. Workers are delighted with the long weekends and the increased time available for family, travel, and many new activities.

While some report disadvantages, the employees of 4-day firms clearly feel that the advantages far outweigh the disadvantages. One hundred and thirty-six of 148 workers report they feel either pleased or very pleased about the 4-day week. Only 12 report feeling: very displeased (2), displeased (5), or indifferent (5).

This high positive proportion (over 92%), like many of the other results reported in this study, is well above the 67% that we can normally expect from the introduction of almost any attempted improvement, regardless of type (The Hawthorne Effect).

Every manager interviewed in this study was pleased (2) or very pleased (18) with the way the 4-day week is working out for him and for his company. When one looks at what the 4-day week is producing for the companies, it is not amazing that so many managers are so pleased. (A separate study by Riva Poor, reported in Chapter 1, which included 14 additional firms, uncovered several managers who indicate they are indifferent or displeased. In fact, in 2 cases, problems with *customers* were so severe that 4-day was discontinued. But the other advantages to the firms and to the employees stated in *this* study are found to hold, even for the firms that discontinued 4-day.)

THE SAMPLE

Managers constitute 12% of the sample. All are males, almost all are 30 years old or over (9 are 40 or over), and 4 are new at their firms. Because the managers' responses are different from the workers' responses in most cases – more positive and more company-oriented

58

– we report their attitudes separately to avoid obscuring the workers' responses.

Workers constitute 88% of the sample (148 people). Fifty-seven per cent are males (84 males and 64 females). Twenty-eight per cent are under 30 years old (41 people) – one third of the males (27) and one fourth of the females (14). About 30% of the workers joined their firms after 4-day began (44 workers). Sixteen are females (11 under 30 years old) and 28 are males (9 under 30).

The 6 supervisors and foremen (2 females) are counted among the workers, because their responses to the questionnaire are more typical of the workers' responses than of the managers'. Almost all of the workers are factory personnel, but there are several each of office, sales, and professional personnel (e.g., quality control).

The firms include manufacturing, service, and retail businesses – 3 of them unionized. Most are located in the greater Boston area, but a few are outside the area, in California, Florida, and Oklahoma.

Whether the responses of this sample are typical of those of the rest of the 4-day workers, we cannot discern. They probably are, though, because they match the responses reported by the managers, in other chapters, and by the other authors who interviewed workers for their reports. The proportions of male and female workers, types of jobs, and so on, are similar. The 13 firms were selected because they were the ones we knew existed at the beginning of the study. (We discovered the other 4-day firms too late to add them to the study.) Almost 700 workers were given a written questionnaire, and received post-paid envelopes so their responses could be sent directly to us. A little over 100 mailed their responses in time to be used in the study; 68 were collected on the spot.

ADVANTAGES AND DISADVANTAGES FOR COMPANIES

Greater Commitment to the Company. One of the greatest benefits for the 4-day firms is an improvement in employees' attitudes towards the firm. Table 1 shows that only 5 of the workers like their company "less" after beginning 4-day, out of 100 workers answering the question. But 46 state they like the company "more". This positive change in attitude may be enough to make any manager ponder the feasibility of the 4-day week.

Both younger and older employees like their company more, although liking the company more is slightly more prevalent among younger workers. Fifty per cent of workers under 30 say they like

TABLE 1. MANY WORKERS REPORT LIKING THEIR COMPANY MORE ON THE 4-DAY WEEK.

Attitudes	Number of Respondents		
	Male	Female	Total
"I like the company *more* now than I did when we were on 5 days."	25	21	46
"I like the company *the same* now as I did when we were on 5 days."	26	23	49
"I like the company *less* now than I did when we were on 5 days."	1	4*	5
Totals	52	48	100

*All factory workers over 40 years old, employed by one firm on a 10-hour-a-day schedule.

their company more, and none likes it less, compared with workers over 30 – 45% like their firms more, but 5% like them less now. Older workers, or workers who have been with a company for a number of years, tend to report liking the company the same. It was a common thing to hear them say in an interview: "I like the company the same – I've been working here for 15 years. I like the 4-day week, but I like the company the same – it's a good company."

The responses of male and female workers are different only in that 4 of the 5 workers who like the firm less now are females. (It should be noted that they all work at the same firm.)

Do the managers recognize accurately how their employees feel about the 4-day week? The managers happily report that the attitude of workers towards their work is better than before 4-day, and that the general morale of the firm is excellent. In a company where there is no basis for comparison (because the firm *began* operations on 4-day) and in 2 companies where managers state that employee attitudes and morale are the same (always excellent), the survey shows that the attitudes and morale of workers is, in fact, very good. In only one firm did the manager's report of employee attitudes overestimate the satisfaction of his workers; this manager reported that the workers were 100% in favour of 4-day, but the actual responses in a sample of 33 out of a few hundred workers and managers show that 25 are pleased, 4 are indifferent, and 4 are displeased. In every other company, the managers either were correct or slightly underestimated the satisfaction of their workers with the 4-day week.

One should recognize that the positive attitude of workers towards the company may reflect a stronger commitment to their 4-day *job*, rather than their 4-day *company*. Our statistics do not make this distinction for us. One worker who says she likes her company more now also states that she probably would quit "if they ever go back to 5 days." The comment may mean she is committed to the job itself, as opposed to the firm. If 4-day jobs were plentiful, and she could choose among 4-day companies, her commitment to the company might diminish or be based on something other than the 4-day workweek. As one manager said: "If all companies did it, we wouldn't have an advantage."

Aids Worker Recruitment. Certainly, until the 4-day workweek is a common phenomenon in American industry, the company that operates on a 4-day schedule has an important advantage in the competition for workers. Table 2 shows that increased leisure as a form of payment is very attractive to workers. This point is demonstrated by the fact that a little more than 3 out of 4 new workers joining firms already on 4-day indicate: "The 4-day week was a very important reason for my joining this firm." Fewer than 1 out of 4 says that it had little to do with their joining, and not even one worker says that the 4-day week is a disadvantage.

Of the 44 new employees who responded to this question, 16 are females and 20 are under 30 years of age. Of the females, 13 out of 16 state the 4-day week was an important reason for joining the firm (81% compared to 67% of the males). Several women say they

TABLE 2. MOST NEW WORKERS STATE THAT 4-DAY WAS A VERY IMPORTANT REASON FOR THEIR JOINING THE FIRM, AND NONE SAYS 4-DAY WAS A DISADVANTAGE.

Attitudes	Number of Respondents		
	Male	Female	Total
"The 4-day week was a *very important* reason for my joining this firm."	21	13	34
"The 4-day week had *little* to do with my joining this firm."	7	3	10
"The 4-day week was a *disadvantage* in joining this firm."	0	0	0
Totals	28	16	44

returned to work because the 4-day week gives them more time at home for family and housework. Of the group under 30 years old, 16 out of 20 say 4-day was important to their decision (80%, compared to 75% for the over-30 group). The long weekend is the most attractive feature of the 4-day week for this group.

Three of the 4 new managers say 4-day was important to their joining. Seven of 16 continuing managers say they like the firm more now, and none of the managers like it less than before although in some cases they have some inconveniences on the new schedule. Ten managers indicate that recruitment is now easier, 2 find it to be the same as on 5-day, and the other has no basis for comparison because they have always had 4-day. Together, these facts illustrate that the 4-day week is a boon to companies that find it difficult to compete in the labour market.

Disadvantages for the Company. The disadvantages of the 4-day week are hard to find. Ten of the 20 managers mention no disadvantages for themselves nor for their company. A few managers mention problems with work scheduling, particularly when 4-day is first implemented, or recount difficulties they had educating customers to the fact that they simply would not be open on Fridays, for instance.

Some managers report having to pay for more overtime work now, but they say it with a smile. As one manager put it: "Anybody knows that if you've got the orders and you need to work your people overtime, you can afford to pay them." And an important advantage of the 4-day schedule is that it provides an *extra* day for overtime when it is needed.

MOONLIGHTING AND OVERTIME

Moonlighting interests many managers. To some companies it is an advantage, and to some a disadvantage. One manager remarked: "If they are caught, they are fired. It takes too much out of them." At other companies moonlighting is positively encouraged. For example, men who work the night shift at one company are permitted to work a day shift as well if they desire – at a guaranteed salary of $200 per week per shift. Despite the differences in managements' attitudes, we found no significant difference in the incidence of moonlighting at firms that oppose it and those that encourage it.

Second-job holders in American industry usually number about 5% of the labour force. A comparable percentage of the 4-day workers (4%) state they held a second job during the 5-day work-week. But the figure more than quadrupled when workers began the 4-day week. Twenty-five out of 141 of the respondents (17%) indicate that they now hold more than one job. There is reason to suspect that even this high figure does not accurately report the prevalence of moonlighting among 4-day workers. One manager states he would be surprised if fewer than 25% of his workers have second jobs. And when workers were asked in interviews about the moonlighting of fellow workers, their responses always suggested a higher number of second-job holders than indicated in the questionnaire survey.

Moonlighting is more prevalent among male workers (20% of the males moonlight on 4-day), but it increased among the females too. While only 2 females report moonlighting on the 5-day week, 6 of 64 report moonlighting on 4-day, a jump from 3 to 10% – 5 times higher than the national average for women on 5-day (2%).

The form that moonlighting takes among 4-day workers is varied. In addition to extra shift work, some companies provide their employees with the opportunity for extensive overtime, ranging as high as 20 hours a week. Many workers consider this an important advantage of 4-day. Some have similar jobs at other firms, a few have their own businesses (especially farms), and others serve as part-time policemen or firemen.

What is the relationship between the 4-day workweek and moonlighting? Although there are problems of defining moonlighting, gathering accurate data, and isolating the many variables at work, it is evident that the 4-day week contributes significantly to moonlighting. But Professor Paul Mott points out that while the shorter workweek is a major factor in contributing to the prevalence of moonlighting in our society, other factors are important too, such as, the presence of shift work in the community, high economic aspirations of the workers, and inadequate opportunities in the community to exercise free time. Especially important, we think, is his statement "the worker must have adequate physical energy and the appropriate psychological traits if he is to be a successful moonlighter."* Since no pay cuts are involved and no other factor emerges to correlate with moonlighting, it appears that 4-day itself makes these attributes *operative* in an additional set of people, amounting to over 13% of our sample. The implication, too, is that the longer days of the 4-day schedule are not unduly fatiguing for many workers, including females – in fact, quite the reverse.

The long-range effect of 4-day on moonlighting is difficult to

*Paul E. Mott, "Hours of Work and Moonlighting," in Clyde E. Dankert, *et. al.* (eds.), *Hours of Work* (New York: Harper and Row, 1965), pp. 76–94.

predict. The increased spending reported below could lead to increased moonlighting. At any rate, at present, about 80% of 4-day workers use their new time for leisure, rather than to gain additional income!

ADVANTAGES AND DISADVANTAGES FOR EMPLOYEES

Bunching of Leisure. The workers are overwhelmingly pleased with the 4-day workweek although there is a slight, but definite difference between male and female reactions. Although most men and women have positive responses to 4-day, more men report a greater degree of satisfaction from 4-day. Of the 96% men pleased or very pleased about 4-day, 82% are *very* pleased; of the 92% of women pleased or very pleased, only 75% are *very* pleased.

Worker satisfaction with 4-day stems primarily from the leisure advantages it offers, rather than from the longer hours of labour on the job each day. Most workers are delighted with the bunching of their free time, inasmuch as it makes the leisure hours more useful for old and new activities. The most frequent response to the open-ended question, "Please name one or more advantages . . . to the 4-day week," is simply "the long weekend!" Others state that they like the extra time it gives them with their families, and some say that it provides a weekday for conducting personal business, such as keeping appointments with doctor or dentist, or going to the bank. A number of women say they like 4-day because it gives them an extra day for housework while still leaving them a 2-day weekend. (This may explain why the women are somewhat less enthusiastic than the men – most of them work second jobs at home.) Table 3 shows the frequency with which advantages and disadvantages are cited by the 4-day workers.

Little Negative Reaction. Eighty-seven of the 141 labour respondents cite no disadvantages, reporting advantages only. Forty-six cite both advantages and disadvantages, and only 8 report no advantages. Although it is the older workers who have all but one of the negative reactions to 4-day (one worker under 30 says he is indifferent to it), oddly enough it is the older workers who report the fewest disadvantages. Almost 65% cite no disadvantages at all, compared to 54% of the younger group.

The disadvantages mentioned most frequently are "longer hours per day" and "too little rest time during the day." Managers and

TABLE 3. THE WORKERS CITE MANY MORE ADVANTAGES OF THE 4-DAY WEEK THAN DISADVANTAGES.

Advantages and Disadvantages	Number of Citations*
ADVANTAGES	
Long weekend or more leisure	65
More time for family (excludes travel to relatives)	25
More time for personal business and errands	14
More time for housework	11
More overtime	11
More time to putter around house or garden	9
More time for travel (includes visits to relatives)	8
More time for shopping	4
Miscellaneous reasons	13
Total	160
DISADVANTAGES	
Longer day is fatiguing	23
Loss of former job or pay benefits** (includes loss of overtime)	11
Longer day disaccommodates meals, car pools, or other schedules	5
Work load is high on the day after the weekend	3
Miscellaneous reasons	9
Total	51

*87 of the 141 respondents (59%) cite advantages only, while 8 respondents (5%) cite disadvantages only.
**The bonus system imposes a large penalty on those who are late or absent from work without a bona fide excuse.

foremen also mention having to work harder the first day after the weekend. One manager interviewed on a Monday morning pointed to a large stack of mail and remarked: "This is what Monday is like on the 4-day week!"

One significant factor bears mentioning again. Most of the negative attitudes towards the 4-day week are reported by workers of a single company. The reasons for this negative feeling are varied. It reflects discontent with the bonus system which has the effect of a rate cut for those who are late or absent without an important excuse. It also reflects some disapproval of the shift system employed by the company and the manner in which overtime is arranged. It is only fair to point out, however, that 75% of the respondents from this company state they are pleased with 4-day, and also our sample from the company is small.

Some writers have suggested that with increased free time the average worker would be troubled by boredom. This study indicates otherwise. Only 6 out of 168 people report being bored with free time. (Four are males, one is a manager, and none is under 30 years old.) In contrast, 2 report they were bored on 5-day. With the arrival of 4-day, one got a second job and is no longer bored. The discussion (below) of workers' activities during their new free time indicates that most workers do not experience a problem in finding new outlets for their time and energies on 4-day. Whether they would be bored on an even shorter week is a different issue.

Adjustment Problems. In an attempt to learn if the *transition* from a 5-day workweek to a 4-day workweek presents problems for the workers and managers, they were asked if there were problems in adjusting to the 4-day week and, if there were, to give an example. Of 142 labour respondents, only 37 state they experienced adjustment problems. The problem mentioned by nearly half of these workers is "longer hours", but several add that this was just "in the beginning". Some mention that they had to adjust to standing on their feet extra time, but one worker volunteers "O.K. now!"

Female workers report more adjustment problems than male workers; 23 of 61 female workers answering the question (38%) say there were problems in adjusting to 4-day, and 14 of 81 male workers (17%) indicate adjustment problems. But these are the females over 30 years old. Of the workers under 30, 73% report no adjustment problems (the same for females as males). Only 15% of the older males report adjustment problems, while 40% of the older females report problems, and 35% of the managers (7 out of 20) do so as well. It seems that the problems are more related to a person's functions and responsibilities than to age or sex alone.

The thing that stands out is that most adjustment problems are experienced early in the transition and tend to disappear with time while, most importantly, most workers report no adjustment problems at all (74%). Adjustment problems occur primarily with the more strenuous jobs and at the firms that schedule the longest workdays (10 hours, rather than $9\frac{1}{2}$ or 9 hours).

Fatigue. Fourteen per cent of the employees (about $\frac{1}{2}$ male, $\frac{1}{2}$ female) cite fatigue as a disadvantage of the 4-day workweek – which generally has a longer workday. But despite citing fatigue as a drawback, almost every one of these 23 employees is pleased or very pleased with 4-day. Also, as mentioned above, 19 additional employees obtained second jobs after 4-day started, an increase of moonlighters from 4 to 17% of the work force.

It appears that fatigue from the longer workday – which might be expected to be a big problem – is not a big problem for almost all of the workers. Why? For one thing, the new workday is not much longer than before, while the total hours in the workweek is now somewhat reduced. Secondly, morale is now higher. But perhaps most important, the weekend is now 50% longer.

The difference that a longer weekend makes may be explained by a look at the problems found with the shorter weekend of the 5-day week. The following is from an article headed "Five-day Workweek Too Long, Study Claims" (*Boston Sunday Globe*, August, 23 1970):

Associated Press

OSLO, Norway – A Norwegian medical study says the 5-day week fails to provide a relaxing weekend, and people need longer vacations . . .

The study [by a medical association committee] quotes an expert on leisure as saying: "Medically viewed, the five-day week is meaningless, even absurd. It is injurious to health."

The committee chairman, Odd Bjerke, observed: "In a [two-day] week-end people don't get the relaxation they need. The rush to use the leisure hours produces a stress situation like the rest of the week.'

It appears that the 4-day workweek's longer weekend more than makes up for whatever additional fatigue, if any, may result from its usually longer workday.

Employee Evaluation. With all its advantages and disadvantages, its problems in adjusting, and the changes it causes in the everyday lives of the workers, the 4-day workweek is appreciated more *after* experience with it than before. This is seen in the change in the workers' opinions between the time they first heard about 4-day and after they have had experience with it.

Eighty-nine per cent of the workers (125 out of 141) say they favoured the 4-day week initially. Ninety-seven per cent of this group (121 out of 125) indicate they are pleased or very pleased *after* working the 4-day week. Only 1 person reports being indifferent and only 3 say they are displeased. (One complains: "Now I get home too late at night to have supper with my family after $9\frac{1}{2}$ hours a day.")

Of the 16 people who report that they did *not* favour the 4-day week initially, 8 say they are pleased or very pleased now, and 2 report they are indifferent. Five continue to be displeased and 1 gives no opinion. In short, acceptance of 4-day is a little higher after experience with it than before it has been tried – 92% favour 4-day afterwards, compared with 89% beforehand. (Managers' attitudes are omitted here since they are all in favour of 4-day both before and after experience with it.)

While these statistics indicate a very favourable attitude towards 4-day, they certainly do not convey the enthusiasm that 4-day workers express in conversation. An example of this enthusiasm is expressed by one excited young worker who said in an interview: "The 4-day week has been the turning point in the life of my family. Why, it almost made a Christian out of me! I used to go to the tavern every Friday after work, but now I've stopped drinking and smoking – and I spend the weekends with my family. I take care of the kids on Fridays now, and give the wife a chance to go shopping. Then on Saturdays, we go camping. I was a Green Beret in the Army, and I like to teach the kids woodlore and that kind of stuff. . . . The 4-day week is great, man!"

That the 4-day week *is* very important to most 4-day workers is clearly seen by the positive responses of both males and females, regardless of age. As one manager put it: "You probably couldn't get this high a percentage of our workers to agree on anything else. But they like the 4-day week!"

CHANGES IN PEOPLE'S LIVES

New Spending Patterns. During the pilot interviews with workers it was discovered that many were spending more money since beginning the 4-day week. In an effort to discover how widespread was the increase in spending, employees were asked: "Do you find that you are spending more money for free-time activities since you began the 4-day week?" One third of the workers (44 of 137) replied "yes." One worker said that the problem became so severe for his family that he and his wife "had to sit down and talk it over". They began to plan their activities in order to keep their spending within limits.

In his case the increased spending resulted from too many weekend trips, but other items are mentioned by other workers. Increased spending for recreation in general is the item mentioned most frequently. Travelling is cited often, as are such things as eating out, going to the beach, boating, dating, and shopping. Nine people purchased vacation homes. This figure appears very high considering that most have experienced 4-day for less than a year.

Although two thirds of the workers do not report increased spending, it seems likely that the *patterns* of spending for almost all

68

employees are now changed somewhat, because most report spending their *time* differently (reported in the next section).

Increased spending seems to be some function of age. None of the 6 respondents over 60 years of age reports increased spending, but one fourth of those 30 to 50 years old report increased spending, 40% of those under 30 report increased spending, and 60% of those 50 to 60 years old spend more (mostly the men). Spending is also a function of income level: 65% of the managers say they spend more money now.

Changes in Leisure Activities. One way in which the 4-day workweek is effecting changes in the lives and the spending habits of workers is seen in the ways workers use their increased free time. The workers were asked to indicate on a checklist both those activities in which they regularly participated when they worked a 5-day week and also the activities in which they participate regularly during the 4-day week. All free-time activities increase with the increase in usable leisure time that comes with its regrouping. The results are shown in Table 4 (on page 70).

One important leisure activity for workers is recuperation. Nearly 70% of the workers say they spend some of their new free time resting, relaxing, and loafing. The figure is far greater than the 22% reporting this as a regular activity on 5-day. Whether this recuperative activity derives from the pressure of the 4-day workweek or is simply an activity that workers enjoy and can afford to increase with extra time, one is unable to say. It is probably a bit of both.

Workers increase their "creative" activities (hobbies, reading, and returning to school), and 85% report that 4-day gives them more time to work around the house.

Seventy-five per cent report spending more time with their families. It is very likely that the 4-day week will contribute to the strengthening of family ties in many homes. Thirteen women say that they like the 4-day week because it gives them more time with their families, and 10 males report this advantage. (Several women report that they would not have returned to work but for the 4-day week, because they want more time at home with their children than the 5-day week permits.) The extra day at home will enable many fathers to play a more important role in the family and the lives of their children.

Another example of 4-day's strengthening family ties is that one of the largest per cent increases in activities is visiting relatives (121%). A foreman told how his wife had arranged to get her own job at

TABLE 4. ALL LEISURE ACTIVITIES INCREASE WHEN THE SAME EMPLOYEES GO FROM 5-DAY TO 4-DAY WORKWEEKS.

Activities	Numbers			Per Cent Increase on 4-Day
	Cited on 5-Day	Cited on 4-Day	Increase on 4-Day	
1. Work around the house	94	116	22	23
2. Spend time with family	76	102	26	34
3. Travel	29	73	44	152
4. Go to ballgames, fights, hockey games, etc.	19	38	19	100
5. Fishing and hunting	22	43	21	95
6. Other hobbies	22	49	27	123
7. Engage in some form of athletics (bowling, golf, baseball, etc.)	26	43	17	65
8. Read more	16	41	25	156
9. Go back to school or learned a trade	7	8	1	14
10. Active in school boards, P.T.A., Boy Scouts, etc.	9	14	5	56
11. Got another part time job	5	24	19	283
12. Joined social club	6	11	5	83
13. Engaged in political action work	2	6	4	200
14. Rest, relax, loaf, etc.	26	96	70	269
15. Swimming, boating	16	67	51	319
16. Work on car	17	39	22	129
17. Church activities	9	14	5	56
18. Bought or buying vacation home	2	6	4	200
19. Bored with free time	2	5	3	150
20. Visit relatives	28	62	34	121
21. Watch television a lot	27	44	17	63
22. Attend movies, theater, concerts, etc.	22	44	22	100
Respondents citing at least one regular activity	118	138	20	17

another firm onto a 4-day schedule. Now they visit their son and his family every other weekend, a trip of over 300 miles. Before the 4-day week they were able to visit them only once every 2 or 3 months.

The most striking increase is reported in the category of participant activities (travel, fishing and hunting, other hobbies, athletics, swimming and boating). More than half of the workers state that they travel regularly now, compared to one fourth beforehand. The vast changes that would result from increased travel if the 4-day week were to become widely accepted are difficult to imagine. One can only speculate that the demand for recreational facilities and travel services would mushroom beyond our wildest current imaginings.

The large per cent increase in workers reporting regular participation in swimming and boating (319%) is one of several items indicating that the new leisure class wants recreative action. Regular participation in athletics showed a 65% increase, fishing and hunting increased by 95%, and participation in hobbies was up by 123%. An avid camper exclaimed: "The 4-day week is the greatest! Thursday afternoon when I get home, the wife and kids are packed and ready to go. Thursday night we are in Maine or Vermont or the Adirondacks. When everybody else is fighting the commuter traffic Friday morning, I'm lounging around the camp, or fishing in the lake. And we don't have to fight the Friday crowd for a campsite!"

Although 4-day workers seem action-oriented as individuals, they also indicate that they can be spectators. Compared to 20% on the 5-day week, 30% state that they regularly attend each of the following: ballgames, fights, hockey games, etc. (a 100% increase); movies, theatre, concerts, etc. (also a 100% increase); and watch television a lot (a 63% increase).

The thing which does not seem to "turn on" the 4-day workers is participation in voluntary associations. There is only a small increase in the number who report joining social clubs, working in service organizations, and engaging in political and church activities. (But these are in some cases large per cent increases.)

When one attempts to correlate free-time activities with variables such as particular type of 4-day schedule, job category, firm, or shift, one finds no significant relationships. Whatever the type of worker, and whatever his circumstances, he finds plenty to do with the increased usable leisure time provided by the 4-day week.

Actual vs. Anticipated Use of Leisure Time. In an article in which he discussed the effects of automation upon leisure time,* William Faunce suggested that with increased leisure time workers would probably seek more creative and service-oriented outlets for their energies, inasmuch as there would be a decrease in the proportion of their free time needed to recuperate from work. He further hypothesized that more free time would enable workers to acquire the skills necessary for engaging in participant activities, resulting in a decrease of participation in spectator activities. In an attempt to test his hypotheses, Faunce conducted a study of automobile production-line workers in which the workers were asked how they might use increased free time if it were to become available through longer vacations of a shorter workweek.

*William A. Faunce, "Automation and Leisure," in Erwin O. Smigel (ed.), *Work and Leisure* (New Haven: College and University Press, 1963), pp. 85–96.

The present study of 4-day workers provided an opportunity to compare Faunce's hypothetical results with those collected from actual experience. There are difficulties in comparing the 2 groups, however. Faunce's study was of workers in automated automobile manufacturing plants, considered by some social psychologists the most alienated workers in American industry. To the extent that the samples were drawn from different populations, the comparison is weak. To the extent that the comparison may provide insight into *actual* vs. *anticipated* use of increased leisure, it is of value. The responses of all 4-day workers are included in Table 5, inasmuch as there was no significant difference in free-time activities reported by those on continuous process and other types of jobs.

TABLE 5. PROPOSED USE OF INCREASED LEISURE TIME DIFFERS FROM ACTUAL USE. PEOPLE SPEND MORE TIME ON UNORGANIZED OR RELAXED ACTIVITIES AND LESS TIME ON ORGANIZED OR DISCIPLINED ONES.

| | Per Cents | |
| | Faunce Study (N=125) | 4-Day Study (N=138) |
Activities		
1. Work around the house	96.8	84.1
2. Spend time with family	76.8	73.9
3. Travel	53.6	52.9
4. Go to ballgames, fights, hockey games, etc.	48.8	27.5
5. Fishing and hunting	42.4	31.2
6. Other hobbies	25.6	35.6
7. Engage in some form of athletics (bowling, golf, baseball, etc.)	24.8	31.2
8. Read more	24.8	29.7
9. Go back to school or learned a trade	19.2	5.8
10. Active in school boards, P.T.A., Boy Scouts, etc.	17.6	10.1
11. Got another part time job	16.8	16.7
12. Joined social club	15.2	8.0
13. Engaged in political action work	12.8	4.3
14. Rest, relax, loaf, etc.	11.2	69.6
15. Swimming, boating	4.8	48.6
16. Work on car	2.4	28.3
17. Church activities	1.6	10.1

Note: Items 18 through 22 included in Table 4 are omitted here, because they were not studied by Faunce.

The table shows that 4-day workers somewhat exceed in action the increase in creative activities the workers in the Faunce study anticipated. Whereas 26% of the auto workers said they would spend time with hobbies, 36% of the 4-day workers state hobbies are a regular activity. As to reading more, the results are nearly identical: nearly 25% of the respondents in the Faunce study indicated they would read more, and nearly 30% of the 4-day workers report reading more.

The creative category "go back to school or learn a trade" provides a negative difference between anticipated and real experience. Almost 20% of the auto workers said they might go back to school or learn a trade, but only about 6% of the 4-day employees indicate that they attempt this. Furthermore, most of these respondents are managers, or are students working their way through school. One can only conclude that the "best laid plans of mice and men" too often go astray.

Excluding church activities, the 4-day workers fall short of fulfilling the expected participation in organizations that might be considered service-oriented. Ten per cent of the 4-day workers report they participate in school boards, P.T.A., Boy Scouts, etc., compared to nearly 18% of the workers in the Faunce study who anticipated participation in such organizations. Whereas 13% of the Faunce workers predicted they would engage in political activity, only about 4% of the 4-day workers report this as a regular activity. Although the 4-day workers did increase their participation in organizations, they did not attain the high levels anticipated by the workers in the Faunce study. Although the 2 groups are different, one suspects that the actual use of increased leisure by workers in the Faunce study would also fail to measure up to their anticipated use.

Faunce was correct in predicting that workers with more free time would engage in participant activities to a greater extent than in spectator activities. (This increase may have nothing to do with the job's degree of automation, though.) The most striking difference between the 2 groups was in the number reporting interest in swimming and boating. Only about 5% of the workers in Faunce's study indicated that they would engage in swimming and boating, but 49% of the 4-day workers state that this is one of their free-time activities. (Perhaps geographical differences account for some of this variation.)

While participant activity does increase among workers with increased leisure, spectator activity also shows a marked increase over the 5-day level, while education and service-oriented endeavours do not match expectations. Again, it must be stressed that the groups are different, that the time is different, and that the use of leisure may change as employees experience it over longer periods. But the theme seems to be that the workers choose unorganized, relaxing activities over organized or disciplined ones, and that the use of leisure may not be a function of type of job.

Managers' Use of Leisure Time. Contrary to what some might expect, most managers also report having increased free time as a result of the 4-day workweek. In some companies there is no increased leisure for top management, while in others the 4-day week applies to everyone, or the managers shift their times so that each gets a long weekend once a month.

Also contrary to what one might expect, there is little difference in the overall pattern of use of leisure by managers and by labour. Managers do engage more in "creative" activities (hobbies and reading). The number of managers reporting that they read more compared to the number of workers who do so is significantly different at the .01 confidence level. (Another statistically significant difference at the .01 level is in the greater number of managers who report buying vacation homes. Three out of 12 managers [25%] report buying vacation homes, compared to only 6 of 141 workers [4%].) In participant and spectator activities, management and labour are very similar although labour indicates a higher interest in television and movies. What differences there are are probably more a function of educational level than of type of job.

Informal Group Ties. An interesting speculation about the 4-day week is the potential change it may create in the informal relationships of workers on the job. In some 4-day companies the official coffee break was eliminated; furthermore, most employees work only 36 to 38 hours now (but are paid for 40 hours). When one considers these factors, together with management's desire to increase or maintain the previous level of output, it seems that one result of the 4-day workweek could be a lessening of informal group ties due to a reduction of free time at work.

The fact that most 4-day companies report increased output for fewer hours indicates what every manager already knows: that very few companies operate at optimum capacity. Although many variables are at work, it is obvious that the old production norms established by informal consensus among the workers may have been broken by the 4-day workweek in some companies. As one worker put it: "When you've got that carrot [the 3-day weekend] hanging out there, you just work harder!"

This is not to imply that 4-day is some insidious plot by management to get more out of labour. On the contrary, 4-day is mutually desirable for both management and labour. If labour *can* maintain or increase production, and is *willing* to do so for the extra day off, then it is in the best interests of both management and labour for management to provide the opportunity. But it is still too early to say what the long-range effects upon the informal structure of 4-day companies will be. The increased morale reported may mean the interactions are more intensive as well as more positive, instead of reduced and negative.

Alienation and the 4-Day Workweek. A subject of concern to some American sociologists during the past 15 years has been the so-called "alienated worker". The problem was first brought into prominence by Karl Marx, although his purposes in dealing with alienation were different from those which motivate today's industrial sociologists.

What then do we mean by the alienation of labour? First, that the work he performs is extraneous to the worker, that is, it is not personal to him, is not part of his nature; therefore he does not fulfil himself in work, but actually denies himself; feels miserable rather than content, cannot freely develop his physical and mental powers, but instead becomes physically exhausted and mentally debased. Only while not working can the worker be himself; for while at work he experiences himself as a stranger. Therefore only during leisure hours does he feel at home. While at work he feels homeless. His labour . . . satisfies no spontaneous creative urge, but is only a means for the satisfaction of wants which have nothing to do with work.*

Although we did not set out to study alienation among 4-day workers, the results of our study suggest that workers on the 4-day workweek may be less alienated from their jobs than 5-day workers. We make a distinction here between *job* alienation and *work* alienation. It is possible for a worker to be alienated from work, to view it as a necessary evil in life, to find no sense of achievement or satisfaction through it, and yet to be strongly committed to his job. This is exactly the impression we gained about many workers on the 4-day workweek. It seemed clear that some feel a sense of alienation about work generally. But trade their 4-day job for a 5-day job? Not on your life! Alienated from work they may be; but alienated from their 4-day job or 4-day company, they certainly are not!

*Karl Marx, "Alienated Labor", in Eric and Mary Josephson (eds.), *Man Alone: Alienation in Modern Society* (New York: Dell, 1962), p. 97.

Leisure – A New Salvation. For many workers the increased free time permitted by the 4-day workweek may be a kind of salvation.* The salvation of which we speak is the need every person has to justify his existence, his reason for being, both to himself and to the significant others in his life. (Essentially, the significant others for us are those persons whose opinions and judgements we value highly.)

It isn't difficult for a manager or a skilled craftsman to justify his existence in terms of his work. He is an important member of the management team, or he is an artistic, highly skilled labourer, and respected for it. With the increase in automation and the spread of bureaucracy it is increasingly difficult for some workers to realize their needs for recognition and achievement in their work (Theory Y management notwithstanding).

Many workers may have turned to leisure activities to justify their existence to their significant others. At the lake cottage or mountain retreat they are somebody! In their boat, camping trailer, motor home, or the motel pool they are for real! In his free-time activities, the workingman is accepted as he is, something he seldom experiences on his job. No longer is he a cog; he has become a wheel. He is important to himself and to the others to whom he desires to be important. In short, it is in his leisure that he may find salvation.

It is through increasing this leisure that capitalism may have created the answer to the problem cited by Marx. Our society is wealthy enough to permit an emerging Leisure Ethic to replace the declining Protestant Work Ethic for the so-called workingman, member of the new leisure class.

IS IT WORTH IT?

In conclusion, what are we to say about the 4-day workweek? The effects upon the company are very positive. It results in a more positive attitude among employees, and aids recruitment. Most companies increase production and improve their service to customers. Absenteeism and worker turnover decline or are eliminated, and the attitude and general morale of the workers are excellent. The disadvantages are few and seem to appear mainly in the period of transition.

Employees are delighted with the new leisure, because the bunching of free time provides opportunity for activities that otherwise

*Our thinking at this point has been encouraged by Dr. Raymond L. Gold of the University of Montana.

would not be possible – including just resting, relaxing, and loafing more. While many workers report spending more money for free-time activities, most do not see this as a disadvantage. They report that more time is now spent with their families, working around the house, and engaging in participant and creative leisure activities. They are enjoying life more. That the change was worth it for them is undeniable. They could not be more pleased, and many jokingly ask: "When are we going to 3 days?"

The fact that every manager reports being satisfied with the 4-day

---

CONFIDENTIAL   CONFIDENTIAL   CONFIDENTIAL
(Please feel free to write on the back of the questionnaire)

1. How do you feel about the 4-day workweek? Please check the word or phrase which __best__ describes your feelings about the 4-day workweek:
   ___ very pleased   ___ displeased
   ___ pleased   ___ very displeased
   ___ indifferent   ___ no opinion

2. Please name one or more advantage and disadvantage to the 4-day week:
   Advantages: _____

   Disadvantages: _____

3. NOTE: This question is __only__ for people who were employed by the company when it changed from 5 days to 4 days.
   Please check the statement which __best__ describes your feelings about your company:
   ___ I like the company __more__ now than I did when we were on 5 days.
   ___ I like the company __the same__ now as I did when we were on 5 days.
   ___ I like the company __less__ now than I did when we were on 5 days.

4. NOTE: This question is __only__ for new employees and for people employed by firms which have always been on 4 days.
   Please check the statement which __best__ describes your feelings about your company:
   ___ The 4-day week was a very important reason for my joining this firm.
   ___ The 4-day week had little to do with my joining this firm.
   ___ The 4-day week was a disadvantage in joining this firm.

YES NO
___ ___ 5. Did you favor the 4-day week when you first heard about it?
___ ___ 6. If you did not favor it, did you feel that it might result in a salary cut or worker layoff? Some other reason?
___ ___ 7. Were there problems in adjusting to the 4-day workweek? If yes, please give an example: _____

8. Do you find that you spend more money for free time activities since you began the 4-day week? If yes, please name two things for which you spend more money: 1. _____ 2. _____

9. Below is a checklist of free time activities. Please check __every__ activity in which you __regularly participated__ during the 5-day workweek. Then check __every__ activity in which you __regularly participate__ during the 4-day workweek.

5-Day	4-Day	ACTIVITY	5-Day	4-Day	ACTIVITY
		1. Work around the house			11. Got another part time job
		2. Spend time with family			12. Joined social club
		3. Travel			13. Engaged in political action work
		4. Go to ballgames, fights, hockey games, etc.			14. Rest, relax, loaf, etc.
		5. Fishing and hunting			15. Swimming, boating
		6. Other hobbies			16. Work on car
		7. Engage in some form of athletics (bowling, golf, baseball, etc.)			17. Church activities
					18. Bought or buying vacation home
		8. Read more			19. Bored with free time
		9. Go back to school or learned a trade			20. Visit relatives
		10. Active in school boards, P.T.A., Boy Scouts, etc.			21. Watch television alot
					22. Attend movies, theater, concerts, etc.

10. What is your job(e.g., factory worker, foreman, manager)? _____
    ___ Male ___ Female   Please check your age group: ___ Under 30
                                                  ___ 30-40
                                                  ___ 40-50
                                                  ___ 50-60
                                                  ___ Over 60

THANK YOU VERY MUCH!

Work and Leisure Questionnaire

week, that they do not anticipate any erosion of the gains they have made, and that they would recommend it to other companies is "proof in the eating" that the 4-day workweek has been worth the change for the companies that have tried it. The most threatening disadvantage to most managers is the fact that the 4-day workweek is being adopted by more and more companies. This is a prospect they do not relish!

5

AN INDUSTRIAL PIONEER RESCUED BY THE 4-DAY WEEK
by L. Erick Kanter

L. Erick Kanter, author of Chapter 3, was a Naval Officer in Saigon and at the Pentagon, where he produced Navy publicity movies. He has covered such things as Klan rallies in the South; and is currently working on a novel about his Saigon experiences.

[Lawrence Manufacturing, the subject of this chapter, used 4-day to solve a problem experienced by firms all around the world. Although located in an area of exceptionally high unemployment, its business was being choked by the firm's inability to recruit enough workers to get the work done – until 4-day was tried as an incentive.]

What do you do with a famous and once-thriving company when a changing economy and new social realities are making it more and more difficult for you to meet production quotas, and you have already seen many of your neighbouring competitors relocate or shut down?

That was the dilemma facing Lewis C. Doggett, general manager of Lawrence Manufacturing, a 142-year-old textile mill in Lowell, Massachusetts, in early 1969, as he pondered the squeeze being put on his company by competition from mills in the southern United States and by an increasing difficulty in hiring enough workers to keep his plant at full efficiency because of the low regard that many Lowell area residents had for textile work.

Happily, however, Lawrence has not had to move South, nor will it be forced to go out of business as some of its Lowell neighbours have done. The company's situation has been reversed in less than a year. What happened? Primarily, Lawrence Mfg. has discovered - and learned how to utilize – the 4-day workweek.

THE GOOD OLD DAYS

For a century-and-a-half, American school children have learned that the Industrial Revolution was the prime force in raising the fledgling nation to superpower status, and that it was in the once-peaceful and picturesque river valleys of New England that the revolution got its start with the introduction of textile mills and mass production.

And nowhere were the marvels – as well as the evils – of the new Industrial Age illustrated more vividly than in Lowell, which was laid out along the shores of the Merrimack River some 30 miles northwest of Boston for the specific purpose of becoming a textile centre. A series of canals were dug to provide the mills with water power from nearby Pawtucket Falls on the Merrimack, and local boosters were thus moved to hail Lowell as "The Venice of America", despite some criticism from moralists that the "Lowell Girls" (recruited from the farms and hamlets of New England to run the spindles and looms) were more indicative of moral decline than economic progress.

Seeds of Decay. Even though most of the mills did a thriving business well into the twentieth century, the passing years saw the planting of seeds of decay that would eventually result in the collapse of much of New England's textile production.

The dormitories housing the Lowell Girls and their educational and social training classes gradually gave way to tenements crowded with entire families, who toiled long, arduous hours in the mills for near-starvation wages. Consequently, mill work acquired a bad image and only the lack of adequate jobs in other industries enabled the mills to maintain an ample labour supply and keep their spindles and looms humming.

To further complicate matters, the mills were generally managed by company "treasurers", who lived in Boston and rarely inspected their plant sites personally. Commission agents in Boston and New York, who worried more about their own profits than mill efficiency, frequently took orders for products that their mills were least well-equipped to produce.

The Last Hurrah. Textile production in Lowell reached its apex during the Roaring 20's. More than 1,000,000 cotton spindles and 24,000 looms were turning out ginghams, denims, and chambrays at a record clip. And like the stock market, nobody thought there was any way for mill production to go but up. But the Depression, and changing times, soon transformed optimism into despair. Some mills went bankrupt. Others moved to the cheap labour supply of the South, while some – such as Lawrence Manufacturing – stayed fiscally afloat by gearing production to the new realities of the marketplace.

In 1926, Lawrence Manufacturing had been the world's largest producer of long-handled underwear. By the early 1950's the decreasing popularity of that product and the rapidly increasing use of vinyl upholstery in automobiles and other areas had caused Lawrence to switch entirely to the production of knit backing for the new vinyl.

The building of an electronics plant by Raytheon Corporation near Lowell during World War II signalled the beginning of another new trend that would provide even greater problems for what remained of the textile industry – the mushrooming of the electronics industry in the western and northwestern suburbs of Boston. Even though the primitive working conditions of the previous century no longer existed in the mills, the memory lingered. Besides that, textile mill work was still physically demanding and dirty by comparison to what was required of semi-skilled workers in the sterile, laboratory-like atmosphere of the new electronics plants. Also, electronics was new and exciting – space age stuff. The very identification with history made textile work less desirable.

The Labour Dilemma. During the 1950's and 60's the few remaining textile mills in Lowell were caught in a complicated trap. The newer mills in the South – blessed with ample and cheaper labour – were providing deadly competition in the textile market, while the rapid expansion of the electronics industry in the Lowell area was leading up to a point in the mid-1960's when the textile mills were no longer able to compete adequately in the labour market. It was not just a matter of the price of labour; it was also a question of hiring – and keeping – enough labour to keep production high enough to meet orders.

"The textile business had acquired such a bad reputation that a lot of people who were out of work wouldn't even bother to come and see us," recalls Mr. Doggett, who is also a Vice President of Ames Textile Corporation, Lawrence's parent company. Even though Lowell has in recent years been suffering from one of the nation's highest unemployment rates, the textile mills were suffering from a labour shortage. Lawrence Manufacturing, while desperately seeking new solutions, was approaching a situation where the ability to take orders and fill them adequately was being threatened.

"Our labour acquisition problem was one of quality as well as quantity," states Mr. Doggett. "Many of the workers that we were able to obtain were low in talent and motivation. They usually didn't stick around very long; a lot left before they had even learned their job properly."

Lawrence was plagued by a labour turnover rate of 11% per month, and absenteeism stood at a little over 6%. Increasingly haunted by the twin spectres of falling efficiency and dwindling profits, Doggett became more and more willing to try drastic solutions as the 1960's drew to a close. There had to be some way to attract and hold more good workers so that orders could be filled on time and the company's relatively modern equipment could be more fully utilized.

It was in early 1969 that Mr. Doggett and his top assistants began to hear of the success that another company in the Boston area was having with an innovative programme – the 4-day workweek. It would obviously be risky to attempt such an innovation in their own operation, but management at Lawrence was desperate. And despite the risks involved, experimenting with a 4-day week would hardly be so costly as relocating.

IMPLEMENTATION OF THE 4-DAY WEEK

So it was that Mr. Doggett and the next 6 executives at Lawrence Manufacturing (plant manager, personnel manager, and 4 department heads) held frequent meetings behind closed doors during the autumn of 1969 to draw up plans for switching to the 4-day week.

Since the mill had traditionally operated around-the-clock, Monday-through-Friday, with three 8-hour shifts, an immediate problem was to devise a new schedule of shifts that could be fitted into a 4-day schedule. One obvious solution would have been to continue the three 8-hour shifts, but that would have meant reducing the workweek to only 32 hours, and management did not want to cut back so drastically from the standard of 40 hours.

However, if employees were to work more than 32 hours per week, it would mean shifts longer than 8 hours per day, and thus there could only be 2 full-time shifts. Since housewives and students had frequently inquired about part-time work, the final solution provided for two 10-hour shifts per day (7 AM to 5 PM, and 9 PM to 7 AM) with a 4-hour shift sandwiched in the middle to accommodate the part-timers. Excluding time off for breaks, the new 4-day, 10-hour shifts would give the firm 1 more hour of work per week per person. The regular shifts would run Monday through Thursday, with super-visory and office personnel continuing on their regular 5-day schedule. To make the arrangement even more attractive to the employees, as well as to increase production further still, it was arranged that anyone desiring extra work could voluntarily come in on Fridays and draw time-and-a-half.

The basic system of payment was also revamped with a built-in attendance bonus, designed to discourage absenteeism and tardiness. Employees who did not miss any work during the new 40-hour week would receive payment for 8 bonus hours, a total of 48 per week. Anyone missing a day would lose not only the pay for that day, but the bonus as well, amounting to more than one third of that week's paycheck. There would be similar, but lesser, losses of bonus for tardi-ness. (Exceptions would of course be made for emergency situations.)

Although the payment of 48 hours of wages for 40 hours of work technically means an increase of 20%, it really amounts to a little less than a 10% increase under the new system at Lawrence, since the base hourly scale was dropped about 10% and the total hours actually worked was raised about 3%.

Thus, a person receiving $2.00 per hour under the old system would be dropped back to about $1.80 per hour on his basic rate. However, since he was previously paid only on 40 hours of work, his weekly pay had been only $80, whereas he would now receive almost $88 on the basis of 48 hours under the new system – 10% more for 1 additional hour of work. Any overtime over 40 hours at the plant would be compensated at time-and-a-half, even though it would be on the new lower scale.

Each 10-hour shift would include a $\frac{1}{2}$-hour paid lunch period (lunch was previously not compensated) and 2 15-minute breaks – also paid – which amount to 1 free hour out of 10.

Labour was informed of the new plan a little more than a week before it was begun on December 1, 1969. For two days groups of about 30 workers were brought into a conference room to have the new programme explained by one of the executives. The manage-ment presentations generally lasted about 45 minutes and were followed by about 15 minutes of questions and answers. "At first it would confuse them a bit," recalls plant manager James Dossett.

"It was just too much information to be absorbed right away, and they would keep asking more questions for several weeks after that."

In addition to the confusion, says Dossett, there was a good deal of scepticism at first. "They just figured they weren't being told the whole story; there had to be a catch somewhere." But once the idea began to soak in, the concerns of the workers began to revolve around the routine aspects of the workers' lives away from the mill. About half of the employees are female, and most of them are married. They were mostly concerned about not being home when the kids came home from school, or not being able to cook breakfast for a husband who went to work later. The men in the work force were worried about being away from their wives and families longer each day – and in some cases they would have to quit second jobs that they had been holding. Some of the employees worried about the physical hardship of working the longer shifts, since most of the work must be performed in a standing position.

In fact, a Massachusetts labour statute prohibits women from working shifts longer than 8 hours without special extra rest periods. Lawrence obtained an exemption on the grounds that the shorter workweek was an advantage to female workers.

Despite such concerns on the part of the work force, only two employees quit their jobs as a result of the switch to 4-day. And despite some lingering concern about physical fatigue – and some failure to fully understand the new pay system – most scepticism quickly melted away and outright opposition disappeared as the employees began to enjoy the fruits of their extra day off. (One official estimates that about 4% of the work force was opposed to the plan at first, but that outright opposition has now dropped below 1%.)

Recruitment Dividends. The most obvious and immediate result of the new programme was the impact on recruitment. Although the full-time basic work force was increased only about 15 to 20% as had been planned, the number of job applicants increased by more than 400% during the first 6 months under the new 4-day plan. This was extremely helpful in upgrading the work force. "We have finally been able to start to be selective in our choice of employees," says Mr. Doggett. "As a result our work force is becoming more stable."

Furthermore, the ability to fill the shifts continuously around-the-clock (the third 8-hour shift had frequently been dropped for a lack of personnel during the preceding 2 years), combined with the upgrading of employees on the job, has resulted in a production increase of 15%, and there is no longer a danger of not being able to fill orders on time.

PROBLEMS REMAINING

Because it takes up to 6 months to fully train people to run knitting machines, it is still a bit early to be able to evaluate fully the success of the 4-day week. Thus far, despite all the obvious improvements, some areas of uncertainty remain. Although absenteeism is now down to about 3%, the turnover rate has remained as high as it was initially. Mr. Doggett explains that this is the result of having to hire more people than are actually needed for a trained full-time work force because some will quickly find that they are not suited to the work, while others will not be able to perform at full capability until they are properly trained.

"We are still in the process of taking in people who just aren't right for this kind of work," says Mr. Doggett. "And they aren't going to stay very long. Sometimes they are too skilled for the kind of work we have to offer, but they try it anyway because they want to work the 4-day week. There is still the basic problem of the job itself. It just isn't as attractive to a lot of people as the work in the electronics plants. But the 4-day week is very helpful in overcoming this problem."

"We are confident," says Mr. Doggett, "that once we have trained a lot of the people that have started working for us recently, our work force will become even more stable than it has already begun to be. We do not as yet have the kind of permanent work force that we want eventually to have, but the attractiveness of the 4-day week is making it possible for us to develop it."

Employee Opinion. Generally, the long-time employees of Lawrence Manufacturing like the 4-day workweek as much as the new recruits. One young and childless housewife says that now she gets all her housework done on Fridays and can thus spend the entire weekend on leisure activities with her husband. "We love it," declares a forty-ish knitting machine operator. "The work has actually become more enjoyable with that extra day off."

There appears to be very little moonlighting – probably because of the extra overtime work that is usually available on Fridays. Although occasionally the week's workload does not require it, usually

30 to 40 people come in on Fridays to pick up time-and-a-half pay.

A recent survey of Lawrence employees turned up many comments in favour of the 4-day week, such as: "There is more free time", "You have more time to spend with your children", "There is more time for the home and garden", and so on.

Yet many of the same people also complained about the length of the 10-hour shifts: "The hours are too long; I get exhausted", "Everybody is grouchy from the lack of rest", "Working 10 hours a day can be very tiresome – sometimes", "Ten hours is too long to have to stand up."

Still, such complaints are in the minority, and as one woman in her late 40's points out: "People always want to have something to gripe about. Sure it's harder to work 10 hours than 8, but I really feel that you get more rest overall with the extra day off."

Although none of the office and management personnel seem to mind staying on their 5-day schedules while the operatives work only 4 days, one maintenance person had a somewhat unique complaint. Since he must keep the machines running, under the old system he would frequently have to work on Saturdays, thus picking up some overtime. Now he finishes his work on Friday, and consequently feels that the 4-day week for the other people is depriving him of his chances for receiving overtime pay.

Mr. Doggett is aware of such complaints, but points out that they comprise a small minority of the work force. He says that some people will always be dissatisfied regardless of circumstances. When the new plan was first introduced, he says, two middle-aged ladies complained that the new 10-hour shifts were too physically demanding. Arrangements were made to pair them with 2 person on the 4-hour shift, so that the 2 ladies would only have to work 8 hours each day. Several weeks later they decided to switch back to 10 hours.

"The problem is perfectly understandable," says Mr. Doggett. "If it were possible, just about anyone would prefer to work 8 hours instead of 10 – and 5 hours would be even nicer."

"If it really came down to switching back to the old system," says Mr. Dossett, the plant manager, "most of them would probably walk out on us."

Another continuing problem, even though it is minor, is the failure by some workers to understand fully the new payment system. Several workers that were recently queried, complained of pay cuts resulting from the 4-day week – quite possibly a consequence of the diminished amounts of total pay received by employees who lose out on the bonus because of absenteeism. Company officials say it is still necessary to make frequent explanations of the new system, but that the problem is decreasing; and they emphasize that employees with good attendance records gain pay rather than losing.

The Union Factor. Like a majority of other firms that have thus far tried the 4-day week, Lawrence does not have a union. But considering the enthusiastic response from their employees and the lack of opposition from unions at other firms that had made the switch, it is doubtful that the lack of a union made much difference in the implementation.

More time might have been involved – more discussions, voting by the rank-and-file, and so on – but otherwise the plan could have probably been introduced just as easily, if not more easily, with a union's helping employees to understand the new pay system.

CONCLUSION

Even though profits have risen in recent months at Lawrence, and production has increased, Mr. Doggett says it is still too early to evaluate the success of switching to the 4-day week on the basis of profit figures alone. The recent fluctuations in market prices, the instability remaining in the work force because of the training programme and the search for workers who enjoy mill work, and the fact that the programme is still so new – all these factors make a neat statistical analysis impossible at this time.

Yet, despite this and the occasional grumblings about long hours and the misunderstandings about pay scales, there is no intention at Lawrence Manufacturing to turn the clock back to the days of the 5-day week.

"We don't know exactly how successful we are yet, or how successful we can become with the 4-day week," says Mr. Doggett. "But we do know that things are better than they have been for several years."

In any case, the 4-day week has enabled an original pioneer of the Industrial Revolution to bypass the fate of most of its now defunct peers. By becoming one of America's first companies to try the 4-day week Lawrence Manufacturing has once again become a pioneer of American industry, possibly helping to start another revolution – the widespread shrinking of the 5-day week to 4 days.

6

THE 4-DAY WEEK
AT A 7-DAY HOSPITAL
by Ray Richard

Ray Richard is a staff writer for The Boston Globe *who has covered many major news stories in New England since 1956. In 1967, he won the Sevellon Brown Award for public service writing from the New England Associated Press News Executives Association, for his stories about men illegally confined in the hospital for the criminally insane at Bridgewater, Massachusetts.*

Today there are nearly 3 million workers in hospitals in the U.S.A. – a 20% increase in 3 years – and their swelling ranks have made the field of health-care services the third largest employer in the country. Yet there is a shortage of health-care workers – although their number (2,858,500) was still rising in March, 1969, when the U.S. Department of Health, Education and Welfare and the American Hospital Association surveyed a sample of the 8,157 hospitals in this country.

Simultaneously, the industry faces a big problem of rising costs, as do other industries. Hospitals have been quick to adopt cost-saving techniques that other industries use; but, because they deal in human needs, hospitals cannot use some of the cost-saving methods.* For example, while farms reduce production costs by automation, the health-care industry often cannot. In fact, new equipment can actually increase its manpower needs. Add to the radiology department a radioisotope scanner for scrutinizing digestion, metabolism, and other body functions, and you must add another trained worker as well. And hospitals, unlike many other industries, cannot reduce unit

---

*Since this book publicized the benefits – especially in cost reduction – achieved by this hospital in changing to 4-day, over 60 U.S. hospitals have begun experimenting with it, in many different departments. Results so far are very good.

costs by increasing production. Treating more patients requires adding staff and services.

Aside from recruiting more employees, health-care facilities must also be able to cut costs by increasing their employees' *productivity*. (This doesn't mean driving people harder – which could have the opposite effect.) Some hospitals are, for one example, reassigning work: ward secretaries are doing paperwork which nurses formerly had to do; aides now take temperatures, a function once restricted to nurses; and so on. But further improvement is needed. Improvement of employee productivity has such great potential for ameliorating cost and labour shortage problems that the American Hospital Association is preparing a manual on the subject for its 7,090 member hospitals, to be published in early 1971.

One promising avenue for solving these problems may lie in rearranging traditional work schedules. This is where the 4-day, 40-hour week comes in. While all the results aren't yet in, the plan shows promise of becoming a remedy – and a remedy *without* adverse side effects.

Probably the first hospital to test the 4-day week is Roger Williams General Hospital – a 256-bed hospital in Providence, Rhode Island. Affiliated with Brown University, it is an innovative hospital geared to change – provided it's change for the better.

The hospital is located within handy commuting distance of many nursing personnel, but in an area that does not have trained nursing specialists so readily available as in big medical centres like New York and Boston. To meet the need for specialization and to keep the entire nursing service abreast of advances in nursing procedures, the hospital runs a broad but intensive in-service training programme, presenting lectures and classes on a 24-hour-a-day, 7-day-a-week basis.

For a number of sound reasons, the hospital's director, Jack R. Fecteau, and its director of nursing services, R.N. Lorraine P. Fraser prefer full-time nurses to part-time nurses – because of the heavy investment in training, because of an apparent correlation between the amount of time a nurse spends with her patients each day and her ability to help her patients, etc. But part-time nurses outnumbered full-time nurses 2 to 1 – compared to an industry average of about 1 to 4.

In addition, the director and the head of nursing services found their nursing schedule periodically and unavoidably assigning 4, 5 and 6 nurses to work for which only 3 were needed. "If you lock yourself into a policy of giving your nurses every second weekend off *and* schedule them for 40 hours' work over 5 days," Miss Fraser explained, "then, it is inevitable that you end up with 2 groups of personnel – partially part-time and partially full-time. One will work one weekend, the other works the alternate weekend; but, because both work 5 days a week, there will be 3 days each week when some nurses from each group will be scheduled – providing more than needed at that time."

Furthermore, in order to get every second weekend off (a policy at many hospitals in Rhode Island) nursing personnel sometimes had to work as many as 10 days in succession – or settle for one day off at a time. Neither alternative gives enough time to rest and relax before returning to work – especially for married nurses who have the stresses of family life in addition to the demands of their profession. And the inability of the nurses to get sufficient time off between work periods, Miss Fraser felt, prevented many nurses from working full-time.

Mr. Fecteau and Miss Fraser explained these problems to Russell Moberly, Ph.D., a consultant on management and personnel policies, in March, 1969. Together they pinpointed the blame on the 5-day 40-hour schedule. Dr. Moberly suggested they unshackle nursing services from this schedule, and Mr. Fecteau supported Dr. Moberly in suggesting Miss Fraser abandon it if abandoning it would help her solve the problems.

Generating a variety of ways to match the job requirements of her department and the number of nursing positions available to her, Miss Fraser came up with a neat package of hours and working days that seemed to provide the remedies she sought – not only for one, but for *all* of her scheduling problems. Her schedule calls for two 10-hour shifts a day for full-timers and one 5-hour shift for part-timers. Workers are on duty 7 days every 2 weeks: 4 days one week, and 3 days the alternate week. (For full-timers this averages $3\frac{1}{2}$ working days a week and 188 fewer working hours a year – for the same pay they received under the old pattern.) An employee who works Sunday also works Wednesday and Thursday of that week. The following week, she works Monday, Tuesday, Friday, and Saturday. This means that over each 2-week period, each nurse gets two 2-day "weekends" during weekdays, plus one 3-day weekend during a Friday-Saturday-Sunday period.

Daytime shifts begin at 7 AM and end at 5 PM – 2 hours later than formerly. Part-timers work from 5 PM until 10 PM. The night staff, accustomed to reporting at 11 PM, now comes in at 9 PM, and gets through at the usual 7 AM (Miss Fraser scheduled this overlap of succeeding shifts so that additional personnel are available during the busier period when patients are put to bed.)

Mr. Fecteau, after explaining the plan to his board of trustees, said she could try it. And in December, 1969, nursing personnel in a new coronary care unit began working this variation of the 4-day week.

Before the new workweek was authorized for any nursing unit, a *majority* of the full-time nurses in a unit had to favour it. When first suggested, the plan aroused some opposition. Part-timers worried about the impact it would have on their schedules, and full-timers wondered if a 10-hour shift would be too long; but the benefits had not yet been tasted. Once they were, the plan met overwhelming approval – for the same reasons workers applaud the streamlined workweek in other industries. Occasionally, to fill staff needs arising in units still on 5-day, nurses were transferred back to those units. Often they would say: "I don't know how I can ever go back on the old schedule!" The 5-day workweek now was an anachronism.

Roger Williams General Hospital was convinced it should add more units to the plan. So, in March, 1970, it put the accident room and the self-care unit on it. At first, only full nursing *units* were admitted to the plan, but later *individuals* were permitted to go on it, provided it would not hinder the efficiency of the whole unit. Now, every nursing unit operating 24 hours a day, 7 days a week, has some or all of its workers on the plan. (The administration feels the plan would not add efficiency to units not staffed on this 7-day basis.) Of the 400 R.N.'s, L.P.N.'s, nursing assistants, and clerks in the department, 350 qualify; and nearly 300 are now on the plan. (Two hundred thirty of the 300 are either R.N.'s or L.P.N.'s.)

Last June, Miss Fraser polled the workers on the new schedule. "Can you suggest a better distribution of the 7-day workweek pattern?" they were asked. Of 59 responding, 52 said they could think of nothing better.

The hospital now has more full-time than part-time R.N.'s in units working the new schedule (79 to 75), and more full-time than part-time L.P.N.'s (44 to 32) – more full-timers than ever before. All of the full-time day positions and most of the full-time night positions are filled. Recruiting costs are down. Overtime is almost non-existent. The in-service training programme reaps better payoffs. And there is increased continuity of patient care – meaning *better* patient care.

"We think," says Mr. Fecteau, "that on 35 hours a week we can do a better job with the same basic dollar, because of the continuity of care and everything else. But we can't prove it. We've got to determine effective measurements for judging whether there is a net savings from the plan. It is important for nursing in general, and for other hospitals, that we do."

4 DAYS ON,
4 DAYS OFF
by John L. Schohl

John Schohl, now a consultant on the economics of production, has over the past 25 years been owner-general manager of a screw machine products business and a gear manufacturing business. He invented 4 days on, 4 days off for a jobbing machining business, the Cromwell Corporation, South Bend, Indiana.

[Four days on, 4 days off is a version of the rearranged workweek that is particularly attractive for organizations that want a 7-days-a-week operation. Other variations on 4 on, 4 off are 5 on, 5 off, and even 7 on, 7 off – which means 26 one week "weekends" a year.]

During 1964 I was planning a new jobbing machining business which was to specialize in the production of parts suitable for machining primarily on Warner and Swasey automatic turret lathes. Capital was to be limited, so I wanted to run the small battery of machines this limited capital would provide as many hours as possible.

I knew that a second and a third 40-hour shift with as good men as I could recruit for a first shift would solve my problem. However, the skilled and potentially skilled men one would like to hire can be pretty choosy, even in a soft labour market. Few will accept third shift jobs, and not enough will accept second shift jobs.

Employers commonly lower their standards to fill night jobs. It is true that companies willing to make determined efforts over long periods of time do develop decent second shifts, but these are in a minority. Success with a third shift is rare – but it is the third shift which can make the grand difference economically.

4 Days, 40 Hours

I gave up on the possibility of developing a satisfactory third shift; and, except where the process compels it, so has just about everyone else. But I needed a work schedule which would use as many of the 8,766 hours in the year as I could make attractive to workers.

After considering many possibilities, I settled on one I regard as optimum: two 10-hour shifts a day for two crews of two 10-hour shifts each. One crew (2 shifts) works 4 days while the other is off – alternating in 8-day cycles – 4 days on, 4 days off. Operations go on routinely 20 hours a day, 7 days each calendar week – about 7,000 hours a year.

There is no premium pay for weekend work, but the last 2 hours of each day are paid at overtime rates. This is not very costly, because the base pay rate is established so that a man working under this plan earns the same yearly gross as a man working a conventional 5-day, 40-hour week in the same company.

The idea of my plan is simple. Its ramifications quickly become complex. Hourly direct labour costs are increased, but fixed and indirect costs are spread over so many more hours that they are over-absorbed – with the gain going right to profit. The return on investment in an activity carrying a burden of 250% or more and working 2 conventional 5-day, 40 hour shifts (a situation commonly considered good) can be doubled by going to my schedule.

Advantages include lower investment in relation to output than is usual, increases in the velocities of significant factors like turnover of work-in-process and actual wearing out of equipment for favourable earlier replacement, and much easier recruiting.

The men have more than half of the days in the year free – coming to work 65 fewer days a year than in an ordinary job. A man who will turn down the usual night job and then have no trouble finding a day job can be enticed onto my kind of second shift. Used imaginatively and aggressively, these conditions of employment can attract men to work they would shun otherwise, like foundry work.

It has been a generation since labour unions first set a 35-hour workweek as a sometime goal. It has not come about widely, because sufficient increases in productivity have not been realized. Companies simply cannot afford to shrink their time bases as they would have to do within the context of the 7-day calendar week. My 8-day week plan compensates by giving the company a high level of utilization while giving the worker greater free time – meeting conditions of present economic realities. And there is plenty in my plan for the trades necessary to secure acceptance by a labour union. It is a good thing for hourly-paid men, and they can be brought to recognize this.

The machining business I planned began operations during 1966. I managed it during the start-up period and well into 1969. The version of my plan described here (many variations are possible) was and still is used in this business. The economics of the plan worked out as I expected, and the schedule has been a source of recruiting strength and worker satisfaction.

8

FEWER DAYS OR FEWER HOURS?
THE BASIC ARGUMENTS
by Linda G. Sprague

Linda G. Sprague is Assistant Professor of Administration at the Whittemore School of Business and Economics at the University of New Hampshire. She holds degrees from Massachusetts Institute of Technology and Boston University.

[This chapter outlines the basic arguments people have had in the past about previous changes in the workweek. As Dr. Sprague predicts here, these are some of the same arguments people are using today, as we again experience change in the workweek. But for once, she notes, management is taking the initiative instead of fighting a rearguard action against labour.]

This book is about the 40-hour week and the reallocation of those hours from 5 to 4 days. But 40 hours is not necessarily what comes to mind when a 4-day week is suggested. To many people, a reduced workweek directly implies a shortened workweek.

Since it does mean different things to different people, it should come as no surprise to find an unenthusiastic response to the 4-day week among those not now on it. Any business manager who was involved in the 5-day week disputes may see here the spectre of 40 hours' pay for 32 hours of work.

The 4-day weeks reported here are *largely* reallocations—of the total time at work to a 4-day schedule. And, in every organization we surveyed, the 4-day week was proposed and implemented by management as a solution to current problems. But, "management-inspired reallocation of hours" does not tell the whole story. The 4-day week can readily be viewed as the logical next step in organized labour's

96

ceaseless campaign for a shortened workweek; and, that would inevitably raise the question of how much pay a worker would receive for a shortened workweek.

In 1957, George Meany said: "In effect, the progress towards a shorter workday and a shorter workweek is a history of the labour movement itself." And, almost without exception, management has historically remained opposed to such changes; management has looked upon the shorter workweek movement as primarily a variation on the higher wage theme.

The time-at-work issue has always been intimately linked with labour's campaigns for better wages. Time and money are at the heart of the labour movement, and of management's opposition to it. The earliest focus of attention was the number of hours in the work-day; later, it was the total hours worked each week. Until recently, the distribution of work hours across the week has fallen out of the earlier issue: when the workday is set at 8 hours and the total work-week at 40 hours, the result is a 5-day week.

Now that the 4-day week is gaining currency, we can expect the traditional arguments to be raised again. Over the years both labour and management have addressed the time-at-work issue with moral arguments, and the money issue on economic grounds. The dis-agreements are as fundamental as differing concepts of the nature of man, and as relevant as the pay envelope and the profit figure.

This statement at the Ten Hours State Convention held in Boston in 1852 sets the tone for the next century's crusade for the shortened workweek: "We believe it is the intention of the Great Creator to shorten the time of man's toil, and to extend his opportunities for moral, social and intellectual improvement, by the introduction of labour-saving machinery, and by the powers and mechanical uses of water, steam and electricity . . . If it be God's will to abridge man's daily labour to eight, six, or even less number of hours, we ought cheerfully to submit and say – 'Thy will be done'."

This fundamental argument was challenged by management's position which held that American society, based on the Puritan ethic of work, would crumble if man's labours were curtailed. This was supported with dire predictions of the mischief workers would get into if their work allowed them any free time. Management was highly pessimistic about the "moral, social and intellectual improve-ment" to be brought about with a reduced workweek.

Both sides bolstered their positions with case studies. Labour said that a man released from work before sunset had time to read and be with his family; as a result, he became better educated and more responsible – traits which made him a more valuable employee. Management countered with sad tales of men who, when given the opportunity to improve their minds, headed instead for the saloons and pool halls; in rapid succession, they fell to drinking and "bad habits", were fired from their jobs, lost their new-found "friends", and wound up destitute, a burden on society.

Economic pros and cons also raged. George Brooks, Research Director of the International Brotherhood of Pulp, Sulphate and Paper Mill Workers, summarized some of the underlying motives of the shorter hour movement as: ". . . the desire of workers to make their jobs secure . . . [and] the desire to reduce mass unemployment of the kind suffered during the Depression."

In opposition, management consistently maintained that any attempt to shorten the workweek would result in immediate and intolerable additional costs of production. So, productivity became a major issue, with management insisting that unless productivity increased, they could not bear the heavy losses which would result from cutting hours. Management claimed that this would ultimately force some companies out of business, throwing thousands out of work, and producing exactly what labour wanted to prevent – mass unemployment.

The companies we describe here are partly outside the dispute, partly in it. In one sense, it's almost as though no one had bothered to tell them that some major issues might be raised by the 4-day week. Instead of taking the usual management position – fighting a rear-guard action against a labour proposal, they've taken the initiative and re-packaged the workweek to make it more attractive to their workers and more productive for themselves.

The basic arguments have not changed in substance over the past century. So they will almost surely be re-introduced if a 4-day movement is initiated by organized labour. It could well become a major bargaining issue.

9

DOES ORGANIZED LABOUR
WANT THE 4-DAY WEEK?
by D. Quinn Mills

Daniel Quinn Mills is Assistant Professor of Industrial Relations at the Alfred P. Sloan School of Management, Massachusetts Institute of Technology. He has a Ph.D. in Economics from Harvard University, where he is a Research Associate at the John F. Kennedy School of Government.

[Although 4-day has so far had smooth sailing with unions at some American firms, Dr. Mills expects it to meet opposition from the major unions traditionally committed to pushing for both higher wages and shorter hours.]

The 4-day week is not just an idea – it is a reality. In the past year several companies have gone to a 4-day week with little or no change in the number of hours worked. Perhaps other companies will do so also. It is interesting to speculate to what degree this new work schedule may spread throughout the economy, and to consider its advantages and disadvantages. We are fortunate to have the experience of several firms to guide us in our inquiry. For example, in these companies, who proposed the 4-day week – management or labour? Why was it proposed? Who opposed it, and why? How has it worked?

But beyond the experience of the firms that have adopted a 4-day week, what about those which have not? Will other firms follow suit? Are the unions interested in this new schedule? Will the unions push it, and perhaps spread the 4-day, 40-hour week to many more companies than now use it? These questions cannot be answered by experience alone – but a review of what has happened in those companies with the 4-day week can serve as a valuable starting point.

THE EXPERIENCE OF COMPANIES WITH A 4-DAY WEEK

Several of the 4-day, 40-hour week companies that were interviewed by Riva Poor regarding labour and personnel aspects of the 4-day week, were interviewed further by me. (Profiles of the companies appear in Chapter 2.) This chapter discusses their experience with unions and employees in establishing and operating a 4-day week.

Almost certainly, the companies covered here do not include all corporations using the 4-day week, but these firms are probably a fairly good cross-section of the group. They do not represent a statistical sample because little or nothing is known about the universe of companies which they represent, nor were they chosen in a random fashion. Rather, these are simply the 4-day companies that Riva Poor could find to interview, as described in Chapter 1. (Note: None of the companies included have gone to a 4-day week as a way of generally reducing the hours of work or of preventing lay-offs.)

What have been the labour implications of the experience of companies with the 4-day week?

Are the companies union or non-union? Only 5 of the 27 companies are union. Three are manufacturers and the other 2 are petroleum companies. The unions involved in the manufacturing companies are one independent shop association and two AFL-CIO affiliates. The Petroleum companies are organized by several different unions across the country.

Who recommended the 4-day week? As noted earlier, in every case management recommended the change in scheduling to a 4-day week.

Management's reasons for proposing the 4-day week: The companies had a variety of reasons for proposing the scheduling change. Most often, the companies mentioned the need to recruit or retain better labour. The 4-day week was suggested in the belief that it would be attractive to employees (including, in some cases, management as well!). As described in Chapter 5, one company adopted the 4-day schedule as a device for recruitment in a tight labour market. Another hoped to retain skilled workers by providing 3-day weekends or the opportunity to moonlight. Most firms, however, did not intend to encourage moonlighting. Some viewed the fewer days, longer hours schedule as making moonlighting more difficult for the workers. In another case, the company went to a 4-day week in lieu of a wage increase, hoping that the new schedule would keep it competitive in the labour market.

In only a few of the cases was the new schedule a direct response to production requirements, as, for example, to handle peak loads. An instance of this is the retail tyre company that adopted a schedule of Thursday, Friday, Saturday, Sunday to meet consumer shopping habits.

Were employees consulted about the new schedule before it was implemented? The union companies consulted employees both formally and informally. One company, operating with an open shop, consulted only its union employees as to the advisability of the change.

Half the non-union firms gave employees an opportunity to express their views of the new schedule; half did not. In some cases involving consultation, a formal vote was taken; in others, discussions were held privately with key employees.

Was there opposition from employees to the new schedule? Very little. Opposition to the new schedule came primarily from women with young children and from older men. Some of the women opposed longer hours of work each day because it takes them away from their children. In some cases, these women left the company after the new schedule became effective.

Opposition from male employees was less clearly motivated; some simply preferred to work the 5-day week. In several companies, those persons who wanted to work 5 days were allowed to do so.

Are any employees not on the 4-day week? Not all persons employed by some of these companies have been placed on the 4-day week. Management, other salaried personnel, and sales workers are sometimes excluded. It is interesting that several companies report some opposition or "minor problems" from management personnel when workers went onto the 4-day schedule and they did not. In some cases the firms report that those not on the 4-day week were anxious to obtain it. One firm made the choice it had offered its salaried people a clear one: be salaried, and work 5 days, or be hourly,

101

and work 4. The salaried people gripe, the president said, but they don't want hourly pay.

Many companies reported that employees not on the 4-day week were simply indifferent to it.

What wage policies are followed by these companies? These companies represent a wide range of compensation forms. Before conversion to 4-day some companies paid straight time for hourly work, exclusively; others were on piecework, guarantee plus incentives, wages plus profit-sharing, and piecework plus bonuses. No company felt compelled to switch to another method of wage payment as a result of the new schedule. However in several cases pay rates were changed to provide a pay bonus incentive for promptness and attendance; although these bonuses sometimes increased the total pay package, in most cases total take-home pay remained constant.

In many cases the company reduced or increased (by $\frac{1}{4}$ to 4 hours per week) the weekly scheduled hours when it adopted the 4-day week. In these cases the companies also adjusted overtime payments for the 4 working days to maintain the employees' income.

What have been the results of the 4-day week? With respect to labour and personnel relations, every company but one reports that is is generally satisfied with the new schedule; but most report some disadvantages as well.

Advantages vary greatly among the firms. Most firms report a lessening of absenteeism and an improvement in worker morale. A few firms report increased efficiency and lessened costs under the new schedule. Recruitment of new workers seems to have become easier in many cases. One company reports that virtually all of its newly hired employees came to the company because of the 4-day schedule.

Disadvantages seem to weigh less heavily in the minds of those interviewed, but there are several. Nine of the 27 companies report significant disadvantages. These include worker fatigue from the longer hours and increased overtime due to scheduling work on what had now become a day off (i.e., the fifth day). Some companies report increased labour costs as a result of the new schedule, though these are in a distinct minority.

What happened to union relations in the unionized firms? All firms report continued excellent union relations. In no case does the 4-day week appear to have damaged relations. The companies proposed the change in all cases, and the unions apparently consulted their membership and went along. No difficulties with the unions over this issue are reported.

Note: There has been one case reported in which management has proposed a shift to a 4-day week and the union has refused to agree. The exact circumstances involved are not known, but, as the concluding section argues, unions are likely to be only lukewarm to the 4-day, 40-hour schedule.

THE 4-DAY WEEK IN UNIONIZED PLANTS

This section describes employee-management experience with the 4-day week in the 5 unionized companies included in the survey. The experience of the companies is somewhat varied, each having problems unique to its own situation.

Company 1: In a small manufacturing company in New England both management and the union are enthusiastic about the 4-day week. The union is an independent shop association whose membership includes the 35 or 40 factory workers. The union members were given a chance to vote on trying the proposed 4-day week, and 78% voted for a trial period. A few weeks later, 90% of the members voted to adopt it permanently. The office help appear to be at least as enthusiastic as the factory workers.

There is no loss of pay for any of the employees under the 4-day schedule. The office help now work an $8\frac{1}{2}$-hour day, and the factory workers, 9 hours. Both groups are paid for 40 hours. However, the factory workers have lost their coffee breaks and half of their wash-up period (totalling $\frac{1}{2}$-hour). But workers are allowed to drink as much coffee as they wish at their machines. During the busy season there is often work to be done on the fifth day, at time-and-a-half.

Workers in the plant average 40 years of age with 15 years seniority. Although older workers might be thought to be more traditional and less likely to change their living patterns, the employees in this company have much higher morale as a result of the new schedule; and, according to management, they are "proud of working for an innovative company".

Company 2: A small manufacturing company in Florida is experiencing apparent success with the 4-day week, although it was started only a few months ago. The company is only weakly unionized. Although the union is a national organization, the International Chemical Workers, Florida has a right-to-work law and only 19 of some 54 workers belong to the union. The union employees were allowed to vote on whether to try the 4-day week for a year; the vote was 18 to 1 in favour.

The employees work a 9-hour day, 36-hour week, with the first 18 hours at straight time pay, and the last hour overtime. Coffee breaks have been discontinued. As a result of a wage increase in the new contract, which was perhaps larger than the union would have got if they hadn't been negotiating about the 4-day week, the shop steward feels that the workers are being paid at least as much as, and perhaps more than, they would be if they were still on the 5-day, 40-hour week.

There is no opposition to the 4-day week now that it is in operation. All of the employees except the salesmen are on the new schedule, working Monday through Thursday (except 2 persons who work in the shipping department Friday, and therefore have a Tuesday through Friday schedule). Some minor problems in negotiating the plan have been worked out, and there are currently no difficulties.

Company 3: A small manufacturing company was opened with the intention to convert to a schedule of working 4 days, followed by 4 days off, as soon as production was moving fast enough to make that feasible. The plant is open all week, and plans eventually to have 4 shifts (there are 2 shifts now) for optimum production. The employees in the plant are now working four 10-hour days, at straight time. The original contract with the union, the Industrial Workers, was designed around a 5-day, 40-hour week, and there have been some problems in adjusting the terms of the contract to the new schedule.

One problem of adjustment has been holiday pay. Until very recently, if a holiday fell on a man's working day, he received only 8 hours pay, instead of 10. The man who had a day off, however, received 6 hours pay, in addition to the 40 hours he worked. The contract has been revised so that the man who is scheduled to work gets full pay for the holiday, while the man who has the day off gets 2 hours credit; he receives a cheque for these credits at the end of the year, just before Christmas.

The plant is in a rural community, and one reason for instituting the 4-day week was to attract marginal farmers to employment. The workers are generally pleased with the schedule. There were problems adjusting to the 10-hour day at first, however. The first group of women (the plant now has 50 to 60% women) had great turnover. The next group started working only a half day until they became acclimated, thus decreasing the turnover. Apparently turnover is fairly low now, particularly for a new plant. While some of the women complain about having to work 10 hours at a time, they are also glad to have more full days at home with their children.

Companies 4 & 5: As described in Chapter 1, many of the major oil companies have been utilizing a 4-day week for their drivers in some cities for approximately 30 years. Two major companies were interviewed. They both are characterized by having relationships with a large number of different unions – some affiliated with the AFL-CIO, others independent shops, and an independent union operating in a group of several states.

Representatives of management and the union were interviewed at a plant in Massachusetts. All drivers at the plant (about 73) are on the 4-day, 40-hour schedule. There are 3 different shifts, with different days off, and the shift preference depends on seniority. The drivers also get 5 weeks paid vacation.

There seem to be no problems involving the 4-day week at the Massachusetts plant. According to management, "they love the 4-day week".

A Different Situation: One of the unionized manufacturing plants with the 4-day week recommended the 4-day plan to a steel foundry in California. The California plant wanted to try the 4-day week in a few of its departments on an experimental basis, but met a great deal of opposition from the international union representing the plant workers. Although apparently some workers themselves and the union representatives in the plant were fairly interested, the international union balked. The international representatives' stand was that they had worked very hard to attain the 8-hour day, and that this plan was a reversion to the old 10-hour day. They did not see any benefit to the workers.

THE ATTITUDE OF UNIONS AT OTHER FIRMS

In the companies described, the 4-day week has been a success. Apparently it has been popular with both management and labour.

4 Days, 40 Hours

Given its popularity in these instances, can it be expected to spread?

In fact, the idea of the 4-day, 40-hour week will perhaps be less popular among workers generally than might be imagined. Certainly many groups of workers have been or may be attracted to the 4-day schedule, but others would prefer other schedules. And there are a large number of different schedules available. It would appear from the experience of the companies discussed above that simple distinctions, as between men and women, or between older and younger workers, do not explain interest in or opposition to the 4-day week. It is, therefore, hard to generalize. Furthermore, up till now the companies with the 4-day week tend to be small, non-union companies, so what can be discovered about the probable attitudes of the workers and unions in larger scale enterprises?

Most unions have been pressing for a shorter number of hours worked by the worker per year. Many different formulas have been developed to achieve this goal, some of which are described below. The 4-day week is a popular concept if it is combined with a fewer number of hours worked each week, and with the same pay as before. A 4-day week at less pay or for the same number of hours as before has much less attraction to labour, although it may be desirable to some groups in some areas.

Labour's current interest in a shorter work year arose in the early 1960's with the automation scare. Fewer hours of work were recommended as a means to spread the falling volume of work among the labour force. The high-employment economy of the mid-1960's reduced fears of automation, and increased the unwillingness of employers (faced with labour shortages) to shorten the workweek. Recently, rising unemployment and desires among workers for increased leisure have reawakened interest in the shorter workweek.

Labour's goal of a shorter number of hours of work per man for each *year* may be met by several means, and different groups of workers prefer different mechanisms. In some cases the average hours of work each week are reduced. In others, the number of days of work is reduced. For example, the Steelworkers have negotiated extended vacation provisions by which certain workers receive a 13-week vacation once each five years.* Also, in steel and aluminium, by joint labour-management agreement, some workers have received more days off on a consecutive basis. This is done by scheduling a

---

*See Richard L. Rowan, "The Influence of Collective Bargaining on Hours," in Dankert, Mann, and Northrup (eds.), *Hours of Work* (New York: Harper and Row, 1965), pp. 29–30.

worker for 10 consecutive days of work followed by 4 consecutive days of vacation. Other means of reducing total hours worked include a larger number of holidays and longer vacations. Finally, substitution of double-time instead of time-and-a-half for overtime often discourages additional overtime hours.

Therefore, the 4-day, 40-hour week, or any change to fewer days which leaves total hours unchanged, has only limited attraction to labour. It provides no lessening of the work year, but merely rearranges leisure and working time. Further, a standard 9-hour or 10-hour day conflicts with deep-seated attachment to the 8-hour day, which has been strongly supported on grounds of worker efficiency, health, and safety.* Yet interestingly, the less-than-8-hour day has not been widely popular when coupled with a longer workweek. For example the 6-day, 36-hour week (practised in rubber manufacturing in Akron since 1936) has not proven generally desirable to workers.

Where the 4-day week can be coupled with an hours' reduction or an increase in pay, the shift to the 4-day week becomes more attractive. Thus, four 10-hour or 9-hour days may be attractive when the hours after 8 are paid at time-and-a-half. At least one company which has instituted a 4-day week has adopted a 4-day, 40-hour week on this basis, which yields the equivalent of 48 hours straight-time pay. Collective bargaining agreements have in several instances established a standard workweek of less than 40 hours with mandatory overtime of some number of hours daily.†

Even where a 4-day week may be proposed at an unchanged weekly pay, and perhaps at fewer hours, there may be opposition. Some groups of workers prefer the 5-day week or, just as importantly, give the 4-day week little priority in their desires for improved working conditions. The 4-day week may be opposed for the following reasons:

First, a family with a large number of 3-day weekends each year may spend more than otherwise, so that the 4-day week increases the strain on the worker's pocketbook.

Second, the 3-day weekend may mean little to persons who have limited leisure-time interests. Probably this group is small, but it does include some union people.

Third, workers often feel they cannot earn enough in a 4-day week,

*See Floyd Mann, "Shift Work and the Shorter Workweek," in Dankert *et al.*, *op cit.*, pp. 111–127.
†See Richard L. Rowan, *op. cit.*, pp. 27–28.

and will actively seek additional employment regardless of the rate of pay. In some cases, the rate of pay cannot reasonably be expected to be so high that workers will prefer increased leisure to the opportunity to spend previously scheduled days at other jobs or at overtime.

In summary, workers are interested in fewer hours of work each year, and in maintaining and increasing their earnings. The 4-day week itself has little appeal unless it is coupled with fewer hours or greater pay. Where fewer hours can be obtained with the same or greater pay, the unions and workers normally are very interested.

FUTURE PROSPECTS FOR THE 4-DAY WEEK

Companies which have initiated a 4-day week without reductions in the total hours of work will probably remain a rarity in the economy. They have been, generally, small- to medium-sized firms with special scheduling opportunities and with weak or no unionization. However, many different types of corporations have gone to a 4-day week, which indicates that technological conditions (excluding scheduling problems) have not been a major determinant of the number of days a week scheduled (continuous production facilities are a partial, but major, exception).

Companies that are amenable to lessening the number of hours in the workweek, involving no loss of pay to workers, should have little difficulty in obtaining the 4-day week. Most companies are not anxious. However, the recent resurgence of interest among workers and unions in fewer weekly hours may cause companies to find themselves pressed in this direction. The experiences of the 27 firms described above indicate that companies may be able to adjust more successfully than they had imagined to a 4-day week.

On balance, in my judgement it is unlikely that the 4-day week will become a characteristic feature of our economy unless it is coupled with a reduction in hours generally. This is likely to occur only if major labour organizations push strongly for this result. Such a push for shorter hours was made in the late 1950's and early 1960's, including calls by the AFL-CIO upon Congress to amend the Fair Labour Standards Act to provide a 5-day, 35-hour week. The union initiative was met by both President Kennedy and Johnson with the argument that the 40-hour week remained essential to the nation's economic welfare.* In consequence of that political rebuff and also of

*Paul Pigors and Charles A. Myers, *Personnel Administration* (New York: McGraw Hill, 1969, 6th ed.), p. 479.

improving economic conditions, the impetus to shorter hours was dissipated.

It is not difficult to foresee a similar process occurring in the current recession. As unemployment worsens, unions will turn to shorter hours as a means of spreading work opportunities. Yet the sluggish economy of the early 1960's was not accompanied by rapidly rising consumer prices, as is the case in 1970. Today, unions are caught between demands for large wage increases to keep abreast of rising prices, on the one hand, and the need to moderate wage demands and conserve job opportunities, on the other. Currently, workers are generally opting for increased wages, improved vacations, and security provisions, with reduced hours a low priority item. Only a prolonged recession and a deceleration of price increases would appear likely to affect this pattern of preferences. In consequence, fewer days in the workweek (with or without shorter hours) will probably not suddenly mushroom throughout the economy.

BREAKING THE 5-DAY MOULD:
ARE YOU A CANDIDATE FOR CHANGE?
by Linda G. Sprague

Linda Sprague, author of Chapter 8, is an Assistant Professor at the University of New Hampshire. She is also a Doctoral Candidate at the Harvard University Graduate School of Business Administration, doing research in the field of health care.

[After pointing out that the calendar is an often neglected management tool, Dr. Sprague spells out the *primary* scheduling tasks in any organization, showing ways to determine whether your firm is a good candidate for a calendar change. Included is a format for blocking out scheduling. (Another format can be found in Chapter 16.)]

In 1926 the National Association of Manufacturers published a *Pocket Bulletin:* "Will the 5-day-Week Become Universal? It Will Not!" Today the 5-day week is, if not universal, the "standard" American workweek. With the 5-day week has come the 2-day weekend – Saturday and Sunday for most people. And over the past 30 years, we have come to think of this work pattern as a fact of life – not always particularly convenient, but just there.

However, the 5-day week is a man-made artifact, the result of more than a century of strife and negotiation – as the NAM's booklet might suggest. It is now so commonly taken for granted that it might seem impractical to suggest breaking the tradition. Why would any company willingly stir up the kinds of dispute that the 5-day week brought on by changing it?

The answer is: because some companies have discovered how to use the calendar as a strategic weapon in the competitive labour market. They are using the 4-day week to help them attract and keep a reliable and loyal workforce, and to solve the problem of regular but highly variable demand. The old moral and economic arguments which revolved around the 5-day week are still there, but today's companies simply are not using them. The 4-day week is being proposed by management as an attractive solution to current problems.

Is the 4-day week a "free" solution that any company can pick up and instal, with immediate and heartwarming impact on profits? Of course not. The 4-day week *can* provide a company with increased employee satisfaction as evidenced by lower absenteeism and turnover, with improved productivity, and increased customer satisfaction *only* if management finds, after thorough analysis, that its own operations would benefit from such an innovation.

A warning is in order here: the analysis I am about to suggest may well show that a 4-day week would be disastrous for your firm. On the other hand, some extraordinary arrangement – for example, an 8-day "week" with three consecutive days off; or a 17-day "week" with 2-day and 3-day breaks – may prove to be exactly what you need. The 4-day week is offered here as but one example of breaking out of the 5-day mould – although it will probably have wider applicability and acceptability than such variations as I've just mentioned. Indeed, it is now working successfully for a number of companies across the country. But don't overlook the potential advantage of other unusual packages, including those that completely break the 7-day cycle.

ARE YOU A CANDIDATE FOR A CALENDAR CHANGE?

Before seriously considering a calendar change, take a critical look at your relationships with the outside world in 4 important areas:

1. **Demand pattern:** The 4day Tire chain in California is open Thursday through Sunday because that's when the demand for tyres peaks. Management chose to forgo possible sales on Monday through Wednesday in return for full staffing when demand is high.

   Do *you* face wide cyclical variations in demand? Don't make the common mistake of examining your production orders; go back to raw demand. How much of your demand variation is due to your own advertising and promotion activities? Is any of the variation the result of your own operating problems –

are your Saturday part-timers as competent as your regular workforce?

2. **Requirements of your technology:** The aluminium smelters at Alcan's Arvida Works in Quebec have been in continuous operation since 1957; Children's Hospital in Boston has provided around-the-clock patient care for over 100 years. These are two disparate examples of industries with technological requirements for continuity. However, within each there are non-continuous operations which can be identified. For example, only emergency surgery is performed after the regular operating schedule has closed – the technological bottleneck for this aspect of the hospital's activities is its scarcest resource, the surgeon.

What does *your* technology look like? What parts of your process are continuous and what segments are not? Are there statutory limitations on the length of time your process can run? For example, in the food industry some machines must be shut down and cleaned periodically. Are your present batch sizes based on anything more concrete than tradition? In short, what *real* patterns are imposed by your technology and what patterns are you imposing for other reasons?

3. **Labour market:** The Geo. H. Bullard Co., manufacturer of industrial abrasives, wanted to attract and keep an improved workforce, and to reduce absenteeism and turnover. They did it with a week of four 9-hour days.

Would a different packaging of the workweek make *your* firm more attractive to your workforce? Do you hire women who would prefer one weekday off to catch up on shopping and housework? Are you in a rural area where many of your employees could use an extra day on their farms? Would rearranging your employees' schedules to avoid traffic snarls let your workers make better use of the workday?

4. **Deliveries – yours and your suppliers:** The Lawrence Manufacturing Company, otherwise on a 4-day week, is not so in the shipping room. Three men work there on Friday to meet customer's shipping requirements.

What about *your* customers. Could they accept a shortened delivery schedule – especially if you were able to say, "We can't send it out on Monday, but how about the Friday *before*?" On the other side of the picture, what kinds of delivery schedules can your suppliers meet? If your present suppliers could not deliver under a new schedule, perhaps one of their competitors could.

Once you've examined these four broad areas, you will have a general idea of the feasibility of a calendar change – to a 4-day week, for example. You must next thoroughly analyse your internal operations.

YOUR INTERNAL OPERATIONS

In any organization, there are a variety of scheduling activities going on which in fact comprise one complex joint scheduling problem. Let's take a brief look at specific scheduling tasks, and then talk about their interrelationships.

The diagram on the next page is a representation of the primary scheduling tasks in any operation. We are most interested in 3 of these:

1. **Order scheduling** – the aggregation and allocation of incoming demand to the available means of production, including physical and manpower resources: the best-known example of this segment of the scheduling problem is job-shop scheduling, in which the objective is to assign jobs rationally to special elements of the means of production so as both to maximize the utilization of resources and to satisfy customers' demands.

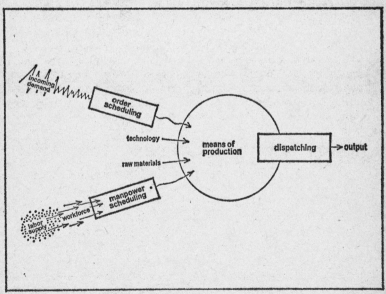

Primary Scheduling Tasks in Any Operation

113

2. **Manpower scheduling** – the allocation of labour resources to the physical resources in light of the demand: a good example of this aspect of the problem is the scheduling of ward nurses so as to provide a hospital's necessary coverage around-the-clock. Any organization, in the service or goods sector, which requires 24-hours-a-day, 7-days-a-week staffing knows what a headache manpower scheduling can be.

3. **Dispatching** – on-line, real-time scheduling within the production process in order to take advantage of local conditions within the overall schedule: the police dispatcher is a classic example. Prowl cars are assigned to specific routes or districts; the dispatcher receives incoming requests and makes the last-minute exact assignment – "Car 37 to 120th and Spruce." This is frequently one of the foreman's most important tasks, just as it is part of the operating room head nurse's job – exploiting the knowledge of local conditions to solve the operating problems which arise, bearing in mind the overall schedule.

Now you can see why I referred to this as a complex *joint* scheduling problem – each of the separate tasks assumes the successful completion of another. Orders are scheduled against the means of production, but that implies that the workforce has already been assigned with an eye to incoming orders. And, as if that weren't difficult enough, the problem doesn't hold still while you solve it; if your marketing and personnel departments are doing their jobs, they will continuously compound the problem by adding orders (not in any neat sequence) and employees (who will need training). The overall scheduling problem is not only interactive, it is also dynamic.

UNDERSTANDING YOUR SCHEDULING PROBLEMS

If you are investigating the feasibility of a calendar change, there are 2 points to bear in mind:

1. In real organizations, particularly smaller ones, you will not necessarily see these scheduling tasks separated out. One department, or one man, will usually be doing both order and manpower scheduling and, in many instances, the dispatching as well.

2. However, if you're considering a move to some other work schedule, it is extremely useful to think about these as separate tasks.

For example, if you can identify – or create – a 4-day demand pattern, you can then schedule your manpower around it, as the 4day Tire Company has done. What you are doing here is taking a common way out of that complex joint problem: you freeze one segment (in this case the demand pattern) to give you a base from which to do the manpower scheduling. This is not always a bad way of handling the problem, as long as you *know* which part you have arbitrarily locked in. If you, or your predecessor, locked the organization into a 5-day work pattern so that order scheduling could be carried on, presumably you can unlock it and lock it back into a work pattern more appropriate to your current needs.

Fortunately, in most companies, one of the scheduling tasks dominates, either by accident – or design. The easier case to handle is the one just mentioned – domination of the demand pattern, thereby essentially determining the nature of the manpower schedule. If this describes your situation, you have these questions to answer before moving to a 4-day week: Do I have, or can I create through an advertising and promotion campaign, a demand pattern – for example, 4-day? If not, then are the requirements of my demand amenable to 4-day schedules for my workforce?

Some Examples. Let's take a company which faces steady demand 6 days a week as an example, and say that they require a staff of 40 at any time. This is a general description of many retail stores. If their workers are on a 5-day week, then the company has a number of alternatives. For instance, it could have a regular staff of 40 working Monday through Friday, with Saturday covered by a combination of regular people on overtime and part-time help; or it could have a regular staff of 20 working Monday through Friday, another crew of 20 working Tuesday through Saturday, and 20 part-timers hired on for Monday and Saturday. Or there could be other alternatives along these general lines.

What happens if this 6-day firm goes onto a 4-day week? Here's one possibility: the company hires 60 regular, full-time employees and divides them into 3 crews whose workweeks look like this (each crew is 20 people). (See page 116.)

This schedule requires more regular, full-time people than the suggestions mentioned under the 5-day week. There are 60 here, and there were 40 before. However, no overtime or part-time work is required. And your demand is always covered by regular employees; as far as your customers are concerned, they will see a regular staff

Days on Crew	Mon.	Tues.	Wed.	Thurs.	Fri.	Sat.
A	20	20	20	20		
B			20	20	20	20
C	20	20			20	20
Total Staff	40	40	40	40	40	40

of 40 regardless of what day they deal with you. Your total labour bill will not increase; you are still paying for the same labour coverage, but have reallocated your workforce.

Let's change the situation slightly now, by peaking the demand on Friday and Saturday, with very low demand early in the week. A 4-day schedule might look like this:

Days on Crew	Mon.	Tues.	Wed.	Thurs.	Fri.	Sat.
A			20	20	20	20
B			20	20	20	20
C	20	20			20	20
Total Staff	20	20	40	40	60	60

If, in addition, each crew is working a 9-hour or 10-hour day, you will have further extended your coverage on the days when you do have demand coming in. This staggered crew scheduling can apply to daily as well as weekly manpower planning. A restaurant which has demand growing steadily from 4.00 PM onto a peak at 8.00 PM does not *have* to bring all waitresses in at 4.00 p.m., as is frequently done. The work force can be planned to build as demand does.

If the incoming demand pattern dominates in your operations, take a hard look at it. And remember that there is a difference between a 4-day *company* and a 4-day *workweek*. Don't dismiss the 4-day workweek out of hand, just because your organization must maintain 24-hour coverage.

AROUND-THE-CLOCK

In most operations which must be staffed around-the-clock, the manpower scheduling problem dominates. And, if this describes your organization's operations, the chances are good that, while you may *say* you're on a 5-day workweek (which implies a 7-day week), you in fact may not be. The crux of your problem is the fact that there are twenty-one 8-hour shifts in one week. If each of 4 crews takes its 5 shifts/week, you're covered 20 of the required 21 shifts. That one additional shift each week is your scheduler's constant aggravation and the reason he has had to come up with strange packagings of the calendar, particularly if you need highly skilled personnel and can't cover a shift with part-time help on an occasional basis. Six- and 7-week scheduling cycles are common in continuous process industries – which is what most health-care institutions are. These organizations have already taken such liberties with the calendar that the 5-day week hardly applies at all.

Moving a "continuous coverage" organization onto a 4-day schedule allows a variety of alternatives. For example:

The Allen Country Nursing Home in Fort Wayne, Indiana, is on a "4/2" schedule. Their employees work 4 days and then have 2 days off. The cycle repeats itself, of course, every 6 weeks.

The Roger Williams Hospital in Providence, Rhode Island, has about a third of its nursing staff on an experimental 4-day week, but has changed the traditional 8-hour shift: there are two 10-hour and one 4-hour shifts each day. This gives the full-time nursing personnel four 10-hour days followed by 3 consecutive days off; while the short, 4-hour shift allows the hospital to take advantage of nurses who want to work regularly, but on a reduced schedule.

BREAKING THE 7-DAY CYCLE

Obviously, the possibilities are endless once you look beyond the 5-day week. In fact, it would be well worth your while to find out just how many of your workers are on a regular 5-day schedule. If you are facing severe problems in labour supply, high absenteeism and turnover, you may in fact be supplementing your regular work force with part-timers and overtime work. Are your regular employees in fact working 6-day weeks while the part-timers put in 2 or 3 days? Consider the possibility of increasing your *regular* staff by offering a 4-day week; companies who have tried it have found that reduced

117

absenteeism, lower turnover, and improved worker morale are the results.

It should be clear by now that the 4-day week is a viable alternative for many organizations, not just the few who can completely close down 3 days out of 7. Nor is it necessary for your entire workforce to be on a 4-day week. You can use it where it is appropriate within your organization, as many of the 4-day companies we surveyed are doing.

If, after looking carefully at your internal operations, you find that a 4-day week would help you, what problems can you expect if you put in a 4-day programme?

1. **Communication:** You must explain thoroughly to your employees and/or your customers exactly what you are planning. Many companies have installed a 4-day week on a trial basis at first; employees' acceptance of the programme is, of course, critical. After trying it out for several months, almost all employees have been enthusiastic. Some companies cite minor problems in "educating" their customers and suppliers to this new pattern; all of these companies report successful resolution of the problem.

2. **Scheduling:** More than three fourths of the companies we surveyed said that they found they had to schedule both work and manpower more carefully. A few wished they had paid more attention to scheduling problems *before* making the move. Several found that they had to beef up their scheduling departments.

3. **Supervisory coverage:** This is a particularly irksome problem for companies who are on mixed 4-day and 5-day schedules. The solutions are as wide-ranging as the types of organizations. Some move supervisory personnel with the work crews, others appoint assistant supervisors to cover the odd hours after regular supervisors have left – and point out that it has provided a training ground for new supervisors.

4. **Legal restrictions:** If you move to a workday of more than 8 hours, you may run up against regulations which prohibit women from working on such a schedule. At the present time, some firms must apply to the appropriate state agency for a waiver. In any case, if you are extending the workday, pay careful attention to rest periods, lunch, and coffee breaks, to prevent *any* of your employees from becoming overtired.

SUMMARY

Reorganization of the calendar can help management balance manpower needs and the requirements of their demand. If you have demand that peaks and drops each week, if you are experiencing labour shortage, high turnover and absenteeism, consider the potential of a 4-day week. The calendar has traditionally been viewed as the manager's deadly enemy; it can be turned into a strategic competitive weapon.

11

INTERFACE
WITH THE OUTSIDE WORLD
by Grant Doherty

Grant Doherty is Sales Promotion Manager at Kyanize Paints, Everett, Massachusetts. He was in advertising and sales promotion at the E.I. DuPont Co.; and for 5 years before this, was a sportswriter for the Philadelphia Daily News.

[Four-day pioneers must recognize and cope with the fact that the rest of the business and social institutions they interface are still geared to the traditional workweek. Here's how one firm turns potential disadvantages into real advantages.]

Seamstresses have been dealing with "interface" for centuries, mathematicians for decades, electronic and computer engineers for at least a score of years. But they had only to deal with two different kinds of fabric, opposing two-dimensional planes, or direct current in relation to alternating current.

Now there's another kind of interface, and it bids to be the most intricate of all – the interface of the 4-day workweek – a collision of tradition and innovation.

This is interface of recent vintage – come to ferment in the late 1960's when the pioneer 4-day week firms were first trying their "thing". In those days, interface was a nebulous area of the overall planning, like the early New York Mets – in the league but not taken seriously. But even as the Mets became the "enfants terrible" of baseball, so did interface make many stalwart 4-day week planners tremble with indecision.

Take, for example, the case of the raw material salesman and the Fourth of July.

The salesman was new in the territory and, obviously, thoroughly unbriefed on the habits, peculiarities, and idiosyncracies of the manufacturers in his new domain. He made his first call on "X" company on Friday, July 3rd. However, "X" company has inaugurated a 4-day workweek and, naturally, was closed. Puzzled, the salesmen rescheduled his call for Monday, July 6th.

But "X" company's contract with the union called for 10 paid holidays a year, one of which was July 4th. In 1970, our nation's birthday fell on a Saturday – and to honour contractual obligations, "X" company's employees celebrated Independence Day on Monday, July 6th. The raw material salesman again called on a factory that was locked up tight!

Because he was new, and light on experience, the salesman continued his pot-luck procedure and scheduled yet another call – this one for Friday, July 10th. When, for the third successive time, he found the "X" company plant dark and silent, he filed a trade report with his home office that "X" company was "out of business".

You can imagine the confusion of the "X" company president when his opposite number at the salesman's company called him at home to commiserate on his bad fortune!

And for each firm or organization adopting the 4-day work week, there will be at least one interface problem peculiar to that firm alone and germane only to that firm's implementation.

CUSTOMERS ARE PERISHABLE

From the very beginning of your planning you must keep foremost in your mind that group known variously as patients, clients or, most probably, customers. They are, after all, the whole "raison d'etre" of your corporate existence.

The watchword of all interface planning must be: "*Customers are perishable*." Your plans must be shaped and moulded to discommode this most important portion of the outside world as little as possible. And, once you have determined that the 4-day week is your "bag", tell your customers *first*, tell them *often*, and always brag of success (if it's a failure, they'll know soon enough – and you'll be back on your former schedule!).

Dear Kyanize Dealer:
The attached press release is being sent to you in advance of its release for publication.

4 Days, 40 Hours

There are some big plusses for you in the new Kyanize schedule, too.

First, by working a more efficient four day schedule we have already increased our production of all products. This, of course, means fewer back orders – particularly at the height of the season.

Secondly, we are shipping paint orders more quickly than ever before because of a longer "shipping day". Orders which used to be sent out on Fridays are now leaving our plant on Thursdays (or even earlier). Such orders, therefore, arrive at Kyanize dealers' stores on Friday or Saturday – in time for the week-end business. Long haul orders travel over the week-end, most arriving at their destinations Monday, instead of setting around a truck terminal on Saturday and Sunday and starting their journeys on Monday.

Thirdly, this more efficient work schedule ensures faster processing of advertising requisitions, credits, laboratory requests and other inquiries – means you get faster service all along the line.

I'm sure that you will receive tangible proof of the value of this more efficient schedule, time and again, in the near and in the continuing future – and that our association will become mutually more cordial and more profitable because of it.

Very truly yours,

This letter was the first notification to Kyanize paint dealers that their paint supplier was taking the 4-day plunge. (The "press release" will appear further along.) The word "plusses" was deliberately misspelled so as not to present any impediment to complete understanding of the *whole* letter by *all* customers.

The letter was oriented solely to "what's in it for Kyanize dealers" – and it was 100% truthful (don't *ever* lie to a customer).

After this letter went out, Kyanize executives waited – if not with bated breath, at least with omnipresent anxiety – for dealer comment.

First reaction came not from a dealer in the concrete jungles of megalopolis but, surprisingly, from a northern New Hampshire resort area – swimming and boating in the summer, skiing in the winter. The dealer remarked to the Kyanize salesman (in typical, laconic, Yankee fashion): "Wish all companies would do this – we'd have the 'weekend people' for 3 days instead of 2, which means we'd make more money!"

This country storekeeper had found yet another customer benefit – one that hadn't even crossed the minds of the professional thinkers at Kyanize.

After sixteen months, Kyanize has not, yet, had one unfavourable dealer reaction from any account in the 41 states its distribution

covers. On the contrary, many retailers feel that the publicity resultant to Kyanize's innovative move has helped their own image in the
marketplace.

Similarly, Lewis Doggett of Lawrence Manufacturing Co. (textiles)
in Lowell, Mass., reports that customer relations are as good as ever.

And a data processing firm in Massachusetts literally was forced to
put its key punch operators on a 4-day week because punch cards
produced by those operators on Fridays could not be further pro-
cessed quickly enough to ensure that customers' Friday payrolls
would, indeed, be ready by those customers' closing times on Friday
afternoon.

The implementation of 4 longer workdays instead of the former
5 shorter days moved the work peak up earlier into the week and
solved the problem to everyone's satisfaction (most especially, the
key punch operators).

On the other side of the coin, however, a New York City architectural firm had to abandon its proudly heralded 4-day plan after 6
months because clients wanted to be able to consult 5 days a week.
Since clients had been assigned to individual draughtsmen or teams of
draughtsmen and only one draughtsman or team of draughtsmen was
familiar with any given client's problems, if that client persisted in
demanding 5-day-a-week consultation privileges, the 4-day week was,
obviously, unworkable.

In an entirely different vein, a Cushing, Oklahoma, precision casting firm has most successfully implemented a 4-day, multi-shift
operation that keeps the plant humming 7 days a week. The Dalton
Precision Division is one of those very rare firms that was founded
with the 4-day workweek in mind. Located in a rural area, many of
the employees spend at least as many hours per week working their
own small farms as they do at the casting plant.

And, in a modernized version of the mountain coming to Mahomet,
the Dalton 4-day week plan resulted in the Oklahoma Attorney
General's office declaring that Oklahoma's laws limiting the number
of hours a female employee may work in a single day, "null, void
and unconstitutional", and in conflict with precedent-taking federal
legislation.

OTHER CUSTOMER RELATIONS PROBLEMS

Drivers of the big tank trucks that haul fuel oil and gasoline out of
many oil company terminals in the north and northwest United

States have been on a 4-day week for years, this being the most workable solution to the companies' problem of giving 7-day, 24-hour service to accounts. And the daily schedule has built into it two 2-hour periods to service and maintain the big rigs, a company benefit that would be unattainable under any other plan.

Then, there's that aptly named 4day Tire Co. in Los Angeles that does a thriving retail tyre business on just Thursday, Friday, Saturday, and Sunday (you can't buy a tyre from them the other 3 days because they just aren't there). This is squarely in the area of calculated-risk enterprise – the principals of the firm realize that there *are* some lost sales on the 3 days they aren't open; they also calculate that the additional sales they would get by being open those other 3 days would not make the game worth the candle. It is these very forgone sales that make the whole thing an economic success – if payroll and start-up expenses were to be budgeted across a 7-day week, results might be far less spectacular – if, indeed, profit were shown at all.

You must also take cognizance of local custom in your planning.

Another tyre company with a plan similar to the 4day Tire Co., had to go back to more conventional retailing methods.

"People in the Southeast just don't want to conduct business in this weird way – and that means both our employees and the customers we hoped for and didn't get," said a spokesman for this Atlanta firm. "The 4-day week just didn't do enough for our sales. At the retail level, to carry this sort of thing off, you need extensive advertising and promotion – we just couldn't afford it."

As if to bear witness for his colleague across the continent, a 4day Tire Co. spokesman indicated that promotion and advertising was the only way to make this type of gambit succeed, and said that his firm's advertising budget was in excess of $100,000 per year (much of it expended in newspaper advertising).

Coincidence: in a previous existence, the guys who call the shots in both Atlanta and L.A. had worked together for a discount clothier in a practically antediluvian 4-day week experiment in Miami almost a decade ago (it failed).

One parting shot on customer relations: If a sales force calling on customers is a part of the operation, brief that sales force thoroughly and in a most positive fashion at the very outset. Make certain that they present an attitude of complete assurance. And don't let the salesmen feel sorry for themselves. Even though the very nature of your selling effort may preclude putting the sales force on the 4-day schedule, whoever heard of a salesman who didn't arrange his agenda to include frequent, ex officio, afternoon rounds of golf?

SHIPPING AND RECEIVING: FULL SPEED AHEAD!

Well, not exactly. Interface with those rugged individualists known collectively as the Teamsters and individually as truck drivers can be unsettling, to say the least. And then, without doubt, there'll be the usual outspoken opinions of your own shipping and receiving departments (no direct quotes; this is a family article).

Many corporate 4-day planners faced with such a Hydraheaded confrontation have finally surrendered to what they consider an impossible situation and have kept shippers and receivers on the traditional 5-day schedule.

Other, more pedantic, planners have formulated what they regarded as perfect examples of their art only to have the executives who had to implement such planning gnash their teeth in despair upon running aground on such reefs as blizzards, wildcat strikes, and, in one case, a rockslide.

While such problems of logistics have been the bane of military planning since the days of the Caesars, they did not forcefully affect the industrial community until the advent of automation. A human can be diverted to other duties when there is a lack of raw materials – a machine can only sit there, a non-productive capital investment.

Most of those firms that have successfully implemented a 4-day workweek have found that facing the shipping-receiving problem squarely is the best method. And, ultimately, they came up with one of three solutions:

1. Work half the department on Friday, half on Monday and the full department on Tuesday, Wednesday and Thursday.
2. Keep shipping and receiving departments on the old schedule.
3. Four-day full steam ahead.

Geo. H. Bullard Co., abrasives manufacturer, chose the first alternative for its shipping department and the second for its receiving department, according to Bullard's Kenneth Ferguson. Meanwhile, Interstate Incorporated's president, Jerry Silverman, reports that his firm bit the bullet at the beginning and put both shipping and receiving on the 4-day schedule. The shipping of Interstate manufactured paint rollers and other paint sundries continued smoothly, but it took about a month for raw material suppliers to get their gears meshed into a Monday through Thursday delivery schedule.

Milton Machine Co. gave both suppliers and trucking firms plenty of advance warning, and the transition went most smoothly (although salaried help had to man shipping and receiving departments the first 4 Fridays).

At Crocker Co., aluminium fabricators, the 4-day week resulted in a fifth, 6-hour, overtime day for the shipping department.

Lawrence Manufacturing courted the status quo, while Kyanize opted for the split week.

And, in what appears to be dreamy-eyed summation but may indeed be Orwellian prophecy, an executive of New England Metal Spinning Co. says, "It would work much better if everyone, raw materials, truckers, everyone did it; as it is, our management has to work on Fridays."

Of course there's still the problem at Dalton Precision Division where they ship and receive 7 days a week. The Dalton plant needs a 7-day-a-week flow of raw materials, and this switch puts the onus on the raw material suppliers to fill these needs. Spokesman for the firm, Matt Dalton, commented that, "once our suppliers understood that we *had* to have their cooperation, things worked out very nicely."

If there's a 4-day week in your firm's future, give a good, long, hard look before you make any irreversible judgements in the areas of shipping and receiving. Next to customer relations it can be the stickiest wicket of the whole concept.

WHAT PRICE RECRUITMENT?

Many of those companies that have gone on the 4-day workweek have done so in a practically last-ditch attempt to facilitate recruitment of new employees.

Be on notice that this ploy succeeds most times – but the opposite also can occur. And so long as people are people, this boomerang effect is unpredictable and, largely, indefensible.

If you find your firm is at a disadvantage because of higher urban pay scales or because of a small discretionary labour pool in your vicinity, the 4-day week just might turn the trick for you.

There are other nuances of new employee recruitment inherent in the 4-day week carrot, also. At Roger Williams Hospital in Providence, administrators and medical staff agreed that the "ne plus ultra" in intensive care might be possible if ICU nurses could be assigned as teams. Everyone, nurses included, took to the idea immediately; only trouble was that the work is extremely demanding and that absenteeism took its toll with almost predictable regularity. Substitute nurses on the ICU teams just didn't work out because they weren't members of the "in-group".

So officials at Roger Williams tried a unique approach. They recruited enough nurses with top experience to form teams that worked 3 days one week and 4 days the next week – teams of top calibre nurses working what prorates out to 35 hours per week (there is a slight overlap between shifts to pass on doctors' orders, medications, etc.). Absenteeism dropped sharply and the plan became a viable entity that guarantees the finest intensive care possible.

There is, however, the reserve side – the cloud whose lining is pure brass. There were few detractors at Company "Y" when the 4-day week was begun. But those who did oppose opposed most vociferously. One employee did not get along well with his wife and would have preferred a 6-day week; another dropped his wife off at her secretarial job each day and the 4-day week meant that he had to make two 50-mile round trips on Friday, since his wife did not drive. Ultimately the dissident spouse received permission to work on Friday if he so desired (he had an executive post), and the wife-secretary got a driver's licence, so neither employee was lost.

But another firm lost five hard-to-replace female employees because of insurmountable family problems – children who had to be gotten off to school, in conflict with earlier 4-day starting times; 5-day-a-week husbands who objected; and so on.

Kyanize Paints, conversely, has collected a large backlog of job applicants in spite of the fact that paint making is, at best, a dirty, sticky, malodorous way of earning one's daily bread.

There is also the possibility of moonlighting on the part of some of your employees – that is, part-time jobs over the long weekend afforded by the 4-day week.

The oil company drivers are summarily dismissed if they are caught with a second job. Their employers feel that their regular jobs are demanding enough and that another, part-time, job will decrease the efficiency level of any given driver sharply. There is even a case on record of one moonlighting driver having lost a vehicle as a result of being overly tired from working at a second job.

But you probably won't lose any employees if new 4-day hours interfere with moonlighting efforts. At Milton Machine Co., for instance, where second-job hours were in conflict with the new 4-day schedule, it was the second-job hours that got adjusted.

And at Kyanize Paints they received a phone call from an

enterprising temporary help firm asking that a notice be posted on the Kyanize bulletin board to the effect that any secretarial help wanting a second job on Fridays call such and such a number. There were no takers.

At Rex Paper Box Co. they worked out a most ingenious way of putting everyone on the 4-day week and still staying open 5 days a week. Under the Rex Plan the most senior employees work Monday through Thursday; those with medium seniority report Tuesday through Friday; while the least senior employees work a Monday, Wednesday, Thursday, Friday schedule. Rex also works a Saturday shift manned by "semi-voluntary" workers, who are paid overtime for all hours over 36 worked in any one week.

One requirement to keep in mind: demand a quid pro quo from your workers in exchange for the 4-day week. This will, in all probability, mean the establishment of different work norms. "Z" company leaped before looking and now is burdened with $5\frac{1}{2}$-day shipping and receiving, staggered shifts, monstrous administrative problems – and the same work norms as before the new programme started.

THE CORPORATE IMAGE – ONWARD AND UPWARD

The area of community relations is also an important one, albeit full of variables and difficult to measure. Some companies have found no measurable reaction; some have found highly favourable reaction. In no case, however, has there been any lowering of the corporate stature in the community.

At Geo. H. Bullard Co., the corporate image soared – "innovators, that's what they call us," reports Kenneth Ferguson. Milton Machine Co. says its home town of Weymouth was "pleasantly surprised". And at Kyanize Paints one executive was elected to the board of directors of the Everett Chamber of Commerce – a direct result of the 4-day week.

Most companies, however, report that it is next to impossible to measure community reaction to their adoption of a 4-day workweek.

There will, however, be certain indicators of increased community stature. Your firm will be approached by the community's service organizations to "help with this", or to "participate in that". Since the obvious "beneficiaries" of this increased interest on the part of the community's service organizations will be your executives, caution should be the watchword until several months' 4-day week experience have been accumulated.

Another indication of your community "good guy" index will be a disproportionate number of new approaches by charitable groups (both reputable and suspicious) for contributions. The best, if not the only, course to follow is that which was company policy before you achieved your present 4-day "notoriety".

While it may seem relatively unimportant when compared with other aspects of the 4-day week, community relations are bound to be bettered.

TURNING YOUR COMPETITORS ON

There is one interface area which can be exciting or a pain in the neck, depending on your approach – interface with your competition.

Actually life isn't nearly as much fun for monopolies (such as utilities) as it is for people in competitive industries. If you're first in your general area to go on 4-day you can, if you play your cards right, drive your competition crazy.

Almost immediately after your announcement of a 4-day week, your competitors will be abroad in the land pooh-poohing your progressive step and intimating darkly that it was something far removed from innovation that prompted the move. You will practically hear the hearse backing up to the corporate door.

Competitive representatives will have their sharpest "needles" unsheathed at trade and technical association gatherings; a pre-dinner cocktail party can turn into a star chamber proceeding.

But keep smiling, because if they weren't hurting, they wouldn't be reacting in so violent a fashion. And if a competitor is unionized, forget smiling and laugh out loud – your vociferous antagonist shortly will be merely a "me-too'er", docilely following the trail that you have blazed.

You will also benefit by being first, because (1) you will have first call on most of the skilled labour of your type in the area; (2) you will have first call on all of the unskilled labour in your area; and (3) you will almost certainly get some local publicity which is as good as or better than advertising – and it's free! – sinking the barb even deeper into the competition.

AND, OH THAT WONDERFUL PUBLICITY!

The last facet of interface with the outside world is all fun – publicity.

Once you decide all systems are "go", the first to know (outside of your own personnel) should be your local city editor followed immediately by every other city editor, TV station, radio station, and trade publication you can think of. If you've got an ad agency, turn it loose on the project, too.

Interstate president Jerry Silverman reports his firm got extensive publicity in the *Quincy Patriot Ledger* and the *Braintree Star*. Geo. M. Bullard Co. sent out local news releases and was mentioned prominently in the *Worcester Telegram and Gazette*, the *Framingham News*, and the *Westboro Chromotype*.

Milton Machine Co. was written up in the *Quincy Patriot Ledger*, while Lawrence Manufacturing Co. benefited from stories in *Newsweek* magazine, *The Harvard Business Review*, and local Lowell newspapers. 4day Tire Co. shared the *Newsweek* article with Lawrence, as did Roger Williams Hospital and Kyanize.

But it was Kyanize that really hit the jackpot, publicity-wise. They figured they were first when they launched their 4-day week in April, 1969, and hoped to get some Greater Boston publicity from this press release:

Kyanize Paints Announces Four Day Work Week With Five Days Pay
Kyanize Paints, Inc., Everett, Mass., has become the first major paint manufacturer in the U.S. to adopt a four day work week.
All employees – plant, office, laboratory and management – in the Kyanize headquarters operation will receive five days pay for four work days. The third day of the Kyanize "long week-end" is Friday.
The plan, which goes into formal effect beginning with the week of April 7th, was approved by the Kyanize Shop Association in a vote held April 1, following completion of a trial period which began March 10.
A second Kyanize manufacturing facility in Springfield, Ill., is scheduled to adopt the four day work week in mid-May.

The release was dated April 4th but, by some strange happenstance it was "leaked" to the *Boston Globe* on April 2nd. And, suddenly, there it was – on pages one and two of the *Globe*'s April 3rd evening editions with a huge picture on page one, two equally huge pictures on page two and a 72 point headline, "Four Day Week A Reality." It was enough to make a professional press agent bite his nails in envy.

But this was only the start.

Associated Press newswires picked up the *Globe* story and it appeared in newspapers across the country. WBZ-TV (NBC-Boston) sent a crew over, and that evening's news programme carried a full five minutes of interviews with Kyanize employees (and with the Kyanize logotype in continuous evidence).

There were feature articles in the *Boston Herald-Traveler*, the *Christian Science Monitor*, the *Malden Evening News*. There were stories in the *New York Times*, the *Wall Street Journal*, *R.I.A. Alert*, *Business Week Newsletter*, the *American Paint Journal*, and many, many others.

But the crowning achievement came on a Thursday afternoon in May when a Huntley-Brinkley TV crew came to photograph Kyanize employees at work. The next morning they recorded those same employees at leisure – golfing, canoeing, fishing.

Shortly afterwards there were several minutes of prime-time, national network TV on the Huntley-Brinkley TV report! *for free!*

As a result of all this publicity (estimated at more than half a million dollars' worth), Kyanize has received over 300 inquiries from all 50 states, England, Canada, and Mexico. Each inquiry receives a prompt and courteous reply along with a mimeographed, 3-page synopsis of the Kyanize experience.

And the last paragraph of this synopsis is what the game is all about, after all: "Kyanize Paints, Inc., is as forward-looking in research as in employee relations. We manufacture a full line of the highest quality maintenance and industrial coatings, as well as such exotic finishes as seamless floors, urethanes, epoxies and silicones. *We would appreciate the opportunity to serve you, too.*"

INTERFACE IS WORTH IT ALL

Summing up, the interface areas of 4-day can be most rewarding. You can accrue a great many corporate benefits if you're willing to face up to each problem as it arises. And there are a few general points that, if they are observed, will flatten out many of the bumps on the road to complete accomplishment:

1. Tell *everyone* – the whole world – when you decide to go on a 4-day week. Don't cause a rookie salesman to report that you are "out of business".

2. Most important, *customers are perishable*. Plan your 4-day week to help *them* too, not to antagonize them.

3. Don't be intimidated by your truckers, shipping or receiving department. But *listen* to what they have to say – they may save you from a Senior Grade boo-boo.

4. Never forget that people are people. Don't let employees dictate

131

your 4-day policy but don't be absolute, either. A little flexibility here and there may save your best employee.

5. Your community status is bound to go up as a result of your innovative move.

6. Your competitors will hate your guts – for a while. And you can worry about it all the way to the bank!

7. Get all the publicity you can out of your forward-thinking move. And remember, the more cooperative you are, the more copy you'll get.

8. When you finally get your 4-day week running like a Swiss movement, forget the Ozymandias complex – they're already using the 3-day week.

12

HOW TO HANDLE
A 4-DAY CONVERSION
by Kenneth E. Wheeler and
Philip D. Bogdonoff

This article follows up one that was originally written for The Harvard Business Review (*May/June, 1970*) *by Kenneth Wheeler, President of Wheeler Associates Management Consultants. His associate Dr. Philip Bogdonoff is Vice President of the firm.*

[In this report the authors explain how important *thorough prior planning* is to the success of a 4-day conversion – and they list parameters to be considered. While the Editor notes that very few 4-day firms employ outside consultants to plan their conversions, the authors suggest that in many cases 4-day firms could obtain even better results if they would do so.]

THE IMPORTANCE OF PRIOR PLANNING

Wheeler Associates have now conducted research on a dozen companies that have converted to the 4-day workweek, in some cases, for over a year. Such analysis was generally done by means of personal interviews with the principals of the companies involved. From this analysis we have drawn many conclusions, and one of the major ones is that the importance of prior planning should be uppermost in the mind of any company planning a conversion to the shorter workweek.

Many of the firms that did not plan thoroughly beforehand now wish they had done so. For example, one company was under the misapprehension that it was required to pay overtime to workers after 8 hours of work in any given day, regardless of the total number of hours worked during the week. When it went onto four 10-hour days, it continued to pay an overtime bonus for 2 hours a day, the equivalent of 4 hours of regular pay. This was not a legal requirement for their industry. It was a costly error for the company, inasmuch as the overtime premium was 10% of their payroll.

Another firm completely overlooked the fact that car pools played an important part in the commuting habits of its employees. Consequently, when they attempted to convert to a 4-day work schedule on a partial basis, they found that considerable inconvenience was caused employees who were on different work schedules but in the same car pool.

Prior preparation is the key to successful conversion to the shortened work schedule, but I believe success will be directly proportional to the other increases in productivity which management initiates *before* implementing the shorter work schedule. Applied properly, 4-day scheduling can be a powerful tool for management; the company that plans its move carefully and fully can realize gains that will advance its growth for a good many years to come. As you will see, when management initiates the shorter workweek, it is a most appropriate time for initiating other improvements.

Preparation for conversion basically resolves itself into two main areas. The first is a detailed study of the entire operation to discover where varied problem areas lie and what can be done to correct them. The second area of preparation involves devising the type of 4-day workweek schedule that provides maximum attraction to both employees and management.

Gathering the Facts. What are the other areas that could be improved simultaneously? Naturally, management will be aware of many of the problems. To insure that nothing is overlooked, the following broad categories are suggested as a means of putting all the information together beforehand, in order to come up with a proper plan for implementation of necessary corrections:

1. **Background Information:** such things as the departments to be studied with their organization charts; the union contract if the company is organized; plant and office layouts; job descriptions or evaluations; detailed payroll information.
2. **Current Man-Hour Input Information:** detailed information on hours worked, shifts, pay differentials, overtime hours, breaks, holiday and sick leave policy, absenteeism, part-time worker situations, lateness problems.
3. **Sequence of Operations:** for the entire plant with a flow chart for

each department; a paper-work flow chart with reports generated, distribution, the forms used, and samples.

4. **Production Output:** unit costs, production volumes, peaks and valleys, information as to departmental backlogs and volumes, standards evaluations and performance to standard, ratio delay studies, production variance studies, bottlenecks.

5. **Miscellaneous Costs:** such things as utility costs by department per day, personnel advertising costs, personnel turnover and average cost of training personnel.

It is important that sufficient detail be included in the gathering of the above information, so that management can take an objective and accurate view of the entire situation. From such a view, and from the observations made in gathering such information, it will become very evident where all the problem areas are.

Solutions to the problems may or may not be easy. We have noted in many cases heretofore that solutions to certain problems were not possible because of personnel attitudes – attitudes sometimes generated from the employee's opinion that he is getting nothing out of a change. However, the 4-day workweek is a vehicle that the employee gets something out of; consequently the degree of cooperation in implementing corrective action is astonishing.

Devising the 4-Day Schedule. The type of schedule used in the 4-day workweek conversion is entirely dependent upon the individual operation. The possibilities are infinite and must be tailored to the needs of the particular industry and company. Whether the company elects to use a 4-day, 5-day, or 7-day plant operation depends upon the individual situation, availability of personnel, sales requirements, equipment utilization, etc.

Other options that the company has to decide are the number of hours which each shift is to work, and the particular days of the week they will work. There are many combinations that can be used. A few variations are listed below:

1. One shift: four 9-hour days, Monday-Thursday, Tuesday-Friday, etc.

2. One shift: four 10-hour days, Monday-Thursday, Wednesday-Saturday, etc.

3. Three shifts: two 10-hour shifts for 4 days, one part-time 4-hour shift for 4 days.

4. Three shifts: one 9-hour shift for 4 days, one 8-hour shift for 4 days, one 7-hour shift for 4 days; and so on.

Before choosing the right combination for your operation, there are considerations, some of which are listed below for your information. Management has to consider whether its operation fits any or all of these categories:

1. Continuous process, job shop, batch production.
2. Shipping requirements.
3. Maintenance requirements.
4. Sales requirements.
5. Depth of skills involved.
6. Piecework, other incentive schemes in operation.
7. Start-up, shut-down problems.
8. The type of conversion schedule – do we do one department at a time, in what sequence, etc.

As an example of how the above categories might fit into the decision-making process, consider the following:

1. A batch producer might find that a 10-hour day would give him more volume than a 9-hour shift.
2. The company might find that in order to fulfil certain shipping requirements it is desirable for them to be open on Friday or even Saturday and that possibly other departments need to adjust.
3. Some maintenance jobs may be done much more effectively and with less machine downtime if the maintenance department is scheduled to work when other departments are off.
4. Sales requirements may dictate that it is necessary to have sales department coverage 6 days a week.
5. If a particular skill is decisive and yet staffing is shallow, it may not be possible to schedule on a 4-day basis.
6. Incentive schemes may dictate that it is desirable to maintain operations for 10 hours a day, 40 hours a week rather than 9 hours a day, 36 hours a week.
7. Prolonged unproductive start-up times may indicate the desirability of three shifts rather than two.
8. It may be desirable to implement 4-day scheduling in one department at a time to test the scheme before converting the entire company. In other cases, by integrating the whole company at one time, possibly personnel problems can be avoided.

One the evaluation of problems and ways to correct them, as well as the choice of conversion schedule, are made, it is possible to generate a detailed savings potential. By careful study of the savings potential schedule, management can make a valid decision as to the necessary trade-offs and also the net saving to the company by conversion to the shorter workweek schedule.

Conversion Costs. The costs of converting to the shorter workweek are inversely proportional to the amount of planning that is put into the programme. Consider the following possibilities. Costs might increase due to:

1. An increase in the overtime bill to meet production requirements.
2. The possible addition of personnel, especially supervisory, to cover the new scheduled work cycle.
3. A failure to increase productivity sufficiently to offset a possible reduction in work hours.
4. Improper scheduling which results in poor customer service and resultant loss of sales.
5. Temporary costs during the initial adjustment period, for such things as, filling staffing gaps during implementation; obtaining waivers to legal regulations; etc.

Costs can be decreased by:

1. An increase in productivity.
2. A decrease in absenteeism.
3. A decrease in personnel turnover.
4. A reduction in personnel advertising.
5. A possible reduction in utility costs for a 4-day operation.
6. Stabilization of the work force which leads to improved supervisory effectiveness.

Proper weighing of the cost negatives and positives becomes another important consideration. It becomes obvious that proper planning can reduce the costs and increase the profitability of conversion.

LEGAL CONSIDERATIONS

One of the very first considerations in the feasibility of 4-day workweek conversion is the legality of using the extended workday. Each state has its own restrictions and these must be checked out thoroughly before proceeding. Such things as limited hours for female employees and the time of day that a woman can be required either to report or be dismissed from work have to be considered, as will rest periods. I have found that most states will grant a waiver to employers for longer hours, depending on the circumstances.

One of the prime considerations is whether overtime premiums will be required after 8 hours in any given day. Many states require this, even though the employee is not required to work over 40 hours in the week. Companies that come under the Walsh-Healy Act are required to pay this overtime after 8 hours, regardless of the total hours worked during the week. For example, in hospitals the hours of professional people are federally regulated depending upon the type of workweek cycle the hospital elects. If the institution has elected to use a 14-day work cycle as its base, it must pay overtime to employees under this arrangement for any work performed over 8 hours in any given day. If, however, the same hospital elects the 7-day workweek, then they can work their employees beyond 8 hours without an overtime premium, as long as they do not exceed 40 hours in any given week.

It is interesting to note that U.S. industry will be operating on a 4-day workweek for 12% of the year due to federal legislation. In 1971, 6 of our national holidays will be celebrated on Mondays. The decision whether a company should schedule work Monday through Thursday or Tuesday through Friday should be made with these Monday holidays in mind. If the former option is elected, will they pay for these legal holidays or will they require workers to make up the time on another day of the week?

GOVERNMENT PARTICIPATION

If the evolution of the 4-day workweek continues to spread throughout the country, there will be a definite requirement for government participation in two general areas.

Inasmuch as the federal government is the largest single employer in the United States, the first requirement will be to adjust its own policies as regards daily and weekly hours of government employees. If industry continues to take the initiative and the 4-day workweek becomes more commonplace, competition will eventually force the issue. This applies as well to state and municipal governments, each with its own labour regulations. A good case in point is the regulations which the various states have regarding permissible hours of work for hospital employees. In many cases female employees of a hospital

138

cannot work over 8 hours in any given day unless an "emergency" condition exists. The Civil Service laws will have to be changed at both state and federal levels to accommodate the shortened work-week if longer hours are to be scheduled without engendering an overtime premium. Enactment of such changes in the law might prove to be difficult, dependent upon the strength and desires of the local or federal labour lobbies but this does not appear to be an insurmountable task.

The second area of government participation will be in the form of necessary relaxation of certain labour laws regulating private industry, both at the state and federal levels, existing now in indivi-dual situations. Regulations that require overtime pay after 8 hours, that prohibit females from working over 8 or 9 hours in a day, and other laws which tend to restrict the worker's freedom of choice must all be reviewed. All those companies subject to the regulations of the Walsh-Healy Act will find they must pay an overtime premium on hours in excess of 8 in any one day regardless of the number of hours worked in a week.

These regulations were originally intended to prevent the exploita-tion of labour. Such laws were enacted at a time when the 54-hour week was commonplace. Present labour laws, in fact, both restrict progressive innovations that benefit labour, and also impose needless burdens on business.

Even though these regulations are subject to waiver when a firm presents a valid petition to demonstrate the benefits of such a waiver, obtaining a waiver is time-consuming. When the 4-day workweek becomes more widespread, we can expect the regulations to be re-written and/or abandoned.

CONSIDERATIONS FOR SPECIFIC INDUSTRIES

Fundamentally speaking, the two major types of industries involved in converting to 4-day workweeks are manufacturing and service. The aims of both are similar, but the immediate objectives may vary. There are many reasons behind the varied goals and it is well to point out some of the main ones.

1. **Productivity:** In the manufacturing organization our experience shows that overall productivity averages from 60 to 65%, whereas in the service organization it is generous to say it averages 50%. We do not imply that one type of industry is better or worse than the other; one explanation is that in service

industries the functions which the average individual employee performs are extremely varied, thus causing some difference in productivity.

2. **Personnel turnover:** We have found the average annual personnel turnover in production industries is 15 to 20%. Many service industries average 30 to 35% annually and can go as high as 60%. One reason for this tremendous variation is that service industries generally employ young, female labour.

3. **Absenteeism:** Although not particularly attributable just to a service organization, inasmuch as such things as geographical location, type of industry, and skill required have a direct bearing, we do find that service organizations generally have higher absentee rates than the typical manufacturing industry.

4. **Hours of operation:** The production manufacturer generally regulates hours of operation according to the hours required to produce a forecast volume of product. A relatively stable and uniform production flow can therefore be established and, with adequate planning, higher productivity and utilization of personnel can be achieved. Not so in the service organization. The hours of operation here are controlled more often than not by the marketplace, and the service organization maintains hours which are more closely governed by the requirements or whims of its clientele. Thus, the emphasis shifts from utilization of personnel to availability.

5. **Overstaffing:** By virtue of the fact that a service organization relies on availability of personnel for its very existence, we find most service industries overstaffed. This is further aggravated by the three previous conditions: that is, lower productivity, higher turnover of personnel, and absenteeism.

It is ordinarily easier to convert to 4-day scheduling in a manufacturing operation than in the service organization. This is primarily due to the more varied functions required of the service business employee, plus the other factors cited above. It by no means implies there are too many problems confronting the service group, but merely points out that more thought has to be given in this area due to the larger number of variables involved. To illustrate my point, consider the following case examples of two companies. Company A is a typical manufacturer. Company B is a service organization. Both have extremely successful applications of the 4-day workweek.

Company A: A company making a mix of a fairly uniform product for inventory. It is open only 4 days a week, and the plant employees work for 9-hour shifts, 7 AM–4.30 PM with a ½-hour lunch period. The office works 8 AM–5 PM. All the employees have agreed to abolish formal coffee breaks and to reduce wash-up times in order to increase productivity. Workers receive 40 hours' pay for actual work of 36 hours. The difference of 4 hours is labelled "attendance bonus" and in order to collect it, the employee must be present all 4 days of work. The results over a period of 20 months are: productivity up at least 15%; absenteeism has dropped from an average of 7% to less than 1%; the company has a waiting list of skilled applicants; and utility costs are down.

Company B: A hospital, typically service-oriented, and open, of course, 7 days a week, 24 hours a day. Conversion is being made on a gradual basis, and approximately one third of the employees now are under the programme. Three shifts are in operation with an hour overlap between two shifts where the workload is highest. Full-time workers are employed for the day and night shifts, hours being from 7 AM to 5 PM and 9 PM to 7 AM respectively. Part-time employees are utilized to fill in the evening shift from 5 PM to 10 PM. Employees are scheduled so that no one works more than 3 days successively without 2 days off, and every other weekend is a 3-day weekend. Short-term results over a period of 8 months have shown that: absenteeism has dropped to nil; the hospital has a waiting list of qualified professional applicants in a tight labour market; personnel turnover has plummeted; and employee morale has never been higher and is reflected in noticeably better patient care.

Thus we see that the aims of the manufacturing and service industries are the same – basically they both desire to improve profitability. However, the objectives do vary in that the objective of the manufacturing operation is primarily aimed at the increase of productivity. On the other hand, the objectives of the service industry are to decrease absenteeism, personnel turnover, and attract employees; and by so doing increase the availability of personnel to offer its services. In view of these facts, the prime objective of the service organization is of secondary importance to the manufacturing organization, although still important.

The 4-day workweek can be successfully adapted to retail establishments as well. While we will not dwell on the possibilities, consider the modification we developed for a Service Department of an automobile agency. Currently the department operates on a 5-day, 40-hour week. We have designed a schedule so that by adding a maximum of 10% to the staff, service hours can be extended by 35%. They can now operate on a 6-day, 54-hour week, and no individual is required to work more than 4 days each week. This potential for increasing service volume cannot be overlooked easily.

SOME "DON'TS"

In my role as a management consultant, I've naturally had occasion to investigate companies that have used 4-day scheduling, and all have been successful – to a degree. This experience does give me several warnings for companies contemplating the use of the shortened schedule. This advice follows in a broad list of "Don'ts."

1. Don't use the 4-day workweek as a gimmick. In other words, considerable thought, as we have expressed in previous articles and in this book, should be given to the feasibility of using this technique. In actual practice I have seen a company decide on Monday they would start the 4-day workweek for all their employees the following Monday. This decision was made in order to attract labour in a fairly isolated geographical area. Needless to say, labour was attracted, but on reflection the company realized it had, in fact, squandered savings of several thousands of dollars which would have been realized had it done correct planning and instituted the necessary procedures to improve productivity *before* introducing the shortened work schedule.

2. Don't tell all your employees, or even intimate, that you are planning to go into the 4-day workweek. This holds true especially if your plant is organized. It is just common sense to do your planning and investigating before any announcement or intimation is made to employees.

3. Don't fail to take the necessary corrective actions to improve your productivity. Otherwise, all you really do is compress 5 days' inefficiency into 4, and the gains are minimal.

4. Don't be guilty of dismissing the 4-day workweek potential as being foreign to your type of business. So many variations are available for this technique that a complete investigation is most certainly warranted.

5. Don't labour under the misapprehension that all your employees

have to be on a 4-day work schedule. Although it is not usually the most desirable situation, there are cases on record where some employees are scheduled on 4-day workweeks and others on 5-day or even 6-day.

6. Don't expect your salesmen to be ready for a 4-day workweek schedule until such time as the bulk of their customers are also on a 4-day workweek. This is especially true when salesmen depend upon their remuneration in the form of a commission and this, again, is proportionate to the number of potential customers they can see in a week.

7. Don't feel that the entire organization has to be converted to the 4-day workweek at one time. It is very effective to do the conversion on a piecemeal basis in that employees who are not on the 4-day week will voluntarily look for ways to improve their productivity so that they can become part of this new schedule.

8. Don't overlook the possibility, especially if you are in a retail business, that by proper scheduling of your employees on a 4-day basis you might be able to extend your total working, or "open", hours to a longer period of time, with a very small increase in payroll.

THE CONSULTANT'S ROLE

For any company considering conversion to a 4-day workweek, the assistance of an experienced consultant can be of immeasurable value. In its search for a competent management consultant in this field, the company should seek out the generalist and not the specialist firm. The reasons for this should be obvious in that the client company is looking for assistance in pointing out areas which need correction. While the specialist may be extremely competent in his field, the company should be thinking about using the 4-day workweek conversion as a vehicle of problem-solving in any number of broad areas. For this reason it is, again, much to the advantage of the company to work with a management consultant who does not confine his activities to specialized areas.

To the average company without its own internal consulting staff, the management consultant can be of great value in making sure that nothing is overlooked in the preparatory stages. Apart from this insurance, the consultant also offers a third-party or outside viewpoint in relation to the problems which should be solved prior to any implementation. Such problems should be very clearly defined in the consultant's report, and recommendations as to methods or solutions to the problems should be also treated in detail. The conclusion of the consultant's report should give precise details as to the potential cost reduction available as a result of the conversion.

The company should work closely with the consultant to insure that company policies, etc., are incorporated into the general thinking before conclusions are drawn and recommendations made. The company also should insist on at least two alternate schedules to 4-day workweek conversion, along with the advantages and disadvantages of each in order to determine the best possible schedule for its particular situation.

Generally speaking, the consultant's role is dependent upon the size and complexity of the company involved. For the smaller business it may be advantageous to have him analyse and make plans for the entire company. However, for the larger company with several hundred employees, it may be extremely advisable to confine him to a pilot project involving possibly half the employees. This plan not only has the advantage of holding down costs, but when this pilot project becomes successful, it will permeate throughout the rest of the organization. Success breeds success; and most companies will find that other departments and/or employees will be eager to take advantage of the benefits they have seen their co-workers receive. I have seen such motivation generate truly worthwhile suggestions from employees to improve their own productivity so that they could take advantage of the benefits available.

Naturally, the time and fee of the consultant will vary, depending on the size and complexity of the company as well as on the individual consultant involved. It is interesting to note that in our own experience we have found that by reducing absenteeism, for example, from 10% to 5% the resultant saving to the client in increased productivity and/or equivalent wages will amount to a minimum of 5 times the fee for the service.

In a recent analysis of a dozen companies that had converted to the 4-day workweek, I can categorically say that had a consultant been used, the saving by such conversion would have been multiplied by three or four times. In a third of the companies investigated no appreciable saving was generated, due entirely to neglect of proper planning.

In summary, it can be stated that the consultant's role in conversion to the shorter workweek can best be described as one that adds considerable mileage to such a programme in terms of cost-saving potential.

4-DAY WORKWEEK RESULTS

As stated earlier, the effect on the employees generally is good, and we find that approximately 90% are totally in favour. This new approach of offering additional time instead of pay, fringe benefits, etc., is a plus for employee morale and motivation.

The customers of companies who are utilizing the shortened workweek schedule are generally content with the situation. This is especially true if increased productivity can insure on-time delivery of products. It is interesting to note that one manufacturer realized a short-term gain by filling in his normal summer slump in sales with an increased demand for his products during these months. He attributes this phenomenon directly to the fact that many of his customers thought the 4-day schedule would prohibit full production, and therefore ordered during these months to insure an adequate inventory.

As far as competition is concerned, I feel the shortened workweek does make the company practising it more competitive in that they presently can capture more skilled employees, can increase productivity, and can increase employee morale. During our research, we have been fortunate to compare 2 manufacturers engaged in the same type of production, and with approximately the same annual volume and in the same geographical area. Admittedly, there are differences in marketing and production techniques, but, for our purposes, the two were close enough for a good comparison.

The comparison indicates that the manufacturer using the 4-day workweek is manufacturing approximately the same annual volume of product with 40% fewer employees! To enjoy this competitive edge, he must be doing something right. The "right" in this case was proper planning to insure that utilization of personnel was improved *before* he converted to the shorter work schedule. An almost immediate result which can be realized is a dramatic drop in absenteeism. Although subject to erosion, such has not been the case to date and absentee rates average 1% or less over a period of 18 months.

Proper planning and implementation of the 4-day workweek can correct poor use of time. Improved labour utilization can be achieved on a sustained basis, without imposing fatigue on individuals. In fact, it is possible to design schedules so that the worker contributes less time to fulfilling the same work commitment and responsibilities to the company.

Those readers who have participated in labour negotiations and have suffered through grievances and arbitration procedures will immediately recognize the value of the 4-day workweek as a bargaining tool. The 4-day technique affords a unique departure from the vicious wage/price spiral. Thus, the benefit to both labour and management can be a significant one – one which will not be quickly eroded by inflation.

GUIDELINES FOR DECISION-MAKERS

I am sure that most executives reading this text have decided that many of the subjects discussed here do apply to their organization. However, there are still questions that only the executive himself can answer, such as: "Will this technique really make my own company more profitable?" or "Our productivity (or absenteeism or turnover or overtime) rate isn't so bad; where does one draw the line?" or "Are there really any *valid* reasons why I can't do this?"

Obviously the answers to these questions cannot be found in a book. The decision-maker, with all the facts at hand, is the only individual who can do this. By studying key statistics of companies that have converted, I have devised a formula which can serve as a guideline. The "Decision Track Analysis" (below) will give the reader some broad areas in which he can compare his situation with Before and After results of the organizations using the technique.

DECISION TRACK ANALYSIS

The following Decision Track can be used as a guideline for any enterprise considering conversion to the 4-day workweek. Obviously, this formula is broad in scope and individual conditions will necessarily require variation.

Below are four conditions common to most organizations. Circle the point value under each category which is most representative of conditions in your company. Total the point values and note the recommendation.

I. **Productivity:** an estimate of worker utilization. Averages 60–65% for manufacturing and 50–55% for service-oriented companies.

Range	Value
85–100%	1
70–85%	2
*50–70%	3
*Below 50%	5

II. **Absentee Rate:** should reflect absenteeism average for 12 months to eliminate seasonal variations.

Range	Value
0–2%	1
2–5%	2
5–10%	3
10% or more	5

III. **Annual Personal Turnover:** averages 15–20% for manufacturers and 30–35% for service-type organizations.

Range	Value
0–10%	1
10–20%	2
20–30%	3
30% or over	5

IV. **Overtime Rate:** rate computed by overtime hours divided by total hours worked.

Range	Value
0–5%	1
5–10%	2
10–15%	3
15% or over	5

Total the point values circled; then compare this sum with the ranges and recommended course of action outlined below;

Total Value	Recommended Course of Action
0–4	Maintain the positive thinking. Even though conversion would not materially benefit in the basic areas, you would get many advantages in others, such as extended working hours, improved employee morale, union bargaining tool, etc.
5–8	A conversion to 4-day work scheduling would be an excellent vehicle for modernizing your systems. Don't expect drastic savings in either of these first two categories but breaking even will lead to long-term gains.
9–14	The conversion would be very worthwhile, resulting in substantial short-term and long-term gains.
14–20	Nothing to lose and everything to gain by the shorter workweek *if* considerable planning and corrective actions are taken *before* conversion.

CONCLUSION

The movement to the 4-day workweek is frequently credited to the Kyanize Paint Company which made the conversion in 1969. By evaluating its own situation with respect to labour shortages, absenteeism, and outdated systems it discovered that by extending the daily shift to 9 hours from 8, and by obtaining certain labour concessions and cooperation, production could be increased 33% daily.

*Productivity in these ranges indicates a positive need to initiate corrective action *before* conversion.

4 Days, 40 Hours

It is not known where the idea first sprang up, but it is probable that management can claim only secondary credit inasmuch as it seems to have been really started by a small group of production workers in a Massachusetts firm in 1956. This group recognized that in their particular situation, units produced per week could be achieved in 4 days instead of 5 without affecting the company's sales operation. They asked for Fridays off in exchange for working 10 hours a day, Monday through Thursday. Management approved, and they are still doing it.

The management orientation of 4-day programmes is perhaps one of the most important elements of this evolution of labour utilization. I feel strongly that the aims of management and organized labour in guaranteeing security for the individual worker are, in fact, very close.

Conversions to 4-day are, to date, still primarily confined to the small business community, but I definitely expect to see big business take the plunge before the end of this year. This expectation is based, in part, on negotiations currently underway, in which my consulting firm will participate in several major conversions of large organizations.

Current organized labour activity towards the shorter workweek is accelerating rapidly, too. In the words of one corporate executive from the "Fortune 500": "The 4-day workweek is here and we'd better get into it *today* before it is crammed down our throats *tomorrow.*"

13

THE 3-DAY REVOLUTION TO COME:
3-DAY WORKWEEK,
4-DAY WEEKEND
by Millard C. Faught

Millard C. Faught is Chief Economist at The Timewealth Corporation Houston, Texas. One of the youngest Ph.D.'s to graduate from Columbia University, he is also an avid stonemason, poet, explorer, and public speaker.

[Dr. Faught has been trying to alert audiences to the usefulness of the 3-day week for some 30 years. Now that his teachings are vindicated by time, he tells us why he thinks 4-day is just a step towards a 3-day week that will keep costly capital equipment employed a full 6 days a week – and he describes the end of the rat race.]

I note and applaud the phenomenon of a 4-day workweek, emerging roundabout in the American economy, with perhaps an extra dollop of appreciation. As an avocational observer of man's time-use patterns, I have been waiting now for about 30 years for this "step in the right direction". But the ultimate and optimum goal of this shorter workweek trend will be, I am convinced, not a 4-day, but a 3-day workweek.

That is to say, I think the emergent examples of the 4-day workweek will not become a general pattern; rather, they will serve to accelerate transition to a new basic pattern of working and living arrangements in our socio-economy wherein there will be a 3-day workweek for jobholders – and a 6-day workweek for the job-supporting machinery or facilities. Indeed, after 3 decades of continuing inquiry into modern man's use of time and his changing attitudes

149

towards time values, it is my present conviction that the 3-day work-week is not only coming; it is imminent.

Possibly I should temper this initial declaration by noting immediately that the logic of economists and the data of statisticians are not likely to have nearly as much to do with bringing about this revolution in our working/living patterns as will human nature and social crisis.

BACKING INTO PROGRESS

Taking the latter as a relevant point of departure, history affords ample evidence that a society seldom proceeds logically forward into new patterns of technologically permissive progress; rather, the progress often comes from "backing away from crisis". We have a classic illustration of this right now in our sudden, though long overdue, crash programmes to prevent environmental deterioration. We have had growing *means* for environmental repair and orderly management for some time; but we lacked the motivating crises.

Technologically, we could have afforded a far shorter workweek for jobholders in this country years ago.

Indeed, John Diebold and other of the automation authorities have been a steady source of evidence that by all-out application of advancing technology, fewer and fewer workers could do more and more of our work. There is even one such "formula" in wide circulation: that 10% of our manpower using 100% of extant technology could do 80% of our work. In any case, the relevant point is that this dynamic economy can certainly free up a lot of our present job-time for allocation to various forms of "consumption time" any time we decide, as a matter of socio-economic policy and practice, to do so.

Obviously, we have not; there have even been some periodic gain in the average length of the workweek since its low point in the Depression. And the dominating reason is that we have been traditionally, and still are, a highly job-centred society. We have taken the fruits of technological progress in the forms of more money and more goods and services; but, up to now, we have been reluctant to take much of this permissive progress in forms of more non-job consumer time – what I choose to call "Timewealth".

Where trimming has taken place in the total workweek we have concentrated in the main on cutting the length of the workday. Ironically, this trend, which may have seemed logical as it developed, has now become a prime causal factor in what I believe will soon

150

become a major and basic overhaul of the temporal working pattern. It is certainly long overdue. So much so that when history affords some real retrospective perspective, analysts will probably conclude that the 5-day short-houred workweek was one of the stupidest compromises with progress ever made by man; especially so, because he has by now tolerated the rat race it produced for so long.

Synthetic Reasons: A Real Rat Race. We may work only 40 hours a week, but what a struggle we have doing it. The fact that millions of us patently and desperately want out of the resulting rat race now has become, in my view, the greatest source of pressure moving us towards a shorter work*week* – not a shorter work*day*. As a matter of plain fact, thousands of us are already making our own short work-week by just not showing up Friday or Monday.

As far as any real meaning for the human condition is concerned, the present "40-hour workweek" is an absolute fiction: so is the "new leisure" it is supposed to produce. We may be present on the job only 7 or 8 hours, true; but on any given workday for any given worker – especially the 70-odd per cent of us who live in or near mega-lopolis – the home-to-home "workday" is more like from 11 to 15 hours long. Consequently, our non-work leisure is more like 2 beers or a TV programme short – not really long enough for any useful time application of our own motivated choosing.

In short, our present job-pattern compromise with technological progress wrecks five-sevenths of the week, as far as the human job-holder's private life is concerned. What it does to his weekend, during which he tries to "compensate", is sometimes even worse.

High Priced Tools. From the frame of reference of production economics, the 5-day short-houred workweek is an even stupider pattern. American jobs are the most expensively equipped in the world in terms of the tools and overhead essential to creating them. Few of our jobs are capitalized at under $50,000 and many have more than $250,000 invested in providing them. How absurd, then, to use this great, complex, and costly machine 8 hours a day or less; and how costly it has become to run it longer hours at over-time rates.

Ample Crises for Leverage on Change. On the theory that social progress can derive from backing away from crisis, then, we certainly have ample current crises:

151

1. We have inflation endemically adding to high costs, because we operate our incredibly efficient (potentially) economy so ineptly.
2. We have jobholders living in a time-consuming rat race, because their abundant non-job time is eroded by the 10-trip backing and forthing to work.
3. We have the whole mess congealing into ever larger globs of megalopolization; because, in a job centred socio-economy, job and home can be only so many miles apart.
4. And now, finally, we are becoming harassedly aware that such job-centring is not only a nuisance, it is environmentally inimical and is getting dangerously worse.

It is not only that we have an ample supply of socio-economic crises and attendant problems to back away from, the more constructive way to put it perhaps is that never were Americans in a more amenable mood to question old ways or try new solutions. On balance, I believe we have generated a pressure structure which is about to force, and will also accelerate, a drastic change in the time dimensions of the work pattern in this country. And I believe that, once started, the pressures for a *shorter* workweek will force right through to a 3-day workweek, rather than stop at a 4-day week.

My main reason for so thinking is that the 3-day week offers some really basic, new solutions to many of our socio-economic crises, whereas the 4-day week offers only palliatives – and some new problems, when viewed as an economy-wide solution to our major job-related problems.

Nor that I have any quarrel with a 4-day workweek per se. I'm confident that many more smaller companies, or those with unique processing or marketing patterns, will find it an advantageous alternative to the status quo. I am impressed by all of the pluses its innovators have reported to date.

Nevertheless, as related to the big and basic companies and industries that will be the bellwethers and backbone components of any basic new job structure, the 4-day week has too much gravity of economic facts and social mores to defy.

7-Day Habit Pattern. In the first place, we are not likely, even in a revolutionary mood, to abandon our traditional 7-day week, of which Sunday is the cornerstone, whether one is religion-minded or not. Yet we would really have to do so, de facto at least, if we were to make the 4-day workweek a basic pattern for the economy. Moreover, if we cannot afford to spread our costly overhead over a 5-day week as now, we certainly cannot afford to work it only 4 days. And two 4-day weeks buckled together would make the traditional Sunday, a workday.

Admittedly, an increasing amount of marketing is being done on Sunday in various areas of the country. However, I think this reflects far more the fact that people want to include more shopping and other consuming in their expenditure of their non-job "Time-wealth". It doesn't prove that people want to work on Sunday, or that they want to change the basic nature of Sunday.

NO HALFWAY REVOLUTION, PLEASE

One reason I thoroughly applaud the appearance on the scene of the 4-day workweek is the impetus it gives to a national dialogue on how best to evolve towards the right kind of a *shorter* workweek. Towards this goal of wider discussion, I have written many articles and made many speeches over recent years and also have a current paperback book on the market.* I mention this in order to make a reportorial point; namely, that unless my mail and my audience response is totally out of step, there is certainly a wide and strong public concensus in favour of a shorter workweek. And they want it *now*!

Therefore, and I now drop from public to personal opinion, if our technology now makes it possible, and the people want it, and it will open up new approaches to solving many major job-related socio-economic crises – then what are we waiting for? Also, if we are going to perpetrate a peaceful revolution by changing our job structure, why stop halfway to achieving its real potentials?

3-Day Workweek. Why not for once take advantage of the opportunity to do something the easy, practical, and logical way . . . and go *directly* to the 3-day workweek? For openers, let's put Saturday back in the workweek for our costly machinery, plants, and other overheads. And while we're about it, let's run them on longer shifts, even 10 to 12 hours. For discussion's sake, let's say we go to a 6-day, 60-hour straight-time week. This would provide a 50% increase over present straight-time use of the tools of production.

Now, on the human side of the scale, let's finally harvest our really great potential for taking some of our technological gains in the form

*More Timewealth for You (New York: Pyramid Books, 1970).

153

of non-job, human-use time. As noted, I prefer to call this "Time-wealth" rather than "leisure" – the latter being an amorphous and often historically invidious term without any real definitive meaning.

Let's then split this 6-day, 60-hour production week into two job periods – that is, two 3-day workweeks. One set of jobholders would work Monday, Tuesday, and Wednesday; one set would work Thursday, Friday, and Saturday; all to have the traditional Sunday off.

The economic readjustments of such a shift could be considerable, depending on the individual company situation. But the incredible increases in productivity from running our facilities, which are the real source of our economic wherewithal, so much longer and steadily make this revolution economically permissive. I have found little dispute on this point in years of discussing the 3-day week. Ironically, I find that more concern revolves around what employees would do with all that extra time than on whether the employers could afford to provide it. Actually, a lot of workers would have to moonlight during the transition period; that is, hold two 3-day jobs; else we would not have enough manpower to provide the double work forces required. For sure, this kind of change will generate no technological *un*employment!

There will be adjustment problems, both minor and serious, because this will be a basic revolution in the job structure and productive use of the economy. However, for perspective's sake let's not lose sight of the fact that so massive a change is not going to be an everywhere-at-once and overnight phenomenon. Various sections of the economy will follow their own adaptive paces.

ADAPTIVE CHALLENGES*

It should also be noted that so much more Timewealth so soon will undoubtedly have some attendant nouveau-riche problems, and it may well take longer to adapt to it socially than economically. There is no question, for instance, that many *will* choose to moonlight, holding two 3-day jobs until their useful interest in more time exceeds their long-houred interest in extra money.

Part of our current social turmoil stems from an apparent desire of some among the younger generation to lessen the job-centredness

*Many changes in leisure use anticipated by Dr. Faught for the 3-day week have actually begun to happen in the case of the 4-day workers; see Chapters 1, 3, and 4.

of our society. Certainly a 3-day week would accelerate shifts of emphasis to other than work-centred time-use patterns and values. There will be an acceleration of the progress we are patently already making in the arts of Timewealth spending even in the midst of our rat race. However, I think it will take at least 2 full generations after the *economic* transition to this new kind of split-week living before man will really have adapted to it *socially*.

Very likely the key to the adaptive timetable will be determined by how soon our *educational* complex can itself adapt to the new time dimensions of personal lives. Our liberal arts and social studies curricula to the contrary, ours is still dominantly a learning-for-earning educational pattern.

However, by suggesting that this adaption process is going to be both massive and often complex as to its detailed impact on inherited social mores, I do not mean to sound negative. We will be adapting here to a kind of progress with highly positive potentials, both for mastering old problems and for achieving new goals. I think the really exciting short-run potentials of the 3-day week hinge on what people *are* likely to do with their new Timewealth – and quickly. On this new frontier I believe that the people – as individuals, as families, and as communities – are going to outstrip by far many of their yesterday-oriented socio-economic institutions when it comes to adapting to abundant Timewealth.

Split-Week Living. As a prime example, I believe that very quickly large numbers of families will seize on the new time-permissive opportunity of the 3-day week to escape from Megalopolis. That is, the emancipated jobholder will move his family far enough into what I call "Hinterlurbia" to escape the mounting evils of both Metropolis and suburbs.

The worker, probably in car pools with his fellows, will commute to his city job *once* each week. Moreover, he and others will probably rent an apartment or other barrack facility for the 2 nights between his 3 workdays. Another group will use the *same* facilities at the other end of the week. The jobholder is thus away from his family for 3 whole days, yes; but also he is *with* them far more than he is now.

What is really important here is the potential *effectiveness* of the new Timewealth available. If marriage, the family unit, and parenthood have been eroded by the absence of the father under contemporary work patterns; then, if his presence is the key factor, they certainly ought to be advantaged by his availability in full-time

155

stretches of more than half the week every week. Patently, the 3-day workweek will afford today's rat-raced jobholder more time to be a person, a spouse, a parent, a neighbour, and a citizen. I cannot help but believe it will beneficiate all such roles in life.

Not that man and his family has to take to the woods, sands, or hills of Hinterlurbia to exploit these new Timewealth potentials. For those who prefer urban life, and perhaps for many of the job-holders who are women or sans family, the less-crowded cities should certainly offer living amenities over today's Megalopolis. Nor is it inconsequential to note that a less-pressured urban environment will be more hospitable for industrial and commercial functions (which gave rise to urban centres in the first place) if the function of housing people has been reduced.

New Personal Participation in Life. Irrespective of the new geography of living which The Timewealth Revolution will make possible, by cutting the time and distance tethers of our own job-centred living geography, many new and interesting possibilities open up. As an example, I am optimistic about man's inventiveness in putting his new Timewealth to work at what might be called the do-it-yourself level. Indeed, I envisage a veritable resurgence of all of the traditional self-help and group-help patterns of frontier life out there on those new frontiers in Hinterlurbia, when these 4-day-weekend pioneers get there. And the market impact for everything from hand tools to pickup trucks will be reverberative. After all, Veblen called it man's *instinct* of workmanship. Give man some real time to use his tools, and some room, and I believe all those Yankee craftsmanship traditions, skills, and incentives will reflower in a Time-wealthy world.

Urban Readjustment. What concerns me more as an adaptive problem is what may happen back in Megalopolis, where now there is too little of everything – from schools to parking places. Not that there won't be need for a lot of planning to accommodate the migration to Hinterlurbia, but it will be in the nature of more orthodox *growth* planning. I think it is a greater question whether the cities will wake up in time to the need for wise "*shrinkage*" planning as many of their citizens (and taxpayers) depart.

As previously noted, it may well be one of the ironies of history that, as people no longer have to *live* in cities just to be near their jobs, cities can do a better job of *providing* jobs, since the cities will be better suited to their original function of accommodating the needs of commerce and industry.

One thing is certain: accommodating the needs of the redistributed population will virtually amount, not just to rebuilding the cities, but to rebuilding America before this revolution is over. As just one illustration which grows out of a frequently asked question about education: no, the schools will not operate on a 3-day week. We will really have to rebuild our educational system.

Tomorrow's children will grow up in an increasingly complex world. They will need to know more and more to cope with it. If also they are going to have far more Timewealth for living their lives, aside from working, then obviously the educational function must grow both in its quantitative and qualitative dimensions. Whether this means more school hours per day, or more days per week, or both, I am not the pedagogue to say. But I have this conviction: education will have to become a more intensive process and it will have to *continue* through life, else the true potentials of the Timewealth Revolution will be sold short on many fronts.

It may be only the least intrinsically important of all the aspects of the above fact, but facility-wise we will virtually have to rebuild the nation's school structures – new schools in the Hinterlurbs and highly rearranged facilities in the cities. This massive readaptation of facilities to the new demography will affect all kinds of man's facilities, from hotels to hospitals, from supermarkets to churches.

HOW SOON?

As a concluding notation it might be helpful to report that, over years of audience exposure of such thinking as is set down here, I have found few people who doubt that the 3-day workweek will arrive someday. Having watched the signs perhaps more closely than most, I feel quite safe in predicting that "someday" is about here. The appearance of significant precursors, such as the number of companies trying the 4-day workweek, should serve as alerts to the beginning of the Timewealth Revolution.

Timewealth Revolution. That the shift to a 3-day workweek will indeed set off a revolution of required adaptations is by no means an exaggeration of terms. And because it will be so all-encompassing as to its impact – on everything from social mores to land values, from municipal management to market modification – the risk of ignoring it, even as a mere possibility, increases.

157

The probabilities of the $5-day seemed quite unlikely (and impossible), too, until "all of a sudden", thanks to Henry Ford, it became a widespread reality. The first major precedent of a 3-day workweek will probably spread even faster in our modern concatenated socio-economy.

In my view, the 4-day workweek will serve as a critical fuse for the Revolution; mainly, because it will begin to break the seemingly frozen notion that the workweek is just naturally a 5-day phenomenon.

So far, only a few small companies have adopted the 4-day work pattern. But the AFL-CIO has made it a declared major target of bargaining. Before long, *major* management is going to be confronted with the 4-day gauntlet. Without rearguing the case, I do not believe that the 4-day week has a prayer of becoming a viable pattern for the basic American economy. Nevertheless, it will become a growing demand, and managers will have to have an alternative.

They will have to get up early or stay up late to find a better counter-proposition than the 3-day workweek for the people, and the 6-day workweek for the machinery. It will give them new productivity at one end and new markets at the other ... and a marvellous bargaining position in the middle.

And it will give all of us a new way of life in America.

[*It came to our attention at press time for the original edition of this book that a few firms were trying the 3-day week right then. (Profiles of 3 of these firms are included in the Late Entries section at the end of Chapter 2.)*

These 3-day firms seem to indicate a need to provide more non-wage benefits to employees for purposes of attracting and keeping high-quality personnel, in what appears to be a period of simultaneous unemployment and labour scarcity. (There is even an employment agency in New York, Baeder and Torton, that places personnel on what it calls NEWTIME – a 5-hour day, 5 days a week for permanent, salaried professionals, mostly women.)

At this writing, almost 2 years later, there are now more than 100 firms using the 3-day week. About half of these involve data processing; the rest involve varied functions, especially manufacturing, but also including masseurs at health spas and photographic processors – where primary concern is for timing of output. Generally, the desirability of keeping costly capital equipment in full-time operation for 6 or 7 days a week is most frequently behind the use of 3-day workweeks.

And employees love the 4-day weekends – The Editor.]

Part Two

14

BRITAIN AND THE 4-DAY WEEK: WITH PROFILES OF SOME BRITISH 4-DAY PIONEERS
by Theo Richmond

Theo Richmond, B.Sc.Econ., is a graduate of the London School of Economics. He has directed television documentaries for BBC and ITV, and directed and scripted industrial films. As a freelance journalist, he contributes to The Guardian *and* The Daily Telegraph Magazine.

INTRODUCTION

I first came to the 4-day scene when I investigated it for several months at the beginning of 1972 for an article in *The Daily Telegraph Magazine*. Some of the material in the following report appeared in that article. Subsequently, I widened my research for the purposes of this book.

I found that little had been written in Britain about the 4-day week. The first thing I read was the American edition of *4 Days, 40 Hours*, edited by Riva Poor. It did wonders for my interviewing confidence. Forgetting my own recent ignorance, I was shocked to discover that the people I interviewed did not share my encyclopaedic knowledge. Didn't they know about Kyanize Paints? About AFL–CIO attitudes? About the beneficial effects of 4-day on absenteeism, labour turnover, recruitment, company morale and production costs?

In truth, I didn't really expect a detailed knowledge of the American scene: what did surprise me was the general unawareness of an important new trend gathering momentum on the other side of the Atlantic. It was as though America were some small far away country about which we needed to know very little.

One cannot always assume that what happens in America today,

161

will happen here tomorrow. Nevertheless, many of our economic and technological trends do follow in the wake of the United States. Social trends too. In which case, British management might well find it in their interests to keep a sharp eye on the latest American developments to be ready for their arrival here. Why not benefit from American experience?

Every day more American companies are changing over to the 4-day week. Since the publication of Riva Poor's book, business journals, academic papers, surveys and seminars have probed the subject from numerous angles. The mass media have had a field-day. The 4-day week is no longer dismissed as a passing fad, but accepted as a relentless and significant trend.

In Britain, where we have our own 4-day pioneers, the subject has received little attention so far. Of the people I talked to (not all of whom could be quoted or referred to in this report), only a few were well-informed about the pros and cons of the 4-day week. Many thought of it exclusively in terms of reduced weekly hours, and had hardly considered the possibilities of the *rearranged* 4-day week: the 4-40 principle in other words. Some appeared only too ready to reject change without having analysed its consequences. The words "four-forty" had barely left my lips when one trade union official rapped, "We wouldn't stand for that!" While a management representative, doggedly supporting the industrial *status quo*, said: "Things are working all right as they are." Interestingly, the same reactions greeted 4-day initially in the United States.

There was no road to Damascus on my various journeys through 4-day territory: no blinding light to convert me into a fervent 4-day week campaigner, believing that the good life was only one day away. But I feel convinced that here is a subject of importance to both management and labour, and one that both sides ought to be exploring and discussing. This report might help to get the debate going.

BRITISH EXPERIENCE WITH THE 4-DAY WEEK

Britain can claim a world pioneer of the 4-day week. Years before the movement got going in the United States, a small metal-finishing firm in Batley, Yorkshire, gave the 4-day week a one-month try-out and, finding that it worked, decided to stay on it permanently.

The man behind the innovation was Mr. Frank Spicer, Managing Director of Roundhay Metal Finishers Ltd. Acting on what he calls "just plain commonsense", he saw that there were advantages to be had out of rearranging his 40-hour week. Advantages to him as a businessman and to his work force. In November, 1965, when he switched permanently to 4-day, he changed from five 8-hour days (Monday to Friday) to four 10-hour days (Monday to Thursday).

Looking at the company's case history (see Profile 1 in the second half of this chapter), it is interesting to note how closely it parallels that of American 4-day firms; how reactions from employees in Batley echo those of their American counterparts.

Results at Britain's Pioneer 4-day Firm: Since going over to the 4-day week, the company's productivity has risen impressively. And according to its Managing Director, profitability has increased at a greater rate than it would have done had they stayed on the conventional 5-day week. They have a more contented labour force, firmly wedded to the idea of a 3-day weekend. Absenteeism, labour turnover, heat, light and power costs have all been reduced. Not a single skilled man has left because of the change. Nor has one customer been lost. The company's prices to its customers have remained remarkably stable. All in all, a healthy counter-inflationary situation which, were it to be repeated throughout the country, would do wonders for Britain's economy.

Frank Spicer took exception to one trade union leader saying that his company was "as untypical as you could find". It all depends, of course, on what you mean by typical. Frank Spicer says that Roundhay is "very, very typical" of many small firms in Britain, and that, taken in total, these firms play a vital national role. Having practised 4-day for so many years, he is convinced that larger industrial units could benefit from it, just as he has done. He is sharply critical of tradition-bound management and labour, settled in old ways rather than exploring new ideas.

Other Experiments: CDG Ltd., a leading design consultancy in the West End of London, provides another revealing 4-day case history (Profile 2). It shows that the rearranged 4-day week can work for white collars as successfully as for blue.

In November, 1971, after reading about the 4-day week in the United States, CDG decided to try it out for themselves, initially on a 6-months experimental basis. Their 37½-hour week was rearranged over 4 days, Tuesday to Friday. At the end of the trial period, 83% of the staff voted to remain on 4-day. Various snags which had arisen in the course of the 6 months had been ironed out. Having got over

163

this adjustment period, the company felt it could look forward to reaping the full benefits of the 4-day week.

For many years British firms with round-the-clock shift systems have broken away from the conventional 5-day pattern. These systems, including 4 days on and a variety of days off, usually involve very long shifts – anything up to 12 hours (see Profiles 4, 5 and 6). Operating on a rotating basis, they result in time off falling on different days each week. They abolish the weekend as a Saturday/Sunday concept. These unconventional working weeks, dictated in part by the technology of continuous process industry, are spreading as the need increases to maximize the use of capital-intensive plant.

Another breakaway from the 5-day mould is the swing, particularly strong in the Midlands, towards four 10-hour night shifts a week instead of five 8-hour shifts. Thousands of workers in Coventry can lay claim to the 4-night if not the 4-day week. (See p. 167 and p. 174.)

A number of firms have thought about the 4-40 week, flirted with the idea for a while, but then pulled back. Thomas Hardman and Sons Ltd., a Lancashire manufacturing firm, was intent on going on to the 4-day week (Profile 3). But certain problems, mainly of a trade union nature (about which more later), forced them to put aside their plan. However, the company has not abandoned its 4-day hopes.

Firms like Roundhay and CDG, which have gained 4-day benefits for themselves and provided a regular 3-day weekend for their employees, remain thin on the ground. In their different ways, they say a great deal about the 4-day week in a British context. Obviously they do not represent every sector of the economy. Nor do they illustrate every labour-management situation. But their experience – and success – should be of interest to those who have given the 4-day week little thought. And to those who have dismissed it out of hand.

SOME BRITISH ATTITUDES

The Confederation of British Industry justifiably describes itself as "the spokesman for British industry". Its membership comprises approximately 11,600 companies, 220 employers' organizations, trade and commercial associations, and 16 nationalized industries. A spokesman for the "spokesman" gave short shrift to the 4-day week if it meant a reduction in total hours: "At this particular time industry can't afford a reduction in working hours. It's just not on, unless there is to be a going back to more inflation. In 5 years' time – maybe. At the moment – no."

The CBI, he said, had not yet looked into the 4-40 concept. "But the last thing we want to be is inflexible. Provided that the 40 hours, however permutated, resulted in the same amount of production being obtained, I don't think employers would have any objection. But it's possible that with certain kinds of work – heavy manual labour or concentrated work – 10 hours is more than you can do. It has been suggested that the last 2 hours are not so productive when overtime is worked. But if there was no loss – or no significant loss – in production, I don't think there would be any objection."

If many firms in the United States had *increased* their productivity after changing to 4-day, shouldn't British management be taking the initiative? "Management here probably finds that if it makes the first approach it will meet with a conservative reaction from labour. Therefore the employer is probably reluctant to make the first approach."

The British Institute of Management's main purpose in life is to improve management in industry, central and local government, and other important areas. It organizes conferences, courses and seminars. Had they done anything on the 4-day week? "Offhand I can't think that we have," said the spokesman. "The 4-day week is not an issue that has thrust itself at us."

The Association of Management Consultants: "Personally, I would be very surprised if any work has been done on it in this country. It certainly hasn't reached me, and I read most things currently produced. It's probably a little early in this country . . . Both sides [management and labour] tend to be suspicious. It's like so many things here. If it's new, we don't really want it. I find it quite horrifying how unaware people are of the benefits certain changes could bring them. It would be better if employers looked into it [the 4-day week] first, rather than end up having it forced on them by the employees."

The Department of Employment: "As far as the Department is concerned, there has been no investigation into the subject."

A CAUTIOUS RESPONSE FROM ONE EMPLOYER

The Engineering Employers' Federation is by far the biggest of all the employer organizations. Its 5,000 member firms employ a total labour force of about 2 millions. And because the Federation's line on wages and working conditions is followed by most non-federated firms in the industry, its agreements affect a further 1 million employees. The Federation's Director-General is Mr. Martin Jukes QC.

When we met, his Federation was facing – and strongly resisting – a union demand for a 35-hour week. How did he feel about the idea of a 4-40 week? "Quite frankly, not at all favourably. The history of the unions shows that for the last 30 or 40 years they have fought to bring the working day down to 8 hours. And that does seem quite long enough for an ordinary day. Of course emergencies come along and then you need to have overtime. But there's a considerable feeling that if you have too long a day, people get tired. You do have to remember the productivity of your hours of labour. Once you give a chap a 10-hour day he'll want overtime on top of that." Did he fear that overtime would then spill over to the fifth day? "Yes. At time-and-a-half."

Could he see 4-40 bringing any benefits at all for the employer? "I don't think so. I don't see them myself. Yes, if you closed the place down on the fifth day you wouldn't have to light it, heat it and so on, but then you'd have a lot of expensive machinery standing still." But surely if that machinery was being used for the same total hours per week, there would be no net loss in its utilization? "No, there would be no net loss, that's true."

Did he not think absenteeism would be reduced by a 4-40 week? "I think you'd get Monday absenteeism just the same." He was doubtful whether workers would benefit from having more leisure time: "Would they know how to use it?" And he was certain that a 3-day weekend would inevitably result in more moonlighting, which he regarded as a bad thing, "though" – drily – "I might, of course, get a gardener that way."

He said: "May we talk about women?" By all means. "Well would it be right to make a woman work a 10-hour day? Look at the average married woman who works. She's got a husband to get tea for when he gets home. She has to make the beds. Would a longer day be awfully good for women? I don't think so." If American experience was anything to go by, it did seem as though some women liked getting domestic chores out of the way on Friday, and having the weekend free for more enjoyable activities. Mr. Jukes listened with interest.

We talked about the night-shift agreement to which his Federation had been a party since the 1960's. He recalled that workers in the motor industry in the Midlands had objected to working the Friday night shift. Instead of working five 8-hour night shifts

Monday to Friday, they wanted four 10-hour shifts Monday to Thursday.

"The unions were against it," recalled Mr. Jukes, "but in the end they had to come back to us and say, 'Look, our principle is that we shouldn't work more than 8 hours, but we just can't hold our members.' " And the employers, with all their fears about loss of productivity through fatigue, had agreed to a 10-hour shift? "We had to. We couldn't get them to work the fifth night. They just didn't come in. We didn't welcome the idea. Nor did the union officials. It was the man on the shop floor who insisted."*

In which case, perhaps a similar shop floor pressure might lead to the 4-40 week for day workers? "There are no signs of it." Might the pressure come from management? "I think management would not welcome it and should not be initiating it." But surely there must be something in it for management, otherwise why were American companies initiating the 4-40 week? Was the Federation studying the concept? "It is not. It's true that it takes time to change the attitudes of management, and that it takes time to get new ideas across to them. But with this one [4-40], they would need some very convincing evidence to prove that it was of help to their production ... We as a Federation certainly haven't been thinking about it."

Looking ahead, did he not agree that the 4-day week, in one form or another, was bound to come? "It may," he replied with a lawyer's caution, "It may."

A SCEPTICAL RESPONSE FROM THE DIRECTOR'S SPOKESMAN

Sir Richard Powell is the Director-General of the Institute of Directors, with 44,000 members and imposing headquarters in Belgrave Square. In his outer office hangs a framed cartoon which appeared in the *Sydney Morning Herald* when the D-G paid an official visit to Australia some years ago. It shows Sir Richard, a tall and pukka Englishman, being greeted by a demonstration of disgruntled company directors. Their banners carry fiery slogans calling for "More Champagne Breaks" and "A Three-Hour Week."

When I went in to see him, Sir Richard laughed heartily at the idea of a 3-day week, and he thought the 4-day week was a bit of a joke too – "a bad one at that!" He saw "great dangers" in it, and regarded it as "another route to inflation". He was thinking of a

*See p. 174.

167

reduced working week, but the 4-40 week didn't appeal to him much either. He was concerned about excessive fatigue after 8 hours, and thought there were other factors which might reduce productivity.

He did not think management ought to be initiating 4-40. Nor could he work up any enthusiasm for the 3-day weekend. "I don't think I'm being unduly reactionary over this, but I think the average Englishman actually enjoys his work. I don't think he'd welcome it." There was evidence of this on his own doorstep, he said. The Institute's luncheon club, unlike most West End catering establishments, does not function at the weekend. In theory, he said, a whole weekend off should seem a splendid idea to the chefs, waiters and kitchen porters. "But they don't like it. Not a bit. They spend all their money."

So far as his own members were concerned, he felt they were the least likely to benefit from extra leisure time. The 4-day week might be all very well "for those who can forget about work when the hooter goes", but he thought the whole idea "a joke in poor taste to the hard-worked company director whose responsibilities never stop even when he leaves the office".

Was it worth investigating the 4-40 week since American experience showed that it could benefit both management and labour? "Of course it's worth investigating. But in Britain we're not ready for it."

MANAGEMENT VIEWS VERSUS 4-DAY REALITIES

To judge by what management spokesmen (including those not mentioned here) had to say about it, it seemed that 4-40 had little or nothing to commend it. Indeed, its effects might be positively damaging. One needed to remind oneself of the two British companies that had put it into practice, found it worked well all round, and were recommending it to others. The managing director of Roundhay: "I started the 4-day week because it seemed the sensible thing to do. It's so obvious. And the more you think about it, the more obvious it becomes ... We've looked at it for 7 years and still haven't found anything wrong with it. I can't understand why other people haven't done it. If they looked into it properly, I'm sure a lot of them would."

The sales director of CDG: "I'm amazed so few people are doing it. But then, in America management is on the ball, always looking ahead. British management has never been well known for instigating new ideas."

168

A LABOUR SPOKESMAN'S RESPONSE

Mr. Jack Jones is the leader of Britain's largest trade union, the Transport and General Workers' Union, which has nearly 1¾ million members. We met at Transport House. The mention of 4-40 failed to arouse the General Secretary's enthusiasm. A shorter working week? At once I had his full attention. "If we go down to 35 hours, we could then quickly get a movement towards the 4-day week," he said.

He could see the attractions of a 3-day weekend. "There is a great deal of sense in providing good leisure breaks." If the 3-day weekend came about, did he believe that people would find problems in coping with the extra leisure time? "We were asked the same sort of questions when we wanted to come down to a 5-day week. We said our workers wanted more leisure and that there would be no problems. They wanted Saturday morning for things like do-it-yourself or, if they had caravans, for going to the seaside."

Presumably then, he did not go along with Sir Richard Powell's point about the average Englishman not welcoming more leisure time? "With due respect to Sir Richard," said Mr. Jones, "I think he's talking nonsense. I think I have more knowledge of the average Englishman than he does. People *would* benefit from longer leisure breaks. It's all right for the businessman who can take long lunches and play golf on Friday afternoons."

If 4-40 held out the chance of a good leisure break for workers *now*, wasn't it worth campaigning for? He was more interested, he replied, in "pressing continuously" for a shorter working week. This would help to create more jobs at a time of high unemployment, much of it caused by new production techniques. "I think we must first get a move towards a reduced working week. This is on the cards. It's a number one item on our trade union agenda."

How would he respond if employers came to him with the 4-40 idea? "We would be sympathetic, although a lot would depend on the product, the location and other factors. We are flexible in our approach. We wouldn't say no on principle. We would negotiate it." Then came the predictable *but*. "But we would want some sort of penalty to be applied against the extra hours." In other words – overtime. "There are some industries where it [4-40] *could* operate, but we'd want some provisions regarding overtime."

Some trade unions, he pointed out, would not warm to the idea of a 10-hour day, even with overtime provisions. "There is a traditional objection in Britain to lengthening the working day." He felt a 10-hour day could cause excessive fatigue, industrial accidents, and inhibit productivity.* Nevertheless, if the workers in a given plant wanted 4-40, it would be open to local negotiation. He could see the idea developing, but felt the future lay with a 35-hour week, and he could not view 4-40 as anything more than "a temporary arrangement".

A few months later, in June, 1972, Mr. Jones waved the 4-day flag in public. Addressing a TGWU rally in the Midlands, he appeared to have discarded the 35-hour objective: ". . . we are going all-out for a massive cut in the working year," he said, and that included "the 3-day weekend, with 4 days and a 32-hour week."

MORE RESERVATIONS ABOUT 4-DAY

Going on the investigation so far, the prospects for 4-40 as a widespread movement in Britain continued to look bleak. However, it had been heartening to hear from the TGWU that they were flexible in their approach, and to learn from the CBI that the last thing they wanted to be was inflexible. Who but a cynic would think otherwise?

On April 18, 1972, a conference held in London by the Industrial Society (an independent body which "promotes the best use of people at work") devoted a good part of its time to the question of the 4-day week. The main speakers on the subject were Mr. Frank Spicer, outlining the success of his own 4-day operation (see Profile 1); and Mr. John Frydd, General Secretary of the National Federation of Professional Workers, which has 41 member unions representing a total of 1½ million white collar workers.

Overtime: Expressing reservations about the 4-40 week, Mr. Frydd soon came round to the matter of overtime. In principle he disliked overtime. It was a "foul system", he said. Good management should get higher productivity in normal hours, but be prepared to pay for it. If the working day was to be extended to 10 hours, overtime pay would be expected for the additional 2 hours. He did not like the idea of a 10-hour day, and he disapproved of half-hour lunch breaks. One hour, he claimed, was the minimum necessary to maintain good health. Of course, if employers were to suggest a 4-day week with an 8-hour day, yes, he would be very much in favour of that.

*Mr Jones' union has negotiated 10-hour shifts in the past. See p. 174 and Profiles 5, 7 and 8.

After the conference, he explained why he thought the employer should pay overtime for the 9th and 10th hours, although the total weekly hours remained the same. "If there is a fixed working day without overtime and a particular firm varies its hours for its own convenience, it is up to them to pay overtime." But supposing the change was for the convenience of the employees too? "If there is mutual benefit and both sides agreed, then all one is concerned about is that the extension from 8 to 10 is not used by employers generally to get us away from what we've been fighting for for a century and a half – the shorter working day."*

The 4-40 week presented another overtime problem in his view: "Supposing the employer wants overtime done beyond the 40 hours? Whereas you can add overtime on the end of an 8-hour day, the trade union movement would strongly object to it at the end of a 10-hour day; and I don't think an employer would want it either."†

Fatigue: Trade unionists and employers had both expressed concern about the fatigue likely to be imposed by a 10-hour day. Dr. Robert Murray is the TUC's Medical Adviser. Was he bothered by the idea of a 10-hour day? "It doesn't bother me at all. What *would* worry me is a longer working day *and* a longer working week." He stressed that in dealing with this subject "so much depends on the nature of the work". In those industries where there were special health risks, an extension of the working day would no doubt be ruled out. That apart, the 10-hour day seemed to him to be "all right so long as a chap is getting enough rest – physical and mental rest – in order to recover, and so long as he can come to terms socially with the new hours". He was very concerned about moonlighting – "a bad thing" – and felt that the 4-day week would encourage it. "I'm interested in people having leisure and being able to pursue things they normally wouldn't have the time to pursue."

*A spokesman for the West German TUC (Deutsche Gewerkschaftsbund) in Dusseldorf, quoted in *Stern* (October 24, 1971): "We don't spend a hundred years fighting for an 8-hour day only to find ourselves bargaining now about 10."

†In March, 1972, despite the high rate of unemployment, 29% of operatives in manufacturing industries were on overtime; and the average amount of overtime worked per operative was 8 hours a week. (*Department of Employment Gazette*, May, 1972.)

4 Days, 40 Hours

AN UNEXPECTED REACTION

A significant reference to the 4-day week appeared in the TUC
Review of Collective Bargaining Developments (No. 1, 1972) issued
in May, 1972. Significant in that the TUC was actually drawing attention to the 4-40 concept. And, moreover, pointing out that it might
be to the advantage of employer and employee. Not only did it seem
like an unexpected hint to both sides, but it even quoted an example
of a negotiated agreement for a 4-40 week. Quite a breakthrough –
or so it seemed. After making the point that "the major struggle for a
40-hour week has largely been won and that increasing priority can
now be given to attaining the 35-hour objective", the Review went
on to say:

... attention should also be given to the possibility of securing the
4 day working week [their italics]. Whilst the implications of such a change
would need careful consideration by unions and workers in the light of
particular circumstances, a 3-day weekend is clearly an attractive proposition. Other potential benefits include a reduction in time and money
spent travelling to and from work – especially valuable to long distance
and rush-hour commuters. From a management point of view, where the
4-day week did not need to be "staggered" over 5 days by including Friday
and Monday in the weekend for different workers, costs could be reduced
by saving one day's operating expenses. One example of this development
is the agreement for a 4 day (40 hour) week between TGWU and Christian
Salvesen (Managers) of Grimsby.

The Review gave no details of this agreement. Further inquiries at
Christian Salvesen revealed that there was no such agreement.
(A TUC spokesman, admitting the error, explained that they
depended on the individual unions for their information. Profile 7
explains further.)

Even so, mention of 4-40 in this document could prove useful.
It lent the idea respectability. It suggested that it was worth exploring
by individual unions. According to the TUC spokesman, "The
Review is supposed to create subjects for discussion among
unions."

LABOUR AND MANAGEMENT FEARS ABOUT 4-DAY

It should be clear by now that in Britain neither management nor
labour is actively agitating for the 4-day week. Certainly not for the
4-40 week. Each side appears to have other priorities, as well as its

172

own fears and suspicions. The unions, worried by the unemployment figures, have set a shorter working week as their long-term objective. In 1971, the TUC made it clear that by a shorter working week they meant a 35-hour week. This they claim, would offset the reduced demand for labour created by automation and the continued introduction of capital-intensive production methods. (Looking to the more immediate future, the unions still have a mopping up job to do in those areas where the 40-hour week has not yet been won.)

"Four-forty" arouses various union fears. That it might erode overtime working without at the same time doing anything for basic wages. That management might use it to reduce their labour force. That management might gain substantial economies without giving an adequate *quid pro quo*. Not to be under-rated is the deep-down feeling that condoning the extension of the normal working day is somehow an immoral act for organized labour to commit, a betrayal of those who fought in the past to reduce it.

On the employers' side, there are fears that productivity and profitability would be hit, aggravating the inflationary state of the economy. Raised more often than anything else was the question of fatigue, as though this were the only factor governing productivity. Few considered that a reduction in absenteeism – an old blight on British industry – might more than compensate for the effects of fatigue. Not to mention the extra employee efficiency and effort that might be encouraged by better company morale. While the disadvantages of 4-day working were quickly pounced upon, there was little awareness of its advantages.

One big fear, sometimes openly expressed, often implicitly conveyed, was that the 4-40 week would turn out to be the thin end of a bargaining wedge. Give them 4-40 today and tomorrow they will want to reduce the 10 hours to 8. Several executives, in fact, said they were very surprised that the unions were not demanding the 4-40 week with this strategy in mind.

Just as the figure 10 evokes an emotional response from organized labour, so does the figure 4 from the bosses. One working day a week less? How can this possibly be a good thing?

THE PROBABLE FUTURE

Looking back at the continuous movement since the Industrial Revolution towards a shorter working week, it seems inevitable that further reductions are on the way. For white collar workers the $37\frac{1}{2}$- and 35-hour weeks are already a reality.*

For industry, the 35-hour week is still some way off. Exactly how far off is anybody's guess. But once it has been achieved, the unions will not take long to discover the attractions of the 4-day week. A working day of $8\frac{3}{4}$ hours would be a mere 45 minutes beyond the present norm. And doubtless there soon would be a union move to lop off that untidy three quarters of an hour. (In some sectors of industry, employers too would want the 4-day week once they had conceded 35 hours. Five start-up and shut-down operations would cease to make sense with only a 7-hour production run.)

With the 35-hour week still some distance away, 4-40 could be seen as a halfway house or, as Jack Jones put it, "a temporary arrangement". If so, why is there not more pressure for it from the workers? If it offers certain leisure benefits now, why are they not demanding it in spite of the reservations expressed by their union leaders? The missing element could be incentive.

EMPLOYEE DEMANDS FOR REARRANGED WEEKS

Every factory of any consequence in Coventry is on the 4-night week even though, initially, it was strongly opposed by the unions. It came about because the man on the shop floor wanted it badly enough. Working a Friday night shift meant there was barely time to snatch some sleep before the Saturday afternoon football match. Sunday was spent resting. Back to work Monday. The result was "patterned absenteeism" on Fridays. The night worker felt discriminated against. He wanted a full weekend like everyone else. If getting it meant working a 10-hour shift, fine. (See Profile 8.)

Why, then, has there been no similar campaign for day-time 4-40? According to Mr. William Lapworth, Coventry district secretary of the TGWU, "it will come, but it's early days yet". At the moment, there is no incentive to press for an extension of the 2-day weekend – although early finishing on Fridays could be seen as a first step in the erosion of the fifth working day. On Fridays, Coventry starts grinding to a halt at 3.00 PM.

Since 1970 most of the night sub-editors on Fleet Street's national

*On 1st May, 1972, Camden Borough Council in London shortened the working week of its 2,000 white collar staff from $37\frac{1}{2}$ to 35 hours; this will probably lead the way for similar concessions from other councils affecting more than 1 million employees in local government.

morning papers (manned 6 nights a week) have switched their 35-hour week to 4 longer shifts. Their cause was backed by the National Union of Journalists. No increase in staff was needed because of the rota systems which were instituted with 4-day working. "The night subs had been asking for this for some time," explained Mr. Gordon McLean, central London branch secretary of the NUJ. "It was a way of ameliorating the effects of their working hours on their personal and social life . . . Looking at it from a long-term perspective, I have little doubt that sooner or later the 4-day week will come in generally, and maybe soonest of all in journalism, as an extension of the 4-day week as it is already happening for our night people." (Journalists have never negotiated for overtime pay – extra time worked is covered by time off in lieu. This removes one of the obstacles in the way of the rearranged 4-day week.)

In 1970, employees of Plasticisers Ltd., a manufacturing firm in Drighlington, Yorkshire, wanted to work a rotating shift system of 3 days on, 3 days off, with shifts 12 hours long (Profile 6). Their union, the National Society of Brushmakers, advised against it. The union's general secretary, Mr. T. B. Thomas, went to Drighlington to address the men. "They nearly kicked me out of the meeting," he recalled in an amused way, "I was a very unpopular chap. In the end I said, if you're happy with it, all right."

THE LEISURE INCENTIVE

What these cases (and there are others) show is that breaking away from the traditional working pattern needs some strong incentive. If it exists, union opposition will not prevent it happening. What about the 3-day weekend? On the surface, it seems an attractive enough carrot, especially at a time when the Puritan work ethic has given way to the "fun quest". It is; but you need other things to go with it. Mobility, for example. The English worker is less mobile than the American, though he is beginning to catch up as car ownership spreads.

You also need money. Most leisure pursuits depend on residual spending power: what is left after the food and clothing bills have been paid, after the rent or mortgage payments have been settled. Higher spending power will increase the demand for more leisure time. As it is, the sound of the so-called "leisure explosion" grows ever louder. It is evidenced by newspaper supplements for domestic swimming pools and tennis courts, the acquisition of second cars and holiday homes, the spread of gardening centres, the boom in sales of caravans, camping gear, sports equipment and boats. Many leisure activities like golf, horse-riding and water-skiing are ceasing to be the exclusive province of the middle class.

The major entrepreneurs in the "leisure industry" are putting up new multi-purpose leisure complexes, convinced that more playtime will bring more profits. There are signs of a rapid expansion in hiring facilities for sports equipment – "rent-a-leisure" as one promoter calls it. And a similar development of leisure on hire-purchase – never-never leisure. Local authorities are becoming more leisure conscious. Teesside, setting the pace for the rest of the country, is investing a great deal of public money in leisure centres offering a whole range of facilities at low prices. "Supply creates its own demand," according to Teesside's Director of Arts and Recreation.

All these developments must make the idea of a 3-day weekend increasingly attractive. It must also appeal to big city commuters as they find fares rising and no improvement in rush-hour conditions. Thousands of people working in London would probably be glad to work a longer day to save themselves two exhausting journeys a week.

Some would barter their extra leisure time for extra income, as they have done in the United States. Indeed, there is a fear in many quarters that increased leisure opportunities would have a self-defeating effect: in order to pay for them, people would have to earn more, which would lead to more moonlighting.

Increased leisure time is bound to create new social, educational and environmental problems. Perhaps just one of them might be mentioned here: Britain's small territorial space. The 4-day week needs to be considered in the light of Britain's limited *Lebensraum*. Michael Dower has provided an eloquent statistic in his report, "The Challenge of Leisure": "If everyone in England and Wales went to the seaside at the same time, each would get a strip of coast $3\frac{1}{2}$ inches across." And he goes on to ask: "Can we make space for our leisure without ruining these islands?"

HOW WOULD 4-DAY COME ABOUT HERE?

If the 4-day movement gets going in Britain, it is likely to do so initially (as in the United States) among small to medium-sized, non-unionized firms. Once a significant enough number of companies have taken the plunge the word will spread: others will be encouraged to consider 4-day. Similarly, 5-day employees, enviously observing those with a 3-day weekend, will be encouraged to demand it for themselves. Managements and unions will find themselves having to yield to these demands. Four-day agreements will come about as a result of plant bargaining.

Existing industrial tensions, unforeseen crises, entry into the Common Market, and the future state of the economy will all affect the pace at which the 4-day week develops, and the most popular form it finally takes.

One also has to reckon with the national love of precedent. Britain, as the travel brochures always remind us, is rich in tradition. This does great things for the tourist trade, but is cramping in areas where innovation is a rule of survival. "We British," said Batley's 4-day pioneer, Frank Spicer, "are slow to accept change. In 1812 we employed a man on the cliffs of Dover to keep a look-out for Napoleon. We only abolished the job in 1946."

[*Mr. Richmond suggests that Britain has a strong resistance to change. While as an American I cannot have the familiarity necessary to comment on this, I can comment that resistance is a fairly natural reaction to change, and is even a healthy reaction if not carried too far.*

What I find particularly noteworthy about Britain, from reading this article, is that so many British firms have been using 4-day contentedly for so long now that one can call 4-day quite traditional *at these firms. The British news, for me, is not so much that Britain too has 4-day pioneers, but that Britons may be starting to notice the 4-day firms around them, to generalize from their experiences, and to apply the principles to improving their own specific circumstances – The Editor.*]

Here follow profiles of 8 British firms using or considering some form of the 4-day or 3-day workweek.

PROFILE 1

On 4-Day
Roundhay Metal Finishers (Anodisers) Ltd.
Batley, Yorks.
(PROCESSING)

Description: Roundhay is a family firm, employing about 40 people, run by managing director, Frank Spicer, and his daughter. It occupies a single-storey grey-stone building, formerly a mill. The 4-day week was introduced in 1965 shortly after the company moved to Batley from nearby Leeds.

Before going further, one ought to say something about Frank Spicer. In his mid-50's, he is stockily built, has a quietly forceful personality and a dry sense of humour. He has come up from the factory floor, and has a close personal relationship with his employees. In his spare time he runs an antiquarian book business – rare first editions lie around his home. He has visited factories in Russia and – ultimate impudence – has lectured on the 4-day week in America.

He is always on the look-out for new ideas. He was the first in his trade to employ women sales reps, an innovation which caused great amusement among his competitors – until they found that it worked.

Purpose: He invented the 4-day week for his own firm many years before the movement became noticeable in the United States, a great source of satisfaction to him. The idea came to him like this: "Going home one evening in October, I drove past a bus stop at which most of my Leeds workers were waiting. It was 4.40 PM and it was raining. I had to return to the factory 15 minutes later and they were still there, getting wetter and looking more miserable. Two buses had gone past full. I thought – how stupid. If they have to catch a bus home, why not do it 4 evenings a week instead of 5, and out of peak travelling hours?

"I turned this over in my mind during the evening. I could see the advantage to the employee, but the more I kicked it around the more I realized the company could benefit too." He wrote down the advantages and disadvantages as he saw them:

Advantages:
1. Travel time would be reduced for people travelling from Leeds.
2. They would have more leisure time at weekends.
3. We had already decided to operate transport to take employees to and from Leeds City Centre: this would need to operate only 4 days.
4. The possibility of the skilled people who had come with us to our new location leaving us for employment in Leeds was always present. If we could work 4 days instead of 5, this

would be an incentive to them, providing the pay packet was not affected adversely. It would have been difficult to replace these people in our new location – this had been foreseen prior to our move, although we felt our higher rates of pay in relation to others in our industry would counteract the problem of travelling. This had so far proved correct, but the coming winter would be our testing time.

5. Our costs might well be reduced in several ways, such as on services, i.e., heat, water, power, etc., although our lighting bill during the winter period would be higher due to longer hours of work during darkness; but we thought the main saving would be in fuel. We use a coal-fired boiler: most of our vats of chemicals require heat, and as some of these are 2,000 gallons capacity, the heat input was fairly high. We would save almost a day's coal each week.

6. I would also be able to attend to my antiquarian book business on Fridays.

Disadvantages:
1. Would the longer working day affect production due to operator fatigue?
2. Would our customer relationship be upset? We are metal finishers, providing a service to industry, both on long run production and in the short order field. We were specialists with a high reputation for quality and service. We were normally the last operation before assembly or dispatch, and delivery was of the utmost importance.

Implementation: Frank Spicer held a meeting with his employees the next day, and the subject of the 4-day week was thrashed out in detail. Finally it was decided to try it out for a month, with the proviso that if either side did not like it, they would revert to a 5-day week.

Daily working hours before the changeover were 8.00 AM–4.30 PM, including an unpaid half-hour lunch break. The new hours were 7.55 AM–6.25 PM. The half-hour lunch break remained, but two 10-minute tea breaks were abolished. Instead people were free to have tea at times of their own choosing. Maintenance staff, previously on a 5½-day week, switched to 5 days (still at 8 hours a day), so they no longer worked on Saturdays.

"We next had the problem of getting our customers used to the

179

idea that we would be processing on 4 days only, and this applied in our case to 11 major customers in long production runs. Most of these customers considered us to be an extension of their own plant – a phone call would upset our production flow – and we were very often rearranging our schedules at very short notice to keep our production lines going.

"When we told our customers about our plan, they thought we were mad. We explained that we already worked 40 hours over 5 days, and we would still be working 40 hours, but over 4 days. We realized this could well inconvenience them until their production schedules caught up with our way of thinking. We suggested that about 4 weeks would be ample time for them to adjust. In the meantime, we would keep in very close touch with their production control departments. This we did, by phoning at 10.00 AM each morning and asking their requirements for 3 days hence. We also made the gesture that should their production lines get into difficulties for want of finished products, we would work on the fifth day at no extra cost to themselves, even though our own costs would be increased by overtime rates of pay and extra fuel."

Results: When the month was up, the company and its employees decided to remain permanently on the 4-day week. In the next 3 months they needed to work on 5 Fridays, in the following 9 months on 2 Fridays, and after that the average has been about one Friday a year.

"Our customers quickly became acclimatized to our 4-day week and have said it hasn't really inconvenienced them. In fact one or two have benefited. They now have finished goods in their stores awaiting assembly.

"All our maintenance work is now carried out on Friday. We are also open until 3.30 PM on Friday for the delivery and collection of work. In the morning it is taken care of by one of the directors and the anodiser on duty, and in the afternoon by the maintenance staff. My daughter and I take it in turns to stay on Friday until 3.00 PM.

"Our employees became the envy of most of their neighbours. It has also proved popular with the working wives of these people – the old man could help with the housework and do much-needed jobs around the home on Fridays; and as one wife put it, 'It's lovely to have the tea ready when I get home on Fridays.' If the wives were not working, they were able to do shopping on Friday mornings and this left Saturday and Sunday free for visiting relatives or going to the coast – previously, it hardly seemed worthwhile after shopping on Saturdays. Yes, it's been a great success with our employees. As one of them said, 'It's like Easter every week.'

"Day-rate workers were put on to a bonus scheme wherever possible, and where this could not be done the hourly rate was increased. The earnings of pieceworkers have risen by up to 30% since going on to the 4-day week.

"Although we have a slightly smaller labour force [reduced by 5], we produce more, with many hours less of overtime each week. In fact we have very little overtime these days, which makes us wonder how much overtime is necessary in Britain today. I know a lot of people in industry work for overtime because it's the only way they can make a decent wage. You've got to give them the opportunity to make a good wage without working long hours."

Summing up the benefits brought by the 4-day week:
1. Productivity rose by 15% in the first year and has continued rising since, although the rate of increase has tapered off.
2. Profitability has increased.
3. The work force is more contented. Absenteeism has almost vanished. Labour turnover, running at about 25% on 5-day, has dropped to about 1%. No skilled workers have left the company because of the changeover.
4. Fuel costs were reduced by 20% in the first full year of 4-day working.
5. The plant is better maintained and there are fewer hold-ups through breakdowns.
6. The company has 7 vehicles operating against 3 in 1965, and motor expenses have only slightly increased. Although inflation has affected the cost of vehicles, fuel, tyres, maintenance, etc., the extra costs have been absorbed by less journeys per week.
7. Prices to customers have been kept stable.
8. Not a single customer has been lost.

Employee Reactions: Did the employees find the 10-hour day too long? No, they said when I talked to them, they didn't. They might have done at first, but they had got used to it. One man of 64 said he felt no more tired now than when he was on an 8-hour day. There was approval all round for the long weekend:

"Gives you more scope."

"I can go to see the grandkids on Friday and take them to the park."

"You can be on your way to the coast first thing Friday morning."

"I do a bit more sketching now."

Several said they helped their wives at home, and with the shopping on Fridays. Others mentioned playing snooker and going to the cinema. The 3-day weekend provided extra hours for another popular Batley activity: drinking. If Fridays were being spent at the club or pub, didn't this mean they were spending more than in the old days? If so, it didn't seem to bother them. Or perhaps it was personal territory they didn't want to discuss.

The handful of women employed at Roundhay work part-time. Those I spoke to agreed that for a working wife with young children, the 10-hour day might create extra problems, but not insuperable ones.

Many of the Batley workers mentioned one minor irritation: the uncomprehending response they got from 5-day families. "People come up to you on Friday and say, 'What the heck are you doing at home?' They think you're sick or out of work. When you explain it to them they're a bit envious. They can't just grasp that you're still working the same hours as they are. They can't imagine the 4-day week." Asked whether he would consider going back to the 5-day week, one man replied: "Only at double the money."

Final Comments: It has been a smooth transition to 4-day at Roundhay. Frank Spicer has had several things going for him. Not least of all, his own qualities as an employer. He understands his employees' viewpoints and problems – "They know I won't try to pull a fast one on them."

His firm is small and personal. Management is not some remote force, to be regarded with suspicion and resentment. When he thought of introducing the 4-day week, he was able to put the idea to his employees in terms they could understand. If they were uncertain about something, they could put their questions to him and get a prompt answer. Only a few of his employees belong to a trade union – "I pay above the union rates anyway."

He said that none of his employees were using their long weekend to moonlight: "I like to think that if you give a man a fair wage, he won't want to moonlight."

In 1972 he was planning another change in the working week – a reduction of the hours from 40 to 38 before the year was out.

Many other companies have approached him with inquiries about the 4-day week, and he is sure some of them will follow his example.

He does not argue that the 4-day week will work for everyone, but he does feel certain that it could benefit many other companies as much as it has his own.

PROFILE 2

On 4-Day
CDG Ltd.
London W.1.
(DESIGN SERVICE)

Description: CDG (formerly Conran Design Group), one of the largest design consultancies of its kind in Europe, employs a total staff of about one hundred. The firm describes itself as an "autonomous subsidiary" of the Burton Group, better known for its chain of retail clothing stores.

CDG's design work takes in projects like airline terminal interiors, retail shops and "corporate identities".

In 1971, one of the staff pinned up a cutting from *Time* Magazine about the 4-day week in America, and containing an interview with Riva Poor. It caused debate among the staff. "We thought: why not try it ourselves?" recalled Mr. Malcolm Riddell, the company's sales director. In November, 1971, after discussions with their parent group and with their own staff, the company decided to try the 4-day week for a 6-months trial period. At the end of it, so long as the firm's profitability had not suffered, a democratic vote among the staff would decide whether the 4-day week was to become permanent.

Purpose: What prompted them to try it? "The design business is becoming much more competitive," according to the sales director. "If you're going to stay on top – which we are – you've got to employ good staff, and you've got to be creative. The 4-day week allows people to be themselves one extra day a week. It gives them more time to do their own thing, to open up to new influences. This, hopefully, will benefit them and also benefit *us*, because we think it is likely to make them more creative. Also, an important part of our work is the designing of other people's environments. We thought it only right that we should be prepared to experiment with our own."

Implementation: Daily hours on 5-day were 9.00 AM–5.30 PM, with a one-hour lunch break. The 37½-hour week was rearranged Tuesday to Friday, with daily hours 8.00 AM–6.30 PM (6.00 PM on Friday), and the same one-hour lunch break.

Monday was chosen as the extra day off because traditionally it was the quietest. On a rota basis 2 senior staff members come in on Monday to deal with telephone inquiries.

When I first visited CDG, the 4-day experiment had been in progress just over 3 months. Experiences and reactions differed from group to group, and from person to person. One design group was completing its projects more quickly. Another seemed to have slowed down a little. The sales director felt that overall there had been no decline in productivity. With design work, precise evaluation of productivity changes is difficult to make over a short period.

Adjustment Problems: Common to nearly everyone, said Mr. Riddell, was "the tremendous tiredness we feel towards the end of the day. This has been our biggest single problem. We've spoken to the company doctor about this, and he thinks it takes about 6 months for one's metabolism to adjust properly." Many routines were affected. For example, should you make the wife and kids get up earlier too? He said that he himself no longer had a social life during the week whereas before, he did. The longer weekend, on the other hand, was a great boon. "Now there's time to do rather special things – visiting galleries, going into the countryside . . ."

One of the young secretaries at CDG said she just flopped at the end of the day, and had to keep the last hour in the office for un-demanding filing work. She thought there might be some dropping off in her general efficiency by the end of the 4 days. The 3-day week-end had encouraged her to make a trip to Belgium (reduced rates for the Monday return), and she was planning similar trips in the future. She loved shopping on uncrowded Mondays and being "whisked through" at the hairdresser's.

One of the designers explained the extra tiredness this way: "I would measure our productivity in terms of crises. If the week contains, say, 50 crises, there are now more crises between each battery recharge." Does the 3-day weekend not make up for that? "It makes up for Tuesday but by Thursday you're not feeling the benefit." However it had given him time to grapply with various personal dilemmas and emerge with "a personal philosophy of life".

Another designer, father of a young baby said, "Now there's the great plus of seeing him for 3 whole days every week."

For most, commuting had lost much of its agony. There was one day a week less of it anyway, and as the girl librarian pointed out, "You're not having to fight during the rush hour. There isn't that crush, that fatiguing mass."

For some, transport arrangements had become less convenient: trains were less frequent early in the morning. One man was finding travelling a lot more expensive. He used to share a taxi to the station with his wife in the morning. Now he had to hire a separate one of his own.

The designers sometimes had difficulties explaining their working week to friends and neighbours. They met with a baffled response, even "a type of jealousy". Some of the staff who had not been all that keen on the 4-day week when it began in November, were won round to it as the weather improved. Two people had said that if they were offered better jobs with a 5-day company, they would need to think about it carefully.

There appeared to be only one case of moonlighting. And only 2 people had left because of the 4-day week.

Clients had adjusted to the change: "There was the odd irritation here and there at the beginning, but a lot of companies were very interested to know how the experiment was working out, so they couldn't get too stroppy about it." Asked if he thought the 4-day week would catch on in Britain, the sales director said: "I think it will accelerate very quickly."

Results: The staff ballot took place at the beginning of May, 1972. Eighty-three per cent of the staff voted to continue with the 4-day week. The board had previously decided that there had been no bad effects on profitability or the working efficiency of the company. A great deal had changed since my first visit. "The tiredness has ceased being a problem for the majority of people," reported Mr. Riddell. "We're getting over the 6 months metabolism thing. Now we're going to start reaping the full benefits. People are finding a new working rhythm. You can deal with crises more quickly. There's more pressure during the 4 days but there are 3 days to make up for it. It's beginning to have its proper effect. The better weather has made a big difference."

How had the quality of work been affected? "It's terribly difficult to measure. People are generally much more lively, more enthusiastic. At open sessions they're more full of ideas."

What was the feeling of those members of the staff who were

opposed to the 4-day week? "The democratic approach – that's the most important thing, I would say to anyone who wants to go over to the 4-day week. If a company thinks it can just tell people what to do, they're wrong. If it's a common problem, people will resolve the snags. They'll say, 'Okay, we don't like it personally, but so long as the majority wants it – if my friend Joe Bloggs likes it – I'll put up with it.' We wouldn't have had such a helpful reaction from the *no*'s if we hadn't asked them for their views when we started."

He said they had just held an exhibition at their studios showing what the staff had been doing with their 3-day weekend: things like photography, writing poetry, designing book illustrations, silver foil sculpture, painting . . . Others had taken up social work, or used their leisure time going into the country, gardening, enjoying their children and family life.

"It's a fantastically different life. It's a fuller one."

PROFILE 3

A Company that Considered 4-Day But Has Not Yet Adopted It
Thomas Hardman and Sons Ltd.
Bury, Lancs.
(MANUFACTURE)

Description: Thomas Hardman has been established as a company in Bury since about 1812. A heavy industrial fabric manufacturer, its production is small-batch, with different technical specifications for each order. Among its customers are the giant paper-making groups like Bowater and Reed International. It is a capital-intensive firm and recently completed a quarter of a million pounds' worth of new building and plant.

There are approximately 150 employees, including staff. About 90% of the labour force is unionized. (The National Union of Dyers, Bleachers and Textile Workers is the main union.) The 110 on the factory floor divide roughly into 60% men and 40% women. Most of the workers are semi-skilled and on a measured incentives scheme.

The men work a 40-hour week, Monday to Friday. Daily hours: 7.45 AM–5.00 PM (3.45 PM on Friday). The majority of the female employees work a 29¾-hour week: 9.00 AM–4.00 PM (3.45 PM on Friday).

[Ten employees are on a double-shift system: 6.00 AM–2.00 PM, 2.00 AM – 10.00 PM.]

Staff are on a 35-hour week.

Attempt to Implement 4-day: Two young, lively-minded executives were mainly responsible for trying to introduce the 4-40 week. They are David Hardman (his name is only coincidentally the same as the firm's), the works manager; and Eddie Davies, production manager.

It was the power cuts, caused by the miners' strike at the beginning of 1972, which first attracted them to the idea. The cuts restricted Thomas Hardman, like many other factories in Britain, to a 3-day week. On these days they worked 12-hour shifts, with a half-hour lunch break. "We had record efficiency," recalled David Hardman. "We did in those 3 days almost as much as in the normal 5.

"A level income is what most people want. But during the power cut period they earned more than usual, because they overshot their target. It was unfortunate in a way that the crisis didn't last longer. Two weeks were not enough to establish a new norm.

"I was surprised at the size of the increase in productivity. You often find that just before a holiday you get a 'bull week' when people try to make some extra money to pay for the holiday. People *are* able to earn more. You can dangle carrots as much as you like, but if they've decided what level they want, they'll stick to it."

He had been aware before the power cuts of the savings to be made out of working on fewer days: economies in fuel and lighting, and the benefits of having fewer start-ups and shut-downs. "People develop a working momentum. It takes them about 10 minutes to start. They talk about what they've been doing for the weekend and so on. It was during the power cuts that the advantages became very apparent."

When the power crisis was over and the company decided to investigate the possibilities of switching to 4-40 permanently, a complicated situation developed.

At first most of the employees and the shop steward were in favour of 4-40. Subsequently, two union officials, one of them the area secretary, visited the factory. They said that a similar idea had been proposed at another factory some 10 years previously and had been thrown out. With this precedent, they could not support the proposal now. According to the works manager: "They thought (a) it was a backward step to go from an 8 to a 10-hour day – they had fought tooth and nail for an 8-hour day – and (b) they ought to be entitled

187

to overtime rates for the 9th and 10th hours. That ruled it out so far as we were concerned." The union's parting shot was that, even with overtime, they would regard 4-40 as a retrograde step and oppose it.

Benefit Problems: The company had to consider what would happen in the event of short-time working. When, in the past, the company had worked 4 days instead of the normal 5, those workers affected by short-time had been able to claim unemployment benefit from the Department of Employment. If the normal working week was to become 4, and at some point in the future short-time reduced it to 3, would employees still be able to claim one day's benefit each week?

When the company tried to get an answer, they found themselves up against a bureaucratic wall. The official attitude was: "We think it is all right but we can't put it in writing." The local Department of Employment office insisted that they could not pre-judge the case, but would make a firm decision as and when the situation arose. Thus the matter remained unsolved for some time. It was a matter of vital importance to the company since the employees' attitude to 4-40 would understandably be affected by the unemployment benefit situation.

Eventually the company put one man on a permanent 4-40 week and then, for a period of 2 weeks, put him on 3-day short-time working. The Department of Employment did, in fact, pay him one day's benefit for each of the 2 weeks. One hurdle crossed.*

Meanwhile the attitude of the factory floor had vacillated since the 4-day week had first been discussed. At the start the majority had wanted it, then there had been a swing against it, although one particular section of the works was still keen on it.

The most recent report from the company stated that the union had asked for negotiations on new basic rates. The 4-day week would be discussed again and might form part of a "package deal".

Final Comments: Employee attitudes to the leisure benefits of a 3-day weekend varied according to sex and age. The production manager said: "Youngish people leading an active life are all for more leisure time, and are not work orientated. One or two people would think about taking on extra jobs. Some of the anti-4-day feeling is from

---

*The General Secretary of SOGAT (Society of Graphical and Allied Trades), expressing a trade union anxiety about problems that could arise from short-time working and benefit payments, said: "I feel that nobody has really done a coordinating job on the legislation in this country."

older people, very set in their ways, who don't do anything except watch telly.

"We overestimated what people do with their leisure time. A lot literally don't do anything." One man of 63 had said that if he were younger, the 3-day week would strike him as a tremendous idea, but he was quite happy to carry on the way he always had. One or two others felt it would mean another day to spend money. Instead of getting away from a nagging wife, she would be saying, "let's go out shopping" with the result that they would spend a lot more.

The production manager, expressing disappointment that they had so far failed to introduce 4-40 said: "We didn't want to develop an 'us' and 'them' situation. We said to our employees, 'Here's an idea. What do you think of it? It's an extra day off for you, and it will mean certain economies for us.' Even if we only broke even, we'd be quite satisfied if it produced a better working arrangement. We think it's better for all of us."

"We thought morale would be better," said the works manager. "For us it would mean better labour relations, less labour turnover, less training and other fringe benefits." Did he think 4-40 would spread? "Yes, I'm positive it will." He was surprised more companies didn't think about it after the power cuts. "Everyone got this increase." One other firm in Bury was interested in the 4-day week. "They said, 'when you've sorted it out, let us know.'"

He regarded British management's lack of interest in 4-40 as "an indictment. In America they're not steeped in tradition like we are. It is the big disadvantage of having been first in the industrial revolution."

PROFILE 4

On a Rearranged Week: 4 Days On, 2 Days Off
Name Withheld by Request
(MANUFACTURE)

Unionized.
Description: Manufacturer. Highly automated plant. Operates 7 days round the clock. About 230 employees, including staff. About 50 employees are on 4-day, working 12-hour shifts. Of these, approximately 60% are skilled, 40% semi-skilled. Day workers and maintenance men work a normal 5-day week with overtime when necessary.
Purpose: Round the clock utilization of plant.

189

4 Days, 40 Hours

Implementation: The company instituted 4-day working with 12-hour shifts around 1960. Employees work 4 days on, 2 days off, 4 nights on, 2 days off. 3-shift system. Over a 12-week cycle, their average weekly hours are 56.* Average paid hours are 69½.

Results: More efficient use of capital-intensive plant.

Company Comment: "Most of our people like it. It gives them time off during the week. At one time we were on 8-hour shifts, 5 on a trot. They didn't like it at all. They say that if they've got to be there 8 hours, they might as well be there 12. It means they save on transport to work."

PROFILE 5

Many Terminals on 4-Day
Esso Petroleum Co. Ltd.
Terminals in many parts of the British Isles
(DISTRIBUTION)

Union: TGWU.

Description: The terminals are distribution centres for petroleum and industrial fuels.

Purpose: To cover required operations and to maximize utilization of capital equipment. In some terminals this is best achieved by four 10-hour shift working.

Implementation: A Productivity Agreement was made between the Company and the TGWU in 1966, covering in excess of 2,000 operatives who are employed in the distribution function. A key point of this agreement was that shift working was recognized as the normal method of operation for truck and plant operatives and mechanics. It was agreed that the hours in each shift would total 40 hours per week on average over the shift cycle adopted. Some terminals work 7 days a week, while the remainder work 6 days.

*I suppose if one *must* work 56 hours a week, then it is preferable to do so on a 4–2 basis. Nonetheless, 56 hours a week, even with overtime payments, is not everyone's cup of tea. Companies such as this one might do well to investigate the potential of moving to shorter work hours with the idea in mind that the reduced strain could conceivably lead to better work if there is any discretion at all involved on the part of workers. Studies of fatigue and productivity levels on workweeks over 48 hours show less total output than is produced during work periods with shorter hours – The Editor.

Shift arrangements vary from terminal to terminal. Within a terminal, shift patterns are established by local agreement to cover the required operations and workload spread. People work the patterns agreed, which usually remain constant for fairly long periods and are only changed when operating conditions alter significantly.

The normal shift pattern is either four 10-hour or five 8-hour shifts, often combined in a two-week cycle; but other shift lengths and cycle permutations do occur. People on 10-hour shifts normally work on a rota with their days off varying week by week depending on the rota used; this means that periodically a person has 3 and sometimes 4 days off at one time.*

Results: Efficient coverage of operations and high utilization of capital equipment.

Company Comment: Initially there was some resistance to the idea of working 10-hour shifts. Now the pendulum has swung the other way, and at some terminals four 10's has become the most popular shift.

PROFILE 6

3 Days On, 3 Days Off
Plasticisers Ltd.
Drighlington, Yorks.
(MANUFACTURE)

Union: National Society of Brushmakers.

Description: Manufacturers of extrusion machinery and extruded filaments from nylon, polypropylene and polyethylene for brush bristles, rope and packing twine, dolls' hair, carpet staple. About 400 employees, mostly semi-skilled. Sixty per cent of the plant operates 7 days round the clock. Forty per cent 5 days round the clock.

Purpose: Continuous process manufacturing and maximum utilization of plant.

Implementation: The Company instituted 3 days on, 3 days off in 1970, following a 6 months trial period (see p. 175). About 120 employees are on 3-day scheduling, working 12-hour shifts: 3 days 7.00 AM–7.00 PM – 3 days off – then 3 nights 7.00 PM–7.00 AM. Four

---

*Most of the major oil companies in Britain operate similar systems at their terminals, in accordance with productivity agreements made with the TGWU.

shift system. Over a 6-week period, those on 12-hour shifts work on average a 42-hour week.*

Sixty-five employees are on conventional 3 shift 5-day working. Engineering Department and other personnel (220 in all) work a conventional 5-day week.

Results: Before 3-day working was implemented, the plant worked 60 hours per week. Now worked continously. More contented labour force. Easier to recruit labour.

Company Comment: The employees suggested it. They like it without a doubt. They are earning more. During school holidays they see more of their family. People with cars and caravans can go away for 3 days. When they first started on 12-hour shifts, it seemed long, but people have got used to it. They wouldn't want to go back to the conventional system.

PROFILE 7

Previously on 4-day
Christian Salvesen (Managers) Ltd.
Grimsby, Lincs.
(COLD STORAGE)

In the TUC Review of Collective Bargaining Developments No. 1, 1972* reference is made to an agreement for a 4–40 week between Christian Salvesen and the TGWU. Enquiries at the company's head office in Edinburgh revealed that no such agreement existed.

Group Personnel Manager Edward Beaumont explained how the error probably arose. The company in Grimsby *used* to have in their plant agreement with the TGWU a clause stating that the company could work five 8-hour shifts a week or four 10-hour shifts. This clause originated some years ago when certain aspects of the company's work made it advantageous for them to put some employees on four 10-hour shifts, Monday to Thursday. A small number of men had been affected, and the 10 hours had been worked at straight time. Subsequently, the company's trade had altered and four 10-

*Some paper mills in Britain use similar 12-hour shift systems with 4-*day* working and varying lengths of breaks. Employees on such 12-hour shifts have a hidden overtime payment in their wages. This takes into account the average amount of overtime that would have been earned on the normal 8-hour shifts.

†See p. 172.

hour shifts were no longer required. Nevertheless the clause continued to appear in the annually renewed agreement. Eventually the company felt there was no point in keeping it. It did not appear in the agreement commencing February, 1971, nor in that of the following year. There is no intention at present to reintroduce it.

PROFILE 8

4-40 at Night in the Midlands

Every factory of any consequence in Coventry – including the large British Leyland and Chrysler plants – has been using the 4-night week for years. This trend is spreading in the Midlands and is to be found elsewhere in the country.

Four 10-hour night shifts a week, Monday to Thursday, came about in Coventry in 1964, following an agreement between the Engineering Employers' Federation and the Confederation of Shipbuilding and Engineering Unions. The Confederation negotiated on behalf of the engineering unions and the engineering sections of the TGWU, the General and Municipal Workers' Union, and the National Union of Vehicle Builders.

Initially, the union leadership resisted the idea of a 4-night week with longer shifts. But in the end they had to yield to pressure from the shop floor: workers resented the erosion of the 2-day weekend caused by the Friday night shift. Employers had to give in to the workers' demand because of the consistently high rate of absenteeism on Friday nights.

15

PROFILES OF SOME
AUSTRALIAN 4-DAY PIONEERS
by Theo Richmond

The Australian business journal, *Ryge's*, ran an article in April, 1971, on the subject of the 4-day week. Referring to Riva Poor's book, it concentrated mainly on the 4-day scene in the United States. At that time no Australian company had yet ventured into 4-day territory. Explaining why not, the author of the article, Jeremy Webb, voiced thoughts that might equally have applied to Britain:

The neglect in Australia can partly be explained by Riva Poor's finding that without exception, it was the management who introduced the 4-day week. Traditionally in this country it has been the unions which have pressed for radical changes in pay and working conditions and their dialectical battle with management has become an accepted part of the industrial scene.

The 4-day, 40-hour week has reversed this commonly accepted employer-employee relationship and has left both sides in an unfamiliar role. Unions in Australia have never seriously challenged the immutability of the 5-day week and management, with a full plate of industrial disputes, has been content to let the status quo remain. In any event Australian businessmen have not often been noted for innovation and originality . . .

Before the year was out, the same writer was reporting in the same journal that the "first tentative steps towards a 4-day working week have now been taken . . ." They had started in August, 1971, when North Australian Rubber Mills in Queensland introduced the 4-day week.* The press reported the event, and from then on further 4-day developments began to catch the public eye.

*Although this was the first *officially* sanctioned 4-day week in Australia, *The Worker* (published by the Australian Workers' Union) pointed out that: ". . . quite a few outback road workers and perhaps others, have a verbal agreement with their employers which allows them to work a greater spread of hours Monday to Thursday which then allows them to get away Friday morning to travel home."

194

The following case histories show the 4-day week gaining its first foothold in Australia. Will it move on to a more consolidated position? Some of the signs are encouraging. One union (Profile 3) has not only tried out the 4-day week itself but spelt out the important message that here is an innovation that can benefit both management and labour. One 4-day company (Profile 8), employing several hundred married women, has refuted the common criticism that the 4-day week with an extended working day is unsuitable for female workers. The same company has also shown that 4-day working can pay off for management even when accompanied by a 4-hour reduction in weekly hours.

Nevertheless, management generally remains sceptical on this score, as was revealed in a survey conducted by Sidney Technical College's School of Management. Their probing of management attitudes to the 4-day week confirmed widely held views that it would lead to union difficulties, higher costs and problems with marketing and sales, without at the same time producing sufficient compensating benefits.

As in Britain, management suspects that 4-day will bring a higher overtime bill, and enable the unions to make inroads into the 40-hour week. The case histories show that for those companies faced with labour turnover and absentee problems of a sufficient magnitude, such inroads need not necessarily be a bad thing.

In common with other countries, Australia has found that a rearrangement of 40 hours over 4 days holds little appeal for organized labour. The nearer the number drops to 35, the more benevolent becomes the trade union movement's attitude to the 4-day week.

PROFILE 1

On 4-Day
North Australian Rubber Mills Ltd.
Brisbane, Queensland
(MANUFACTURE)

NARM's innovation got off to a flying start, following protracted negotiations with the Queensland branch of the AWU and the blessing of the State Industrial Court. Willingness on the part of Australia's biggest trade union to cooperate with the 4-day experiment (it began on a 3-months trial basis) was an encouraging sign, although this must be viewed in the light of the deal negotiated with the company: this included wage increases and a reduction in the weekly hours for the 250 employees. Day workers were to work 38 hours and shift workers 36 hours, both to be paid for a 40-hour week. The new week would be Monday to Thursday.

Commenting on the event, Patricia Burden of the *Financial Review* wrote: "Many union leaders believe that the 4-day week is not acceptable unless it also means a reduction in working hours. The power and oil industries are involved in campaigns sponsored by the ACTU* for a 35-hour week, which will almost certainly take the form of a 4-day week or a 9-day fortnight."

NARM's management initiated the 4-day week with several aims in mind: to reduce the high labour turnover and absenteeism rates, and to gain productivity benefits from fewer start-up and shut-down operations.

By the end of the first month on 4-day, management and employees were both reacting favourably, the former beginning to see signs of their aims being achieved, the latter enjoying the new pleasures of the 3-day weekend. The AWU's attitude remained cautious.

In March, 1972, after the trial period had twice been extended, a sad headline appeared in *The Australian:* "Shorter week turns out a failure." The paper reported that, "Productivity has not been lifted and the company is considering putting its 250 rubber process workers back on a 5-day roster. 'It has been a great success for the employees,' the company's managing director, Mr. Peter Young, said yesterday. 'But it is another question whether it has been for management.' "

PROFILE 2

On 4-Day
Calsil Ltd.
New South Wales
(MANUFACTURE)

Calsil Ltd. put its brick plant on a 4-day week in September, 1971, after negotiations with the Brick, Tile and Pottery Union. The

*Australian Council of Trade Unions (equivalent of the TUC).

management wanted to make more efficient use of its automated plant.

The company worked a 5-day week before the changeover, with two 10-hour shifts (last 2 hours paid at overtime rates) and a 4-hour shut-down. An extra overtime shift and maintenance were done on Saturday. The new basic week was 35 hours, comprising 3 days at 9 hours and one day at 8 hours, with each of the 4 days made up to 12 hours by overtime. Thus the 4-hour shut-down was avoided. Maintenance was carried out on weekdays.

The new day off was Wednesday for one shift, Friday for the other. The fact that the extra overtime shift and maintenance work were now done on Friday instead of Saturday meant, in effect, that the majority of the employees were gaining a 2- rather than a 3-day weekend. Calsil's innovation was greeted by trade unionists as a valuable precedent in helping their campaign for a basic 35-hour week in other industries. Employer reaction to the 35-hour week was less than ecstatic.

PROFILE 3

On 4-Day
Queensland State Service Union
Brisbane, Queensland
(TRADE UNION)

A trade union trying out the 4-day week on its own staff? This happened in September, 1971, when the Queensland State Service Union (12,500 public servant members) offered its small head office staff (5 men, 5 women) the chance of going on the 4-day week for a trial period.

They were already on a 35-hour week. Two members of the staff voted to continue the existing 5-day pattern: 9.00 AM–5.00 PM with one hour for lunch. The remaining 8 opted for a 4-day roster with daily hours: 8.00 AM–5.30 PM and a 45-minute lunch break. The roster provided for a rotation of off-duty days over a 4-week cycle, meaning that the extra day off did not always join on to the weekend. After 3 months, the staff voted to continue the experiment and review it again in the summer of 1972.

In April, 1972, the general secretary of the Queensland State

Service Union, Mr. T. J. Wallace, provided the following progress report:

There is no doubt that the introduction of the 4-day week has resulted in an improvement in job attitude and efficiency, and whilst productivity is difficult to measure in an organization such as the Union, there is evidence of an improvement in this area, and it is certain that there has not been any decrease in productivity because of the 4-day week.

Members of the staff have adjusted well to the extended daily hours; it has been found that the extra time available each day between 8.00 AM and 9.00 AM and from 5.00 PM to 5.30 PM enables a great deal of productive work to be done without the interruptions experienced in the normal office day. The additional daily hours do not constitute a hardship to the staff and everyone agrees that the benefits far outweigh any minor disadvantages.

In the Union's experience the 4-day week has been an outstanding success, but its implementation requires cooperation and flexibility by employers and employees who each have something to gain from this relatively new concept of working hours.

As a matter of policy the Union has adopted this concept of the 4-day week as an objective for the Public Service and submissions have been made to both the Government and Opposition Parties.

No proponent of the 4-day week could ask for more.

PROFILE 4

A 4-Day Plan Opposed by the Union
Federal Match Co. Pty. Ltd.
Grafton and Alexandria, N.S.W.
(MANUFACTURE)

While one trade union was enthusing about the 4-day week, another was preparing to squash it. In October, 1971, the Federal Match Co. proposed a 4-day week for 300 employees at two plants. There was to be an initial 3-month trial period. The company offered a 38-hour week, Monday to Thursday, at 40-hour pay. There would be three 10-hour days and one 8-hour day. The management hoped the 4-day week would reduce their labour turnover rate, which was high.

While the employees were ready to accept the offer, the New South Wales executive of the AWU opposed it. About 75 women are employed at the Alexandria plant. Most of them wanted the 4-day week and rejected the union's advice. Faced with feminine resistance, the Vice President of the New South Wales branch of the AWU,

Mr. L. McKay, visited the plant and addressed the rebels. The union had struggled in the past to achieve an 8-hour day, he argued, and it could not give its approval now to a 10-hour day. He reminded his audience that the State Labour Council had a claim for a 35-hour week before the State Industrial Commission, and that the 35-hour week should be everyone's objective.

He offered to negotiate a new agreement with the company covering wages and working hours. According to the industrial reporter of the *Sydney Morning Herald:* "At the beginning the atmosphere was obviously hostile . . . Gradually the women's attitude changed." In the end they decided to go along with the persuasive Mr. McKay. The match girls' revolt was over.

PROFILES 5, 6 & 7

On 4-Day
New Hunter River Hotel
Sydney, N.S.W.
(SERVICE)

On 4-Day
Orford Bros.
Toowoomba, Queensland
(MANUFACTURE)

On 4-Day Once A Month
Industrial Acceptance Corp. Ltd.
N.S.W.
(FINANCE)

October, 1971, brought its 4-day victories too. Five barmaids at the New Hunter River Hotel, and 10 workers at Orford Bros., a soft drink company, gladly changed over to 4-day. They were joined a month later by 9 more employees at Orford Bros.

On a larger scale, the 1,200 staff of a finance company were given a 4-day week once every 4 weeks. Averaged out over the 4 weeks, the one day off provided a 35-hour week. By arranging its roster so that only one quarter of the staff would be off duty each Monday, the Industrial Acceptance Corp. was able to maintain its 5-day service. The management maintained that the staff preferred this arrangement to the alternative of reducing each working day by half an hour so as to provide a 7-hour day. The organizer of the New South Wales Labour Council was reported as having expressed approval of the company's scheme.

PROFILE 8

On 4-Day
E. E. Whitmont and Sons Pty. Ltd.
Blacktown, N.S.W.
(MANUFACTURE)

In November, 1971, approximately 700 employees (90% female) at E. E. Whitmont's shirt-making factory gave their wholehearted support to the management's proposal that a 4-day week be instituted as from the beginning of 1972. The new working week would be Tuesday to Friday, with a total of 36 hours paid at the same rate as the previous 40. Some sections would be rostered so as to provide customer service on Monday.

The general manager of the company, Mr. Russell Whitmont, explained the reasoning behind the 4-day week:

The staff turnover rate the year before the introduction of the scheme was 127%. Costs of training a new operator average $300 [Aus.]. We reasoned that if our employees had Monday free (most absenteeism occurred on Monday) and worked a 4-day week we could reduce absenteeism, which usually results in costly overtime which, in turn, again causes absenteeism.

We recognized that the reduction of the working week to achieve the objective was impractical unless the reduction of hours was directly related to compensating productivity.

The reduction of 10% hours per week required an additional compensating 11% of production and unless this is achieved there would be no point in our persevering with the 4-day week. To ensure the required productivity is forthcoming, it was necessary for us to increase the individual operating rates accordingly and to measure individual performances.

The company put their scheme and the reasons behind it to the Clothing and Allied Trades Union, who agreed to allow a plant vote to decide whether the 4-day week should be accepted. The employees gave the scheme their unanimous approval.

The 4-day week was implemented according to schedule on January 1, 1972, with review dates fixed for the following June and

December. Female employees interviewed by the press expressed delight with their new 3-day weekend and said they had no wish to return to the old 5-day week. The President of the ACTU was reported to be in favour of the new arrangement. Why not? It came very close to the trade union movement's target of 35 hours.

After the 4-day week had been in operation for 4 months, Mr. Whitmont was also expressing satisfaction:

To date production has been achieved across the board and everybody is happy. The company, by agreement, has the right to return to the 5-day week if production drops. The absentee percentage has dropped significantly whilst overtime and turnover rates have been reduced substantially. The additional free day for family business, household chores or just plain relaxation is appreciated by all and demonstrated by the increased compensating productivity.

Although the scheme has been successful to date, a note of warning must be heeded. The scheme can only work if employees are on an incentive scheme. Rates must not be loose and each individual's production performance must be measured regularly. If compensating productivity is not maintained, costs will be too high.

PROFILE 9

A 4-40 Plan Opposed by the Union
Water Lily Pty. Ltd.
Weston, N.S.W.
(MANUFACTURE)

In November, 1971. another clothing company in New South Wales wanted to switch to a 4-day week, but found its plans frustrated. With the aim of reducing labour turnover and absenteeism, the Water Lily company proposed a 4-40 week. About 40 employees, who supported the idea in the first place, turned it down after a meeting called by the Clothing and Allied Trades Union. The Union, opposed to the principle of a 10-hour day, said it would be prepared to discuss with the management a 4-day 36-hour week such as had been agreed upon at the Whitmont shirt factory. There the matter rested.

16

2 YEARS LATER:
A FOLLOW-UP REPORT
by Riva Poor

The purpose of this chapter is to provide readers with the additional information that I have developed in researching workweeks over the past 2 years since preparing the original edition of this book.

The chapter provides a series of checklists and analyses concerning the following areas that the public has indicated are of particular concern: the specific means whereby 4-day increases productivity; the advantages and disadvantages from the points of view of both employers and employees; items that managers will want to be sure to think about when considering 4-day; items managers will want to think about when planning to implement 4-day; statistics about the growth of the 4-day movement; changes in the attitudes of companies and of workers who have *not* experienced 4-day as yet; clarification of areas of misunderstanding about 4-day (especially "red herrings" that act as barriers to good decision-making); forces which promote and forces that retard the growth of 4-day; additional innovations spawned by the 4-day movement; and implications for society as the movement continues to spread.

Some of my research appears in this article for the first time. Other parts have been published previously in the subscription service published from my Cambridge, Massachusetts, office, called *Poor's Workweek Letter*. Also included are reviews and quotes from field studies by independent researchers who have begun to study 4-day in response to the great public interest generated by our original publication. These new studies began to appear in 1971 and early 1972.

No field research has controverted any statement made in our original publication of this book. Instead, the research of independent

202

researchers has confirmed the findings originally reported, by duplicating our results. These researchers are quoted to provide the confirmation that decision-makers will demand.

Finally, I have introduced a bit of humour here and there (even a drab subject like scheduling has its funny moments), which I hope you will find excusable, if not enjoyable.

On what basis did you decide the topics to include in the follow-up report?

I chose most of the questions on the basis that they are the ones the public has most frequently asked me, (adding a very few of my own, when it appeared that they might be useful).

During the year and a half since the publication of the original edition of *4 Days, 40 Hours*, I have had a great deal of exposure to the public's questions. I have been invited to meet on the subject with numerous segments of the public. Over forty businessmen's groups across the U.S.A. and Canada invited me to confer with them. These were primarily trade association meetings, but there were also several private board of directors meetings (of major U.S.A. corporations) and a few business school seminars. Over fifty television and radio programmes have had me make a guest appearance – often including audience participation. Several *hundred* newspaper and magazine reporters interviewed me. And a few hundred individual businessmen, union leaders, and students have telephoned for information directly to my office.

All this exposure to what is on the public's mind shows certain questions about rearranged workweeks that crop up again and again in almost every group.

If some of the questions included here appear naïve while others appear overly technical, I hope the reader will bear in mind that the questions and answers are here to serve people with a great variety of backgrounds and concerns. Any new innovation raises a certain amount of anxiety about change *per se*, which displays itself in misunderstandings, false reports, and an entire host of other impediments to decision-making. Since experience shows that each of the following questions is frequently asked by people interested in the 4-day week, it strikes me as well worthwhile to put all of them in. The reader can skip to those topics that interest him and can skip over the ones that do not.

4 Days, 40 Hours

Why do you advocate the 4-day week?

I do not really advocate the 4-day week. What I advocate is finding better ways to do things: I am excited by innovation.

Because my research into 4-day shows me that it is an important innovation – well worth looking into – I am excited about it. But I do not necessarily advocate any particular person or company using it, since it might not be appropriate for them. I *do* advocate people's *looking* at 4-day, because so many companies and employees experience improvements with it. But only if it is appropriate for *you* do I advocate *your* trying it.

I would like to make it very clear that I am a reporter and analyst of this innovation, as opposed to being a proponent. After all, no one pays me anything when they convert to 4-day. (Which is unfortunate, considering the number of conversions.) My "profit" comes only through people's buying my information and analysis. And in order to keep information sales in good order, information has to be accurate, and not partial.

I suppose that the reason some people think I am a *proponent* of 4-day is because so much of the information I report about it is positive and so little is negative. But the reason I report so much positive information is that it is what the respondents whom I interview report about their experiences with 4-day.

Most of the respondents – the company managers and the company employees – are enthusiastic about their new schedules. It is *extremely* difficult to locate negative information about 4-day. Even those companies that *discontinue* 4-day are extremely positive about the innovation: many times they say they plan to try 4-day again; and in many cases they do so – after modifying their initial schedules.

Actually, people need not be so amazed with such positive results if only they realized that 4-day is not just four 10-hour days. FOUR-DAY IS REALLY AN EFFORT TO OPTIMIZE WORK SCHEDULING. And after all, *optimization* means doing things better – by definition.

The real innovation is not 4 days, 40 hours, although we call it that because that is its most frequent form. The real innovation is that people are turning the problem of scheduling work right on its head. Instead of doing the old thing – fitting the work into a pre-established, habitual work schedule – – PEOPLE ARE NOW STARTING WITH THE WORK THAT NEEDS DOING, AND BUILDING THE SCHEDULE AROUND THE WORK.

When they build the schedule around the work, instead of trying to push the work into a pre-established schedule, people find they make the schedule work *for* the company, instead of *against* it. People find they have in scheduling itself a new tool for conducting their businesses profitably – they find they need not consider scheduling a barrier that must be suffered and lived with. The results are happy for both the companies' profits and for the workers' lives; so people are excited about 4-day.

But all this is because firms are optimizing scheduling. It is not because Riva Poor makes money on conversions to 4-day. (I only wish I did.)

Why do you say that 4-day scheduling means "optimizing"?

Since most of us are on schedules that we "fell into" rather unthinkingly, it should not surprise us that many of these schedules are not optimal. It should surprise none of us that examination of such unplanned schedules (or even *planned* schedules that have not been reviewed for a long time) could be improved on. And it should surprise none of us that when companies tailor their schedules to meet the *specific* needs of their *work* and their set of *employees*, they will be better off – and enthusiastic about their schedules. They are enthusiastic, because the new schedules work for them better than the old ones did.

Four-day is a very simple innovation with tremendous ramifications. It's simple, because it is merely a new look at the old problem of scheduling: just the idea of rearranging the timing of when we do the things that we do so that we can do them better. It's an innovation, because people are breaking out of the old habit of fitting the work into whatever schedule is habitual at the time, and instead are building the schedule around the work to be done.

The ramifications are tremendous, because companies are quite naturally able to increase productivity when they tailor their schedules to the work that has to be done, and also because employees get a rearranged leisure package that almost all of them find much more desirable, more useful, than the old leisure package.

Thus, both the employer and the worker come out ahead.

4 Days, 40 Hours

Aren't you really behind the times talking about 4-day weeks? Aren't a few companies already on the 3-day week?

Yes, indeed, there are 3-day companies – over 6 dozen of them that I know of. But they are not doing something *different* from 4-day – it's just that 3-day is the appropriate rearranged workweek for *their* type of work, while 4-day is appropriate for other types of work.

Four-day weeks come in a great variety of sizes and shapes. Many 4-day workweeks are 4-day in concept only – being 3-day weeks or some other variation of 4-40.

The basic 4-day concept is that of trading a longer workday for a shorter week – a lesser number of workdays. While the pattern is frequently 4 days, 40 hours, nonetheless, since firms are tailoring their schedules to meet the individual needs of their work and of their work force, there are necessarily many patterns in addition to 4-40. In fact, there are so very many variations that it is apt to call 4-day the "rearranged workweek". Firms are rearranging to increase productivity, and they are rearranging in a variety of ways.

To get at the diversity of rearrangements, first note that each of the components of workweek scheduling can and does vary: the length of the worker's workday, the length of the company's workday (the firm may have more than one shift), the length of the worker's workweek, the length of the company's workweek (the number of days that the firm is open for business), and the number of days in the work cycle (that is, the frequency with which a schedule repeats itself – some schedules repeat on a 7-day-week basis – others may take as much as a year to repeat).

With just these variations, we get the following diversity: 4 on–3 off, $4\frac{1}{2}$ on–$2\frac{1}{2}$ off, $3\frac{1}{2}$ on–$3\frac{1}{2}$ off, and 3 on–4 off. Where there is more than one shift or more than one group of workers ("turns"), the company's workweek does not resemble the company's manpower schedule. For instance, a company using 3-day manpower scheduling may have 2 day-time shifts and 2-night-time shifts (2 turns of workers, one coming in the early part of the week and the second coming in the latter part of the week); so the company may have a 6-day, 24-hour schedule. (It could also use 3-day manpower scheduling to have a 7-day, 24-hour schedule.)

Hours of attendance are different from hours of work. A 3-day workweek generally has 12 to 13 hours of attendance while work-hours themselves will usually total around 11 a day, because of breaks. (Some companies can achieve 12 hours of production while workers work only 11 hours, by staggering breaks and doubling up on coverage of machinery during breaks.) Daily hours of attendance on 4-day weeks range from 8½ through 10 or 11; and with different lengths of breaks, the hours of work each day also vary.

Then there are patterns that ignore the 7-day calendar week altogether, going 8 or more days before returning to the start of a cycle. On these workweeks, one calculates an average of the hours in the workweek, because the hours in the calendar week will vary during different 7-day calendar weeks. These are patterns like: 4-days-on-4-days-off and 5-days-on-5-days-off, and so on. The average workweek depends on the length of the workday (which is usually 10 hours.)

Two firms that I know of have a 7-days-on-7-days-off schedule. A full 70 hours is worked during one 7-day week, and the workweek is followed by a 7-day "weekend". The average workweek here is 35 hours a week. By compressing 70 hours into one week, the people have only 26 weeks of work in a year and have 26 one-week vacations.

Some of the variations arise from the firm's *past* practices. Since many companies have workweeks fewer than 40 hours long, when these firms rearrange their workweeks, their new workweeks usually average less than 40 hours – just as their old workweeks did. (Few companies *increase* the number of hours in the worker's workweek when they convert.)

Also, since frequently the productivity boost for the company is great, the company can and often does offer employees average weeks shorter than the ones they had before – for the same paycheck. (This is a form of profit-sharing.)

Companies open for business 24 hours a day frequently use 12-hour shifts, but many use other schedules. A popular variation is the use of two 10-hour shifts plus one part-time shift. Typical arrangements are: 10–10–4 and 10–2–10–2, the latter being used where machine maintenance is required between shifts.

In some cases, the 10-hour shifts are staggered, so that a longer-than 4-hour shift is obtained. (In some cases, the staggering means *no* short shifts.) In other cases, where shifts remain shorter than normal, so that they are really very much part-time shifts, the companies use "permanent part-time job" slots. The firms separate out the concept of temporariness from the concept of part-time, and consider part-time workers as permanent as full-time workers. (More about this in a later section.)

The days off are another parameter. Some firms give all the off days consecutively (which I recommend, especially where the workdays are extra-long); other firms give some of the days consecutively and other days here and there during the workweek.

Our purposes in mentioning these variations is to alert the reader to the options and to the flexibility that he can obtain and also to provide the background for the forthcoming section on how 4-day increases productivity. Readers will be aware that we mean a host of variations when we use the word "4-day".

What kinds of firms can profit by breaking out of the 5-day mould and what firms can't?

Those firms that cannot use 4-day are those that are already on optimal scheduling – firms for which the 5-day standard workweek is optimal – firms that have never had or have already solved the problems that 4-day addresses.

All other firms are likely candidates to reap improvements from efforts to optimize their scheduling.

The fact is that most firms now operate on schedules that were picked originally in the usual fashion – picked to fit into the standard workweek. It has been the custom simply to adopt the same workweek that everyone else uses, and *not* to look upon the workweek as a vehicle to be designed specially to work for the company.

The exceptions to this customary practice of workweek selection prove the point: they are the firms whose work is so unsuited to 5-day scheduling that they are forced to create their own schedules. There are firms whose work is flying aeroplanes, shipping stock and passengers, carrying out oil and mining explorations, and so on. The rest of us, those who could manage at all to squeeze the work into the standard workweek pattern, did so.

But workweek schedules are a tool for management. They need not be an immutable constraint that management must live with.

Firms that have squeezed their work into the standard workweek simply because the workweek is standard and not because the standard workweek is appropriate for the company's work – these firms are candidates for achieving improvements by rearranging their schedules to fit their work.

These thoughts are confirmed by the data. In reviewing the kinds of firms that are on 4-day right now, it is difficult to find an industry not represented by at least one firm on a rearranged workweek. (And more firms start 4-day every day.)

The following are industries that have *numerous* representatives on rearranged workweeks. They are worth mentioning, in order to give the reader an idea of the diversity of work situations that can profit by tailoring workweeks to their work: printing, police, data processing, garment and textile manufacture, sheet metal fabricators, hospitals and other health services, government services, banks, publishing of magazines and newspapers, insurance companies, automobile dealerships, furniture manufacture, schools and colleges, libraries, architecture-engineering, and advertising.

What's so important about productivity? Innovation? And profits?

Productivity is a crucial issue of our times – although many of us do not recognize it as the critical issue that it is.

Productivity is the key to all progress, to improvement of *quality of life*. Whether we approve of some of the "progress" civilization has made, or not, absolutely no progress is feasible without rising productivity.

It is rising productivity over time that has permitted us to create civilization, beginning with the first technological breakthroughs that permitted us to make tools and to develop herding and then agriculture. The rising productivity we developed as we pursued the art of agriculture permitted us to form cities, with their division of labour and complex cultures. In the past several hundred years, conceptual developments in business and in scientific technologies permitted us to create sophisticated machinery, giving us an enormous and rapid rise in productivity that permitted us to begin to advance to a *world* culture.

But just as rising productivity has been key to our past progress, it is also key to our future progress. Productivity is key to improving *quality of life*, because it is key to providing us the leisure that is necessary to developing our know-how about living as human beings.

What is this critically important thing, productivity? Very simply, it is output per manhour.

This does not mean that raising productivity means working labour more or harder. Far from it. No one worked harder than primitive man with his primitive technology and meagre output – and that, just in order barely to survive. No, on the contrary, increasing

209

productivity gains come through improvements in the technology of work – improvements in machinery and in the organization of men's efforts – from innovation. From learning how to do the things we want to do better than we used to do them.

Now, the reason that productivity is a critical issue in our era is that our *rate of growth* of productivity has been *declining* for the past 5 to 10 years. Decline of productivity is true of the United States of America, and of other countries as well – including Great Britain.

Inflation is one of the results.

Racked by inflation (which means rising prices for the same or lower value of goods and services), we have the choice to lower prices, to lower wages, or to increase output (quantity and/or quality of output) at the *same* prices and wages. The first two methods are impracticable. At a given productivity level, prices cannot be lowered without either lowering wages or jeopardizing business. Wages cannot be lowered without social and political upheaval; and the only way to *raise* wages without increasing prices (which is what most workers would like to see done) is to increase productivity. Without improving productivity, inflation will continue.

Since raising productivity is critical to our material welfare in addition to our cultural progress, and since our rate of growth in productivity has been declining, instead of rising or holding level, productivity is a very serious issue of our times.

Unfortunately, the public is very little aware of the critical nature of the productivity issue today. This is not for lack of concern with society's welfare, but due to a general (and appalling) public ignorance of the workings of economics. (And I ask myself, *why* don't the lower schools *teach* economics?)

In my opinion, it is lack of knowledge of economics that is behind so much of the public contempt for profits that we hear expressed so often today. It explains how we can hear otherwise reasonable people calling for a halt to corporate profit-making – at least in the U.S.A., and probably elsewhere as well.

The public is simply not aware that it is the expectation of profits that induces the capital investment that provides jobs in our economic system. Unless business can hope to make healthy profits, business must close down – and people cannot have jobs. (I am not talking about "robber baron profits", but normal profits – profits commensurate with risk.)

So widespread is general ignorance of the workings of economics that even some businessmen – who certainly ought to know better –

are themselves against profit-making, as amazing as this may be. In my travels across the U.S.A. in the past several years, I have come across dozens of businessmen who feel *guilty* about profit-making – who feel that profit-making is *dirty*, and who actually consider that they should *cease* this activity!

There is a myth going around today that we would be happier if we were to go back to a primitive, bucolic existence. This vision includes retaining, of course, *selected* bits of progress that society has achieved; such as, a few telephones and some of the wonder drugs, and surgery, and small amounts of modern transportation, and law, and modern fuels and ... Well, the point is that some people think that we can somehow have small amounts of the fruits of the world's progress without having the vastly complex economic and social systems that produce and maintain these goods and services. (Whereas, if they would only reason it through, we can have these modern goodies only because there are enough of us buying these things to create a market for them. The practical economics of goods and services is such that one cannot have just a few modern telephones: one must have many or none.)

At any rate, there was a purpose to this seeming digression. Economic facts of life are the underpinnings of the kinds of goods, services, social order, and progress that we can have. And in our society, *profit-making* is a critical underpinning.

Profit-making is a very socially useful activity in a democracy. Profit-making is a function to be proud of. This is what I tell the businessmen who are hearing Circe's call to a primitive dream.

The ill-conceived notion that the profit-making system should be dismantled and that the role of business should be taken over by government (another dream) is no help whatsoever. Anyone can see that government is sufficiently inefficient just doing government work – without our letting government handle business activity as well. And, if this were not sufficient argument, it should be noted that it is business that is one of the balancing forces curbing government power. Without the profit system, without business, we should be like Russia or China in terms of the balance of power between government and citizen. I am not saying that there is no room for improvement: there certainly is plenty of need. But I cannot believe we can find improvement in the direction of increasing government power. (We have gone too far in that direction already.)

For all these reasons, it is critical that we find means to improve our productivity. The problem is sufficiently recognizable that

4 Days, 40 Hours

President Nixon, for one, has responded by creating a National Commission on Productivity, to recommend means for improvement. However, in reviewing the list of Committee Members, I note that only big business and big labour are represented.

I asked the Secretary of the Committee, who is a high-ranking and highly intelligent member of the U.S. Department of Labor, why other important factions are not represented on the Committee – such as entrepreneurs. He answered: "What is an entrepreneur? ... I don't believe I've ever heard that word."

This is one of our problems!

Entrepreneurs are people who take new technologies and spread them. They are people who promote innovation, and who thereby contribute greatly to increasing our productivity and progress. Innovation is one of the most important means for increasing productivity.

(Another means is that of obtaining a resource monopoly. Unlike innovation, there are many negative results to the monopoly method.)

The other important component neglected by the Commission is small business. Over 80% of business in the U.S.A. is small business. Small business employs over 60% of the workers in our economy.* Furthermore, big business has almost always come from small business starts. Why, then is small business ignored on a commission whose avowed aim is to increase productivity?

Why are only big business, big labour, and academia represented? Big business does not represent the majority of business in our society. In the U.S.A., labour unions represent only 25% of the work force,† although one rarely hears this fact broadcast.

*Of the 11.5 million businesses in the U.S.A., almost 9.5 million are small proprietorships; fewer than 1 million are partnerships; and only 1.5 million are corporations. (Source: "Statistical Abstracts of the United States", 1971; from the U.S. Census.)
Only 27.5% of workers in the U.S. work for firms that employ 500 or more workers. Thirteen per cent work for firms with 100 to 249 employees; and all of the rest of the workers – 60% – work for firms with fewer than 100 employees; and a full 40% of the U.S. work force work for firms with fewer than 50 employees. These employment figures give you an idea of the importance of small business in our economy.
†Only 21 million of the U.S.A. work force of 88 million belong to unions, and 2 of these 21 million belong to employee associations, rather than to internationals. This means that 76% of the U.S. work force are not represented by unions of any type whatsoever. (Source: "U.S. Dept. of Labor Bulletin", September 13, 1971.)

Big business and big labour are the major contributors to our declining level of productivity. Through their very size, their achievements are thwarted by an organizational esprit that dampens risk-taking, dampens achieving behaviour, dampens innovation; and promotes, instead, emphasis on bureaucratic behaviours and personal power-seeking behaviours that are unproductive. While I appreciate the role of big business and big labour in curbing the power of government, there is no question but that they operate in a style that retards innovation in our society – and is thereby detrimental to productivity.

Yet we need innovation desperately, to provide the improvements in quality of life that the public wants. And let us bear in mind that the public is the very people who work for and own big business, and the very people who are the membership of big labour organizations. Yet these organizations do not operate to achieve the goals of most of the people.

Somehow, big organizations must learn how to conduct themselves in a more productive manner. For one thing, they must learn to develop new reward systems, reward systems that encourage productive behaviour and discourage unproductive behaviour.

At any rate, productivity is a key issue of our times. In order to improve productivity, we must have innovation.

Four-day is important, because it is one innovation that contributes to improving productivity in an era when such improvements are critically important, to reduce inflation and to promote social welfare.

How do rearranged workweeks increase productivity and profits?

This is a very good question to ask, because there is just so much patience that any of us have with tantalizing statements such as: 4-day cuts our production costs; 4-day gives us better use of our capital equipment; 4-day cuts out overtime; and even, 4-day lets us obtain *more* overtime. If we cannot hear exactly how these benefits come about, we cannot get the full benefit of other people's experiences to apply to our own companies.

The following long list of advantages 4-day brings about, is not intended as all-inclusive; but there is enough here to suggest the range of mechanisms that are involved, and to stimulate your own creative thinking about your own company. As you look for

213

analogies to your own firm, don't be fooled by superficial differences: for example, there are circumstances under which a manufacturing company has more in common with an architecture firm than with some *other* manufacturing company.

Special Advantages for Those with Substantial Daily Set-up Times: Increasing the Real Production Time Available for the Same or Fewer Hours of Worker Attendance. It is probably best to start with an example before beginning a long list. I use the example of Kyanize Paints, because so much data can be found about this firm elsewhere in the book. Kyanize used to make 15 batches of paint a week, with workers working 5 days a week for 40 hours. By converting to four 9-hour days, Kyanize now produces 16 batches of paint a week with the same number of workers working 4 days a week for 36 hours. Kyanize shares the resulting increase in profits by paying 40 hours of pay for 36 hours of attendance (which is an effective increase in payrate) and also by adding an absolute increase in pay. The following are the specific workings that create the increase in productivity:

There is *increased real production time* available for the same (or fewer) hours of worker attendance, because:

1. There are 20% fewer start-up and clean-up periods each week (4 sets, instead of 5).
2. The production runs are longer, because the workday is 9 hours, instead of 8.
3. There are fewer lunch and rest breaks in the workweek, because there are 4 days, instead of 5.
4. There are fewer minutes of daily attendance devoted to rest breaks, because Kyanize workers agreed to disband organized coffee breaks on the principle that they prefer drinking their coffee at home, rather than on the job. Workers still break for coffee, bringing a cup back to the machines whenever they please. It is *organized* work stoppages (which tend to drag on and on) that have been disbanded.
5. There are fewer opportunities to be late returning to work in the mornings and from breaks; again, because there are fewer days.
6. Unit costs are lower, due to the greater volume of paint that can be produced on longer production runs.

How can any of this apply to your work situation; especially, if your company is *not* a batch processor? Well, in much manufacturing there is set-up time. But even in offices, there is set-up time – although it frequently is not recognized as such. Certainly in the professions,

214

in jobs such as engineering, drawing, editing, and so on – it takes time each day for the worker to settle back into the project.

Taking the Sting Out of Overtime and Out of Late Shifts: Gaining More Hours of Weekly Attendance to Increase Utilization of Capital Equipment. When companies have increased demand for output, they usually solve the problem by having workers put in overtime and/or by adding additional shifts.

But, while some firms report that their employees are anxious to work overtime and some companies report that their night shifts work out even better than their day shifts, many firms report that it is difficult (as well as expensive) to get workers to work overtime, and that their added shifts are a big headache both for the firm and for employees. Four-day helps with these problems because:

7. Four-day helps to obviate the need for overtime in many cases. Companies are able to add workers at straight time, on a day shift, by using schedules such as 4 days on, 4 days off. (Also see items 14, 15, and 16.)

8. Where 4-day cannot obviate the need for overtime, it takes the onus out of it, because the shorter workweek permits a worker who works a day of overtime to retain at least a 2-day weekend, and sometimes a 3-day weekend if the workweek is only 3 days to begin with. (Also see item 26.)

9. Four day removes the need for night shifts in those cases where the number of production hours needed is small enough (say, 70–84) so that 2 sets of workers can put that time in entirely during the day – by using longer workdays and using the full 7 days of the week.

10. Where 4-day cannot obviate the need for night shifts, it can take the sting out of night work by reducing the number of nights a worker has to put in to complete his workweek – using 4-day and 3-day shifts.

11. Companies already on 24-hour-a-day production 5 days a week (8 hours per shifts) can and do add another 24 hours of production (a 6th day) by converting to 3-day workweeks or other 4-day arrangements. (Some 4-day arrangements use part-time workers.) A 7th day is obtainable in like manner.

12. Some firms consider overtime and/or adding shifts so onerous that they prefer adding capital equipment to using either of these methods. These companies report that 4-day enables them to get the production they need *without* adding capital equipment.

This principle is particularly important for bottleneck operations. By lengthening work hours for such operations, companies are able to eliminate bottlenecks.

Reducing Numbers of Workers Required to Perform a Particular Function, and Increasing Efficient Use of Both Plant and Personnel Overhead.

13. Four-day permits the company to use fewer workers to perform functions such as driving trucks on delivery routes – similar to reducing start-ups and shut-downs at the plant.

14. Four-day eases maintenance problems. For example, trucks operating on two 10-hour shifts, instead of three 8-hour shifts a day, are brought in for check-up twice a day, instead of three times. Also, when large repairs are required between shifts, there are only 2 hold-up periods, instead of 3 – reducing waiting-around time (and overtime).

15. Four-day reduces maintenance costs, not only by reducing down time (as above), but also by permitting down time to occur at times more convenient and less costly for the company. One company's manufacturing process requires a full day of machine maintenance at the end of the week. Whereas formerly this maintenance occurred on Saturday at overtime rates, the maintenance now takes place on Friday at straight time.

16. Four-day permits a number of accounting boons, among them, the avoidance of unbillable overtime hours. For example, Haines, Lundberg and Waehler (now back on 4-day again) like many consulting, advertising, and architecture-engineering firms, used to suffer from overtime that was unbillable to clients and that had to be absorbed into overhead. HLW reports that overtime charges are now avoided in 2 ways: workers tend to get their work done now without overtime, so as to have the full long weekend; and when extra hours are unavoidable, since the 4-day workweek they use now contains only 34 hours, there is great leeway before overtime pay rates are incurred. (They begin after 40 hours.) Thus, just about all time is billable to specific clients now.

17. Where 4-day permits firms to add production hours that they were unable to obtain beforehand, 4-day cuts down on fixed costs, including both normal plant overhead and also personnel overhead – the director's salary, the accounting department, and so on.

Increasing Service to Customers Without Increased Costs – In Fact,
Sometimes with Reduced Costs: Putting the Firm in a Better Position
with Respect to Competitors.

18. Companies are extending the number of hours that they are open
    each day and extending the number of days that they are open
    each week – increasing customer service without increasing
    costs – by staggering manpower scheduling. Banks adopt 4-day
    to make longer banking hours more convenient for customers,
    thereby attracting more customers. Government organizations
    use 4-day, so citizens can obtain government services without
    losing work.

19. Companies use 4-day to create better turn-around time for
    customers. Automobile sales and service organizations, such
    as many Volkswagen outlets, now give faster turn-around on
    repairs, frequently permitting the customer to wait for repairs
    instead of leaving the car overnight. Extra fallouts are that
    while customers are waiting, dealers have the opportunity to
    discuss repairs and to avoid misunderstandings; also, dealers
    get an opportunity to sell more services and equipment to
    customers.

    Manufacturing companies use 4-day to get the product out
    the door faster, giving customers better delivery time. This
    applies not only to things like paints, but to photographic
    services, and so on.

Better Uses of Capital Equipment, in Addition to Greater Use.

20. In the context of faster turn-around times, reducing bottlenecks
    deserves another mention. A manufacturer of novelty items
    that include such things as ball point pens uses 3-day to get on-
    time output from a bottleneck machine – leaving the rest of his
    operations on 5-day. Another example is provided by key-
    punch installations that use the long workday to make certain
    that data is ready for costly computers on time. There are
    implications in this context for inventories of finished products
    and of raw goods: quicker turnover of inventories.

Increasing Quality of Output for the Same or Lower Costs.

21. Through the use of overlapping shifts, police departments are
    able to get more men in the streets during high crime peaks of
    the day (using fewer men during the crime valleys). The overlap
    during peaks means safety (in numbers) for the policemen plus

greater protection for citizens. For another example, hospitals use overlap to cope with peaks and valleys created by meal times, bed times, admissions, operating room schedules, and so on.

22. Four-day also permits improvements in quality of output that do *not* depend on overlap. For example, one hospital uses the long workday in its food department in order to provide continuity in supervision, planning, and service throughout the 3 serving periods of the day. Formerly, different personnel were on hand during the meal periods; but by using the same personnel over all 3 meals, the hospital wastes less food, and so on.

23. "Creative" employees say that 4-day enables them to work more creatively, partially because it permits more concentrated leisure time for renewal of the creative powers.

24. Managers on 4-day say their staffs develop more ability – by being given more responsibility. Four-day can be an important opportunity to increase depth of management layers at a firm.

25. Another advantage reported is the opportunity to get your own skilled workers to fill in for workers who are absent for illness or for vacations. Workers who will get a decent-sized weekend even when they work overtime are more willing to fill in now and again for other workers who are absent.

Increasing Flexibility.

26. Firms report that 4-day provides increased flexibility to juggle hours upwards or downwards as sales demand requires, without having to hire or dehire existing staff.

Providing Benefits that Employees Desire without Increased Costs – and Often with Decreased Costs.

27. All other things being equal, if their employees prefer the rearranged leisure package, firms are delighted to have an opportunity to provide it.

28. Four-day permits moonlighting that some employees desire, allowing them to moonlight at one's *own* plant, instead of at the plant of a competitor. (And at *straight* time until the 41st hour.)

Soft Benefits. The advantages described above are what I call "hard" scheduling benefits: they derive directly from the rearrangement of work itself, and not from any psychological factor. There is nothing to suggest that hard benefits could erode with time.

The benefits introduced below are what I call "soft" benefits. Although there is no evidence whatsoever to suggest that something like reported increases in employee satisfaction will erode with time, nonetheless employee satisfaction is an intangible. It *might* erode with time: Hawthorne Effect could be at work; although nothing in the research suggests this so far. Some of the items introduced below are *clearly* temporary, depending for their effect on the fact that the firm's competition is not yet using 4-day. (While when competitors start 4-day, the competitive advantage may be expected to deteriorate, there is nothing to suggest that the rearrangement would become a liability.)

Readers are most sincerely urged not to deprecate temporary benefits: a few added years of increased profits is nothing to sneeze at.

29. Four-day companies report that employee satisfaction with the new arrangement and the conveniences inherent to the new arrangement result in decreased absenteeism, decreased turnover, and decreased tardiness – resulting in savings to the company.

30. In cases where firms incorporate attendance bonus or penalty systems, the firm gets to reward suitable behaviour and to punish unsuitable behaviour in a tangible manner, and in a manner appropriate to the benefits that the company receives.

31. Four-day results in improved morale. Obviously, we have no tangible measurement for improved morale; but innumerable companies report it, and consider results rewarding.

32. Offering 4-day enables firms to recruit more workers and more highly desirable workers than they had access to previously.

    Even firms located in areas of high unemployment still experience tight labour markets for certain skills, either because there is a real shortage in the required skill or because the jobs the firm offers are unattractive – so unattractive that people prefer unemployment to taking such jobs. In these cases, the attractiveness of 4-day frequently tips the scale in the firm's favour.

33. A natural fallout of this attractive recruiting situation is that firms get the opportunity to upgrade their *entire* work force over time.

34. Again, because the new leisure package is considered a benefit by most employees, some companies find that they are able to postpone a pay rise for another year – or to offer a lesser pay increase than might have been demanded.

35. Some companies obtain savings in labour costs by introducing new methods of handling national holidays. In some few cases, 4-day companies trade the new workweek for a pay package that includes *no* national holidays whatsoever – sometimes even vacations are discontinued. An example is the 7-day workweek in which every weekend is 7 days long.

36. Four-day companies report that free publicity about their conversions is readily obtainable and very useful to their marketing efforts.

As you can see from reviewing this list, different companies receive their productivity boosts from very different aspects of 4-day, depending on their circumstances and on their goals. Every schedule improvement involves trade-offs of some kind: for example, an architectural firm's 4-day week may lead to a loss of casual overtime; some employees may dislike 4-day enough to quit; supervisors not on 4-day may feel jealous of workers getting 4-day, especially if the new schedule overburdens them, and so on.

The firm's circumstances will change over time, so it pays to review work arrangements periodically to examine whether it's time to strike a new balance in the trade-offs: a firm using a good deal of overtime needs to examine whether to take on a new shift of workers; a firm needs to examine whether it would make more money by being open to customers for longer hours, and so on.

The 4-day pioneers show that there are advantages to be gained by taking a good hard look at the work being done and making sure that the arrangement works for the firm. Periodic review by 4-day firms may continue to locate new opportunities to strike a better balance.

Won't the 4-day week lead to higher labour costs?

Some firms do hire more workers when they go to a rearranged workweek, and, to the extent that they do so, they can have higher total direct labour bills. But the total direct labour bill is not relevant by itself to any management problem: the relevant thing is total costs *in relation* to total value of output. In other words, you have to look at the entire package of costs and benefits – and not make the mistake of looking at only a part of the package.

As you can readily imagine, company managers are not converting to 4-day in order to spoil their management records. Managers are converting to 4-day only when they can improve overall company performance by doing so; or, in a few cases, where they can provide the long weekend benefit to employees WITHOUT harming the overall performance of the firm. But the entire cost package must be considered, and the entire income package, *not* just one part of the package.

Isn't the 4-day week really just for small firms, not for large ones?

No. People are confusing my report that the smaller firms are the first to use 4-day with the idea that 4-day is only for small firms.

Small firms are making the change first, because it is much easier for a small firm to make *any* change. There are fewer decision-makers; the communication network is smaller and more manageable; and the complexities of the work are usually fewer, making for an easier study and planning process.

Also, in smaller firms, the top manager is usually the owner of the firm. He tends to be much more concerned with profits and less concerned with matters of bureaucracy and empire-building which too frequently deflect attention in larger organizations.

But the larger the firm, the more complex the decision, the more complex the decision-making process, and the longer the decision will take. For example, large firms usually have major unions to deal with. In this situation, not only the manager and the group of workers at the plant need to come to a 4-day agreement, but they must also obtain permission from the international before changing. For the international to permit the local to go on 4-day involves creating a *national policy*. Creating a national policy involves time and study. Many large unions are only now beginning to study 4-day, and are not ready to set national policy.

In some cases, however, really backward large industries and really backward large unions are involved. They are loathe to make any change whatsoever – which is the reason they are backward (and in trouble) in the first place.

Finally, the smaller firm has a greater need to innovate, just in order to survive in a world that favours big business.

When you put all these factors together, it is easy to see why smaller firms convert first. But, their converting first does not mean that 4-day is not useful for larger firms. On the contrary, most larger

4 Days, 40 Hours

firms in the U.S.A. have begun serious study of 4-day, and many of them already have pilot programmes in process at this moment.

Firms large or small, if they are not already on an optimum schedule, can reap benefits from optimizing.

Is Bursk and Poor Publishing on the 4-day week?

Yes, but not on the kind with a regular pattern that repeats itself week after week.

And this raises an important point about scheduling: in order to have *any* kind of *regular* schedule, you must have some regularity in work demands. In our office, which is new and very small, the work demands are highly irregular, and unpredictably so. The sensible way to deal with this situation is to have a highly irregular work schedule that *matches* the demand pattern. We use a flexible schedule: we rearrange our schedule continually, to fit our needs as they crop up. It is in this sense that we have a 4-day week. (Unfortunately, my own 4-day week is all too frequently 6 or 7 days long.)

Won't the longer workdays lead to greater fatigue and, therefore, to decreased productivity? And won't there be increased industrial accidents?

This has not been the experience at firms that rearrange their workweeks. The firms report *increased* productivity. And *no* firm reports increased industrial accidents.

How can this be? Perhaps we should examine *why* we expect a longer workday will result in greater fatigue, in decreased productivity, and in increased health hazard.

I believe most of us make these assumptions from having read or heard of studies on fatigue leading to reduced productivity.

But when and under what circumstances were these studies done? Most of these studies were done during the Second World War when workers worked longer workdays 6 and 7 days a week. These workers worked 50 to 60 hours a week without getting long weekends to rest up.

The 4-day workers are not working under comparable circumstances. They work under very different circumstances from the workers who were the subjects of these past studies. Four-day workers get long weekends in between their work stints, and I strongly suspect that these long weekends account for the difference in the reported results.

This is *not* to say that no one reports fatigue on rearranged workweeks. As we reported in Chapter 4, about 14% of the workers report experiencing fatigue – but they also report that the long weekends more than compensate for the fatigue.

Also, some managers report finding some workers experiencing fatigue. But these managers also report that while individual fatigue is a factor to consider, the *determining* factor for the firm's productivity is the overall arrangement of all the elements of production at the firm. For example, a worker may be tired towards the end of a long production run, but the length of the run is the determining factor in the firm's output.

Most workers and most managers report that fatigue is experienced *only* during the transition period, during the period of weeks that it takes a person to adjust to a new schedule, and that after this period, workers adjust and experience the old levels of fatigue, whatever they were.

Obviously, jobs that require standing on one's feet all day or that involve especially unpleasant work conditions (high noise levels and so on) present more potential problem than less physically strenuous jobs. However, no past studies have shown a one-to-one relationship between fatigue and productivity nor between fatigue and accident rates. The relationships are very complex, involving many parameters, including psychological factors.

Whatever the reasons, and we cannot claim *really* to know why, the results of 4-day companies are contrary to public expectation. Both companies and workers report very little incidence of added fatigue and almost no incidence of fatigue becoming problematic. The companies report increases in productivity, not decreases. And no one, so far, has reported an increase in industrial accidents.

Isn't the 10-hour day a step backwards?

I suppose a 10-hour day would be a step backwards if at the same time we continued to work 5 or 6 or 7 days a week. Under those circumstances, there would certainly be much less leisure and much more effort involved. But the rearranged workweek offers a very different situation. Workers spend fewer days at work for the same or greater paycheck, and have more days available for leisure or other home activities. It's all a question of values – how people evaluate the combined pay package of work and leisure. Almost every worker who tries 4-day considers it a big step forward.

Naturally, some workers object to the longer days, preferring the original schedule. No one is suggesting that everyone enjoys the same thing and no one is suggesting that everyone *must* work a 4-day week. On the contrary, we are suggesting greater variety of choice.

Most people prefer the rearranged workweek; and those who do not will, I hope, have the opportunity to work the schedules that they prefer.

However, it is important in a democracy to provide variety. At present, most people have no choice but to work a 5-day week. It is certainly a step forward, as Professor Samuelson points out, to increase the choices of schedule whereby a worker can earn his pay.

When you go to a 4-day week, isn't your absenteeism going to be worse – because one day will mean 25% of the workweek instead of 20%?

While one day's absence on a 4-day week will indeed amount to 25% of the workweek, 4-day companies report that incidence of absence is vastly reduced on 4-day. Many companies report virtually zero absenteeism. This appears to be due in part to the fact that workers now have an extra weekday on which to conduct personal business, such as attending to bank matters, health matters and to family problems.

Where companies institute a bonus system for good attendance, the employee loses his bonus when he is absent, and the company thereby pays out less than the pro-rated time for this absence from work.

Also, the prospect of the long weekend helps to cut down on the psychological need to avoid work. While there have been no studies done on alcoholism rates under 4-day, a few workers have mentioned reducing their alcohol consumption on 4-day, because they fell under less tension with the long weekends available to them. (With alcoholic intake reduced, there would be a consequent reduction in absenteeism since the two behaviours are closely related.)

Won't these 4-day weeks lead to a 3-day week, and a 2-day week, and eventually to a no-day week?

I certainly hope so: if we can get that kind of productivity, I'm certain management will be delighted; and the rest of us can devote ourselves to really learning how to live together.

As to 3-day weeks, though: we already have them. Well over 100 companies are already using 3-day weeks. It is just another variation on 4-day; and a reason why we call it *rearranged* workweeks. The company chooses the rearrangement that creates the best solution for its particular work needs and its particular set of employees.

But won't the 4-day week lead us directly to the 32-hour week?

No. I think we are going to get the 32-hour week whether we adopt rearranged workweeks or not. The only question is WHEN we are going to get the 32-hour week. I don't think we are going to get it in our lifetime, because we simply do not have the productivity to support it. So I cannot generate much concern about it.

While there are many examples of firms now working the 32-hour week in the U.S.A., it does not appear to be a growing trend, despite 2 generations of agitation. Actually, very few of the 32-hour weeks that one observes are "true" 32-hour weeks. Some of the 32-hour weeks that can presently be observed are simply mechanisms for labour to gain regular weekly overtime wages: the workers do *not* work a 32-hour week. In most of the rest of the cases, where there really *is* a 32-hour week, the workers get only 32 hours of pay – *not* 40. These are firms making what they hope is a temporary adjustment to recession conditions – to distressed sales conditions. The firm and the workers prefer to keep all the workers on the payroll, instead of laying people off while awaiting increased sales demand.

The true 32-hour workweek – true in the sense that 32 hours is sufficient to gain 40 hours of output, and therefore sufficient to give 40 hours pay – is almost non-existent. The reason is simple: we do not have the productivity at present to support a 32-hour week.

The only firms that have been able to shorten their workweeks are those that have found a way to increase productivity sufficiently to support a shorter workweek. Some of the 4-day firms have achieved sufficient productivity boosts to be able to shorten their workweeks by a few hours (almost none have been able to get sufficient increases to shorten it to 32 hours). However, where the firms gain sufficient productivity to shorten their workweeks, they have no cause for discontent about the shortening, and they are not discontent. The only source of discontent in shortening the workweek is in the case where the firm *cannot* afford to do so.

At the rate we are going, we are not going to gain sufficient productivity to support a 32-hour week in our lifetime. In fact, our problem now and for the foreseeable future is to raise productivity sufficiently to continue business on a 40-hour workweek! In the meantime, while we attempt to raise our productivity sufficiently to support the 40-hour workweek and eventually the shorter workweeks, innovations such as the rearranged workweek offer us the only practicable means to obtain long weekends in our own lifetime.

The 4-day week wouldn't work for us, because we have to stay open 5 days a week.

First of all, one really should question whether one *must* be open 5 days a week, since so many firms find, when they question this assumption, that they do *not* have to be. Some companies, particularly where customer contact is minimal, stay open only 3 or 4 days a week, and have a telephone answering service to cover the days when they are closed. All depends upon the type of work you do.

But even where you do have to stay open 5 days a week, that is no barrier to 4-day. Firms that need to stay open 5, 6, and 7 days a week still do so on 4-day: they have their *manpower* scheduling on 4-day, but remain open as many more days a week as needed.

In fact, 4-day frequently permits a firm to have 1 or 2 additional days of operation, as in the case of the Thomas J. Lipton Company which used 3-day manpower scheduling to move from 5-day to 6-day plant operation.

Isn't 4-day just for blue collar workers? Surely managers still have to work long hours?

No. Four-day is used by professional and by clerical workers as well, and even some managers are trying 4-day.

The manager or professional who chooses to work 70 to 100 hours a week will not, of course, be able to compress these hours into 3 or

4 days. But some managers are trying the idea of cutting down to 5 days a week for the first time, and a few are trying 4-day and even 3-day. They report they are surprised with the results. The first shock for managers, and foremen too, is that the firm continues to operate without them. This result can be depressing – until they realize this result is precisely what a good manager should be able to achieve. (The place is *not* supposed to fall apart when he is away.) Secondly, they report that a little more leisure makes them much more creative when they return to the job. And thirdly, underlings get an opportunity to exercise some responsibility – giving the company the opportunity to develop its lower echelons of management. In short, the results are highly beneficial.

Some companies report a problem that when lower level supervisors are not permitted the long weekends, they are jealous that the workers under them get the weekends. This is a problem, but not a big one.

Companies that cannot give managers long weekends are those where the management layer is very thin. (These companies might do well to address the depth of their management layers as a problem in and of itself.)

Isn't the 4-day week much harder on women that it is on men? Don't the women object to 4-day?

No. The big problem women have is that most hold down *two* jobs – only one of which they get paid for.

Work is harder for women than men when the women have both the full job of running a household and also the job that they get paid for at the firm.

Whether 4-day work is harder than 5-day work is another question. Many women report that 4-day enables them to join the work force for the first time. They say it is easier to get babysitters 4 days a week instead of 5. They say the extra day off gives them more time with the children and enables them to take the children to doctors and dentists, and so on, without having their pay docked. Also, the cost of going to work is lower, making the work more profitable.

Very few women find 4-day too fatiguing. The ones that do are older women who are working machines that keep them standing on their feet all day. But men object to this work, too. While a few firms report that their women did not like 4-day, just as many firms report that their women like it, but their *men* do not. So there does not seem to be much difference in the attitudes of men and women.

Aren't workers going to spend more money on their long weekends – and then demand more pay to make up for it?

Workers do report spending more money on long weekends – 32% of them report this. Nonetheless, the answer has to be no, so far. No companies have reported pressure of this kind, so far; so all we can do is speculate.

The workers who spend more money report that they find it worthwhile to spend more money on their weekends, because the long weekends are more valuable to them. Of course, spending more money means that they are saving less of their paycheck than before.

To the extent that people spend more money (instead of saving it in banks), they stimulate the economy, which is good for business. Secondly, a full two thirds do *not* increase their spending, so presumably there would be no pressure from people to increase their wages. Thirdly, regardless of what workers demand, companies can and should give only what they can afford.

Most important, the potential or future possibility for an increase in wages demanded should not keep a company from using 4-day if the company can make more money by doing so. If you're making more money, you will be able to afford to pay an increase if and when it is demanded.

On the other hand, 4-day has enabled a number of companies temporarily to forestall a pay rise when they could not afford it.

But whether you give your employees long weekends or not, they will eventually demand a pay increase from you: that's the nature of the inflation game.

The real problem today is that work is boring and unsatisfying to people. Aren't you side-stepping the issue by introducing the 4-day week?

No. The 4-day week innovation makes no claims for improving quality of work. The 4-day week improves productivity of firms and permits workers to gain a rearrangement of their work and leisure package that they prefer. That's all 4-day does. (And that's quite enough for one innovation to accomplish.)

Four-day is not represented as a panacea and is not a panacea. Nothing is. Even something like penicillin which was truly a "wonder drug" that vastly improved medical results was not a panacea. Penicillin, for instance, does nothing for ingrown toenails. No one expects it to, either.

The rearranged workweek is very useful for the type of problems that it addresses; but it does not address all problems, and must not be expected to do so. If there is a problem of leadership at the firm, 4-day will not cure it – you will have to look elsewhere for a cure. If work is boring and meaningless, it will take another method for improving it. Although it is worth mentioning that many workers report they have a greater tolerance for the unpleasantness of their work, knowing that the work is confined to fewer days each week, and is followed by a long weekend.

Won't the 4-day week lead to a lot more moonlighting?

Yes, 4-day leads to more moonlighting, but the real question is: is it deleterious? I believe there are many misconceptions about moonlighting.

Before discussing these misconceptions, we should note that the additional incidence of moonlighting among 4-day workers whom we have interviewed is probably a good deal less than one might expect. Of these 4-day workers, 17% say they moonlight now, as compared with about 4% admitting that they moonlighted while they were on the 5-day week. But this means that fully 83% of the 4-day workers use their long weekends for leisure, rather than for moonlighting, although they have the same opportunity to moonlight. The proportion using their long weekends for leisure is a very high one, and tends to show that 4-day meets a real need for increased leisure time.

Whether this additional moonlighting is deleterious is the real question. On this score, it is worth noting that in the several hundred interviews I have conducted with 4-day managers, not one has complained about the increased moonlighting experienced.

In fact, many 4-day managers report highly positive attitudes towards moonlighting. Many employers recognize that some employees require more take-home pay than one job is able to provide, and welcome on their employees' behalf whatever opportunities to supplement income that employees can find. In other cases, employers are actively proud of the kinds of moonlighting their employees do. I have heard 4-day managers brag, in public as well as in private, about constructive services employees provide with their moonlighting. Moonlighters engage in teaching jobs, athletic coaching jobs, hospital services, farming, and so on.

The key to the manager's attitude, of course, is whether moonlighting interferes with the employee's work at his primary job. Apparently, 4-day managers feel that moonlighting itself does *not* interfere with the primary job. This is a reasonable reaction once one stops to consider that all sorts of recreational activities, including drunkenness, have much more deleterious potential impact than moonlighting has. (Factors leading to non-performance are very complicated, and require complex analysis and treatment.) The point is that performance on the primary job is largely a matter of *willingness* to perform, and moonlighting itself is not a prime cause of inferior job performance.

In fact, most 4-day moonlighters take jobs very different from their primary employment. This is predictable, considering that the 4-day schedule is unlikely to fit comfortably with other standard jobs, and the longer workday tends to preclude secondary employment during the primary job's workweek schedule, leaving only a day or so here and there for moonlighting. The exception to this is when moonlighting is in the form of overtime on a regular job; and this is a form of moonlighting that both management and organized labour appear to approve of.

Some moonlighting should be considered beneficial, actually recreational in its effect on the employee. Since the source of much recreation is simply change of activity itself, where moonlighters obtain very different kinds of jobs from their primary job (and most moonlighters do take *very* different kinds of jobs), the change of activity itself is important, and may be recreational. A machinist moonlighting as a bowling instructor is not only getting a change of pace, but is also very likely getting an opportunity to practise his favourite sport.

The major misconception about moonlighting is that it supposedly takes jobs away from other workers, increasing unemployment. This simply is not true. The idea here is based on the false assumption that jobs are limited in supply and that a moonlighter is using up a limited supply of work that an unemployed worker would get to use if it were not for the moonlighter.

First of all, many moonlighting jobs are not suitable as a primary means of support; because they are part-time jobs, or because they are highly unpleasant, or because they are extremely low-paying. People who fill these jobs are willing to fill these jobs *because* they are part-time means of support, and not *in spite of* their being part-time. They are not taking desirable work away from others.

Secondly, the fact is that jobs are not limited in supply. On the contrary, as each moonlighter works, *he spends money*, and contributes towards creating additional jobs in the economy.

Another reason moonlighting should not be brought into consideration of a weak economy is that, as Professor Samuelson points out in the foreword to this book, governments have the fiscal and monetary policies available to them to create full employment. That they do not use these tools is a political decision, blame for which should not be borne by persons desiring to moonlight. Economically, it would make much more sense to chastise people who bank their money instead of spending it; because withholding this money from circulation dampens a society's economy – which is why President Nixon recently appealed to United States citizens to stop saving and to start spending. Not that I am suggesting that we do chastise these people; the point is that if there are not enough jobs, there are large governmental forces at work contributing to the situation; there are tools available to governments to correct the situation; and it is ridiculous to deflect our attention away from government and onto the actions of individual citizens who are moonlighting.

Let us keep the spotlight on the right spot. The problem is not too much sweat from the worker, but too little sweat from politicians, managers, and union leaders, who are in a position to guide our economic affairs. It is the people who allow a General Motors to operate in such a fashion that 6 million automobiles have to be recalled to the factory for defects. With this kind of mismanagement, there cannot be enough jobs.

Let's not blame the moonlighter who displays enough motivation to sacrifice his leisure to provide for his family what inflation from mismanagement keeps him from providing through working one job alone.

Instead of holding moonlighters in derision, we really ought to extend them some well-deserved praise. They are people who are trying hard for their families. They are people struggling to buy homes, putting children through college, supporting elderly folks, and so on. This sort of behaviour for family is highly constructive and desirable, and should be encouraged.

As to so-called "workaholics", these people have a right to meet their needs as best they can, too. If workaholics find nothing better to do with their lives than to work, perhaps we should question a society that has not developed a culture of living without work.

Finally, we ought not to forget that much work done by moonlighters is economically and socially useful to society – and might very well not be available to us at prices we could afford unless people were willing to moonlight.

In sum, 4-day does lead to higher incidence of moonlighting. But why should that bother anyone?

Won't the long weekends mean too much leisure for people – making them bored and unhappy?

People worry that leisure is not good for people. But notice: they are usually talking about *other* people, not themselves.

The people who seem to have the worst problems with leisure appear to be the experts on leisure. For most of the rest of us, the problem is not what to do with our leisure, but how to get more of it.

First of all, almost no 4-day workers report being bored or distressed by their new leisure. On the contrary, they report being very pleased with it.

This is not surprising, since most of us yearn for more leisure than we have. But perhaps the explanation is that 4-day workers are not getting enough extra leisure to enter into the range in which time becomes problematic. After all, 4-day is not a permanent vacation from work. It is merely a rearrangement of the timing of leisure hours with only a few additional hours added in.

When you get right down to it, when experts complain that people would be lost and unhappy without a great deal of work to fill their lives, the experts are really saying that we have not learned how to *live*.

If that's what they're saying, they may be right. There certainly are a great many unhappy people in the world, and the well-known phrase that "most men lead lives of quiet desperation" looks fairly true.

I think experts would be a lot more useful to us if they would suggest new, more satisfying uses of time – new patterns of living – instead of complaining when we do not choose to spend what little leisure time we have going to night school or doing something else that experts consider constructive, but which people do not find sufficiently interesting to spend their time on. The onus is definitely on the experts.

But the solution is *not* to *avoid* leisure. We have to plunge right in if we are to learn how to live. We are certainly not going to learn how to live full human lives by continuing to divert our efforts away from exploring what living could be. If leisure is a problem, and I think that large blocks of leisure might become problematic, let us confront the problem and solve it. Let us not bury our heads in work methods that are less productive than they need be merely in order to avoid confronting what could be a big opportunity for the human race.

And let us not forget that the leisure problem may not be universal. Almost all 4-day workers report extreme contentment with the opportunity that the long weekends provide to associate with their loved ones and to do the other things that the 5-day routine had kept them from doing.

But even while small blocks of leisure may not create problems, we still need to address ourselves to exploring fully the "quality of living". There is a great challenge to be met. And I think people yearn for more leisure today *precisely because* they want the opportunity to meet this challenge in their own lives.

Aren't people going to fritter away their time on these long weekends – just watching television and doing useless things like that?

Yes, people do watch more television on 4-day, but is that frittering away time? Who is to judge? They also spend more time with their families.

I am very impatient with experts who attempt to dictate public tastes. I think such behaviour is very out-of-place in a democracy. If people want to watch television, that's their business. I think people should be free to do whatever pleases them with their time off from work.

On the other hand, if people have *not* developed the more "creative" ways of spending their time that experts would approve of, it may be either that no one is offering more creative leisure pursuits at a price people can afford, AND in an entertaining enough manner; or it may be that people just have not yet had enough experience with leisure to begin investigating less obvious ways of using it.

We have been for all these past centuries a work culture. Our one day off from work was supposed to be spent on religious observances. So we have no history or culture of leisure, and each of us must pioneer in our own way until we develop such a culture.

In the meantime, if people want to watch TV, or want just to relax – that's *their* choice. I imagine people would not choose to watch TV or just relax if they did not get something more out of doing so than they do from whatever other alternatives are available to them.

Managers who would deny employees an opportunity to enjoy leisure out of some false sense that they should run their employees' lives away from the workplace would be just as out of place as the leisure experts who sneer at how people enjoy themselves. (See Chapter 8 for the basic arguments that have raged on this topic; and see Chapters 3 and 4 for how very much workers enjoy and profit by their long weekends.)

What will 4-day do for the leisure industry?

It looks like 4-day will be a boon, not only for the leisure industry, but for the economy as a whole. Thirty-two per cent of workers we surveyed report spending more money on their long weekends; and, even where workers don't spend more money *in toto*, they do re-arrange their budget allocations, spending somewhat more on leisure goods and services.

Dr. Justin Voss (Washington, D.C.) points out, though, that 4-day is not a motivator, but an enabler, when it comes to leisure. He says that the increased spending of 4-day workers shows that 4-day unleashes a desire for additional leisure – leisure time, leisure products, and leisure services – that has been pent up by the 5-day week. A good point, I think, although I suppose that such leisure opportunity not only unleashes, but also enhances desire.

Isn't 4-day just another management ploy to get workers to work more hours? Isn't it true that it's only the managers who want 4-day?

Just about the only thing in our original text which we would amend is our report that in every case it was management, not employees, initiating the 4-day week. That situation has changed.

In a survey we conducted almost a year ago, employees, not

234

managers, initiated the 4-day idea in 20% of the cases. I would imagine that the incidence of employees initiating the idea today is much higher.

Four-day works well for both workers and managers. It simply took workers longer to hear about 4-day than it took managers, because the management magazines were the first to write up our results, and the more popular media wrote up the results afterwards.

There have even been cases in which union leaders initiate 4-day.

Many managers now report to me that they first heard of 4-day by discovering a copy of *4 Days, 40 Hours* placed on their desks – anonymously. Other managers say that groups of workers came to them with the idea, explaining how management could gain by adopting it.

Since employees clearly gain from 4-day, it is not surprising to find them suggesting the idea to management, now that they know about it. In fact, the situation may soon reverse itself, with workers trying to push 4-day on reluctant management. And if there are enough 4-day companies around when that happens, the need to hold one's labour force could well turn 4-day from being a boon that management now offers workers to a medicine that management becomes forced to swallow.

Does 4-day increase or decrease the number of jobs available for workers?

In answering questions such as this one I am reminded of a childhood fairy tale about the little forest animals who found a stranger in the woods. The animals asked the stranger why he was blowing on his hands, and the stranger replied that his hands were very cold and he was blowing on them to warm them up. Taking pity on the shivering man, the animals invited him into their tree house for some hot porridge, to warm him up. When the stranger received the hot porridge, he blew on it to cool it. Puzzled by this behaviour, the animals asked why the stranger blew on the porridge. When they heard the answer, the animals threw the stranger out of their house. They felt that anyone who could blow both hot and cold was not to be trusted.

Four-day also works in two different directions. Some companies use 4-day to hire more employees and some use it to reduce the number of workers needed at the plant. In either case, the use of 4-day makes the firm more productive.

Here are some examples. Lipton Tea made the following conversion in three U.S. plants, in order to increase the hours of utilization of capital equipment. Lipton went from two 8-hour shifts, working 5 days (80 hours of production a week) to four 12-hour shifts (144 hours of production) – nearly doubling the numbers of workers employed. Lipton management decided that 4 sets of workers on a 12-hour schedule were more economical than 3 sets of workes on an 8-hour schedule – even though Lipton is paying 40 hours pay for the 36 hours of work.

On the other hand, a company may decrease jobs. One U.S. firm, Sealtest, has truck drivers working 10-hour driving schedules, instead of 8-hour schedules. A spokesman explained that the use of the 10-hour schedule for them meant that 20 men now handle the routes that it used to take 21 men to drive.

The union agreed to this change, even though it meant one fewer driver for every 20, because the union understood that *unless* the company was permitted to achieve this economy, all of the jobs of all of the men would be imperilled by the lower prices available from the competition. The company negotiator took a good deal of time explaining the situation and his proposal, and showed the union other cases where price competition had led to dissolution of a branch of a company. (Fortunately for both the company and the workers, the union negotiators thoroughly investigated the company's claims, and agreed that the company's proposed economy move was in the best interest of the workers.)

Since the economics can become complex, and since fears of possible job loss are quite natural, it is important that managers take the time to explain complicated economics to workers and/or union representatives if and when these fears crop up. (There are too many case histories where plants have been forced out of business – with consequent unemployment for many workers – because managers did not properly convey the economics of the situation to the workers' representatives.) Conversely, it's important that union leaders take the time to study the economic complexities of a situation, so that they can deal with long-range interests to their benefit.

In general, whether achieving more jobs or fewer, the moves to rearranged workweeks increase the productivity of the company – whether by increasing utilization of capital equipment or by increasing productivity of workers' efforts through the rescheduling of the work. These increases in productivity increase the profitability of the firm; and *through this increase*, increase the stability of existing jobs and the potential for more hiring in the future.

There is a second way in which 4-day leads to an increased number of jobs. Individual companies' increases in productivity add up to affect an entire country's economy, to strengthen it. The more individual companies optimize their scheduling and thereby increase their own productivity, the greater will be their country's real national product.

Is it true that Mrs. Poor has become Mrs. Rich?

The reports of my wealth are exaggerated – unfortunately.

The whole thing started with an address made by a U.S. Department of Labor official at a public meeting of a few hundred businessmen in New York. It appears he was trying to minimize growing interest in the 4-day week – possibly to minimize criticism of the fact that the Labor Department has not conducted nor sponsored research of this (or any other) innovation. So he quipped to the audience: the most significant thing about the 4-day week is that Mrs. Poor has become Mrs. Rich.

When a government gets caught with its pants down (why didn't *they* come up with the 4-day research, and why do they *keep* quoting my statistics – without attributing them to me?) it is likely to become a little surly.

The fact of the matter is: because our government has not been sponsoring research on 4-day while people are growing increasingly interested in it, I have continued to operate a clearinghouse for 4-day information – out of my own pocket.

Our Cambridge office has the most up-to-date files on 4-day that can be found. The files consist of the most complete list anywhere of 4-day companies (including hundreds and hundreds of interviews), of companies considering 4-day, and of companies abandoning 4-day. We also keep track of everyone else's research on 4-day, and report their results. We maintain a file of all newspaper and magazine articles on the subject; and receive on a daily basis letters and telephone inquiries from 4-day participants, researchers, and reporters.

Before you mistake me for a really wealthy philanthropist, note that the public's familiarity with my work brings this information to me at a much lower cost than someone else would experience. Nonetheless, subscriptions to *Poor's Workweek Letter*, which include the right of telephone consultation, do not cover research costs – even at a whopping $125 a year ($5 more overseas). Any assistance or suggestions from readers will be welcome.

My experience with introducing a social innovation and keeping the public abreast of it has shown me what probably is a general principle of the matter: namely, that social innovations can only be broadcast and made available to the public if someone – a government, a foundation, or a private philanthropist – shells out the money to support the process. One cannot conduct research and analyse a social innovation and make information available to the public on a break-even basis – let alone on a profit-making basis. Although the collection and analysis of information costs a vast amount of money, once the information is available to the public, the public is then free to use it without charge. There is no copyright or patent protection on information – only on one's *phrasing* of information. So there is little or no return to the researcher of a social innovation.

This is not because the public does not want the information, just as the public wants toothpaste and soap; but because once the information enters the public domain, there is no necessity forcing the public to pay for it, as it pays for toothpaste and soap. No shopkeeper charges you for using the information that you hear.

None of this is new, of course; it's just that the situation is too often forgotten. Persons particularly interested in promoting social innovations simply must pay some attention to the economic necessities involved.

What is government doing to promote 4-day?

In the U.S.A., precious little. In Canada, the federal government and many of the provincial branches have initiated research to determine the pros and cons of Canadian experience with 4-day, and to determine how if at all the government should be assisting.

In the U.S.A. it is difficult to determine whether governmental neglect of 4-day involves just a general policy of neglecting innovation or whether 4-day is considered too controversial to deal with.

About a year ago, the Secretary of Labor published an article indicating that he was in favour of further exploration of this innovation, and he has testified at congressional hearings that legislative barriers should not be erected against this promising innovation. But since then there appears to have been a reversal of position.

In the autumn of 1971, National Public Radio (which was currently in congressional hearings on the subject of refunding) taped a half-hour interview on the subject with the Secretary of Labor, an official of the United Auto Workers, and myself. But this programme has never been aired.

During Phase I of President Nixon's economic reconstruction, the Office of Economic Priorities denied petitions by companies seeking to rearrange their workweeks on the grounds that the rearranged workweeks constitute pay rises for workers. Among the 4-day experiments barred during this period were those proposed by the John Hancock Life Insurance Co., Boston, and the United Services Automobile Association, San Antonio, Texas. After Phase I, both firms initiated their experiments. John Hancock put about 300 workers (out of about 7,000) on a pilot programme; United Services put their entire 3,000 workers on a trial term and, after the trial period, announced that 4-day is now permanent.

Of course, to the extent that OEP ruled against 4-day experiments, it was sticking to the letter of the law and not to the spirit of it. The announced intent of President Nixon's programme (cf. his August 15, 1971, speech) was to stop inflation and to encourage productivity and innovation. He even used the word "productivity" – the first time that I can remember even hearing the word from the lips of a government official. As I wrote in *Poor's Workweek Letter*, September 1st.:

> We will have to wait to discover how seriously people will take our national crisis to discover *which will emerge the stronger: protection of old ways and prerogatives that aren't working or encouragement of new ways to succeed.*

But we have to go a step further than this – asking not what government is doing to promote 4-day, but what is it doing to promote any innovation whatsoever?

Again the answer is "precious little". Which is most unfortunate, because unless the government drops barriers to innovation and unless it actively supports experimentation, we are not going to be able to develop better ways of doing things.

What is the reaction of unions to the 4-day week?

Union developments in the U.S.A. have been similar to those predicted in Chapter 9. No major union has voiced a favourable opinion of 4-day – without adding the hooker that there be time-and-a-half payments for work over 8 hours a day.

Clearly, American unions do not want to be deflected from their old commitment to higher wages and shorter hours, regardless of the state of productivity – at least, they do not want to do so with any public fanfare involved.

Many small unions are continuing experiments with 4-day and some large unions have quiet experiments going – some, even without the time-and-a-half after 8 hours provision.

Judging by the telephone calls received in our Cambridge office, a number of unions began to study 4-day only this past winter and spring. The questions they ask us indicate open inquiry into 4-day (as opposed to "arming" for dramatic anti-4-day statements). Many mention contract negotiations coming up soon, and that they want to be prepared either for what they understand will be a company proposal, or for a proposal they themselves intend to initiate. (The unions that telephone us appear to be the more democratic ones and those representing more highly skilled and/or professional labour.)

We have also received telephone calls from locals asking us for ammunition that they can use to persuade their internationals to permit them to go on the 4-day week.

It should be borne in mind when discussing union reaction to 4-day that only about 25% of the U.S. work force is represented by unions. So, while it would be dramatic to have a large union opt for rearranged workweeks (without pay penalties), there is plenty of room for 4-day expansion without any union participation whatsoever – although there is plenty of union participation already. About 15% to 20% of 4-day companies do have union representation. (Many pay the premium overtime rate, but some do not.) And further exploration of 4-day on the part of unions is likely.

I have heard reports that a local of the United Auto Workers Union in Detroit is campaigning strongly for 4-day (plus time-and-a-half pay). They are said to have jackets and hats with 4-40 slogans.

In view of the fact that productivity is by and large much too low these days for unions to maintain any realistic hope of shorter weeks at higher pay in the near future, why then is there resistance to enjoying the benefits of the rearranged workweek in the interim? Two concrete issues not explored in Chapter 9 appear to have emerged.

The first concrete issue is that since 4-day frequently makes worker performance more productive, there may be a reasonable fear that unless there is a concurrent increase in sales, there will be fewer workers required and a consequent reduction in union membership. This notion is certainly not necessarily correct. In many cases, 4-day leads directly to more jobs, and even in those cases where fewer workers are required, there are often advantages in job security to the remaining workers – plus better long-term prospects for more jobs.

The second concern comes from my initial reports that 4-day was being initiated entirely by management. While that report was true at that time, it was not long before workers heard about 4-day and themselves began to initiate 4-day changes. But while people *thought* it was true, the notion undoubtedly led union leaders to suspect that there might be some hidden catch to what appears on the face of it to be a "win-win" situation. And, in a way, this misconception (for which I am, however innocently, to blame) can be an even more powerful negative influence than the first issue, because it feeds into the old history of labour-management relations, which have very definitely been of a "win-lose" character. The following is quoted from *Poor's Workweek Letter*:

ESSAYS ON THE CONSERVATION OF HUMAN BEINGS
Win-Win vs. Win-Lose Games: What's the Future of Labour-Management Relations?

The world has a long history of playing win-lose games. If I win, you lose; if you win, I lose. So we fight. And there are always losers; in fact, the winners are often losers too.

Because we are growing increasingly aware of the dangers and dissatisfactions of win-lose games, there is a very real need today for learning to structure win-win situations, and learning to avoid structuring win-lose situations.

One of the really exciting things about the rearranged workweek innovation is its win-win nature. Both workers and managers see themselves gaining from the change: firms increase their profits and employees get a more useful package of non-work hours. So, employees and employers see themselves as being on the same side of the issue – both benefiting from the change, rather than seeing each other as adversaries.

In fact, one reason 4-day caught on so quickly is its win-win nature; and

4-day could be a harbinger of a new win-win, cooperative relationship between labour and management.

Why are *some* labour leaders so very opposed to 4-day when the leaders of other unions, including leaders of a few really major unions, are taking a more rational let's-look-at-it attitude (UAW and the Machinists, to cite just two)?

Why do some leaders state categorically that members are opposed to 4-day, without polling them? Why do they claim negative effects for 4-day, without studying 4-day cases? Why the concern to discredit 4-day research? Why the denial of the very possibility that 4-day might be useful or desirable in at least some cases? Why the use of emotional arguments instead of factual ones? Why the growing appearance of a split between these labour leaders and their members on the issue – with some locals contacting *us* for information to use in persuading their own internationals?

I feel forced to speculate that it may be the very win-win nature of 4-day that is behind the opposition. I speculate that the development of a cooperative attitude between managers and workers is viewed as a threat by some union leaders.

Where some leaders now call 4-day at non-union plants a kind of "unfair competition", it may be that it is not 4-day itself that is the competition, but the very nature of the relationship between management and labour at these non-union firms that is the *real* competition.

Now, viewing a change to a win-win relationship as a probable threat is very understandable. Win-win is a relatively new possibility, and we have a strong habit of operating win-lose games. We are thoroughly familiar with the win-lose rules, and know how to play these games. We know next to nothing about what it would be like to play win-win games.

Almost all of the history of labour-management relations has been an adversary win-lose relationship. The only major change in the relationship that has come about over the past several thousand years since labourers were actually slaves with no civil rights is the change in the balance of power from that one-sided master-slave relationship to an even balance of power. Thanks belong largely to the rise of organized labour and to its pushing for increased strength.

But now that a balance of power has been achieved (and some feel the balance has turned in the other direction), now what? May this not signal an *opportunity* for a change in the conduct of relations between labour and management, an opportunity to structure win-win situations and to avoid win-lose ones?

The world is changing. The power balance between labour and management is altered. The needs today are different. It's also possible that *a new type of relationship may be necessary in order to respond to the new circumstances under which we now live.*

In my opinion, win-win will become the relationship between management and labour in the long run. The problem now is that we are, I think, in a transition period. We have a habit of win-lose psychology, and it's not amazing that we cling to it. Change is scary and we don't have a clear model for new behaviour.

Union leadership brought about parity in power. Now union leadership will be needed to change the adversary relationship which its own achievements have made obsolete. For obvious reasons, *it takes great leaders to break away from the old and to create new relationships.*

But, I predict, win-win is the trend of the future. And not only in labour-management relations!

What is the likelihood of union leaders' softening their previous negative attitudes towards 4-day?

I think the likelihood is high, for a number of reasons. First, as leaders look at the increasing amounts of evidence available on 4-day, they will become less fearful about false issues (for example, the "management ploy" theme) and more aware of the real, positive results for workers.

Secondly, there is bound to be increasing membership interest in 4-day, as union members hear more and more about the growing number of brother workers enjoying long weekends – and realize that long weekends would be feasible at *their* places of employment, too, were it not for union (or management) resistance.

But perhaps the most important factor is the shift in members' goals, which has been taking place over time – a shift *towards* much more concern with quality of life and *away* from old monetary concerns, necessary in the days when workers were practically penniless. Those days are gone. And although we are experiencing a rather painful period of inflation and unemployment, nonetheless, most workers today are vastly more affluent than ever before even *dreamed of* in the world's history.

As wages rise, though, it just so happens that each added unit of income becomes less important to people – and each unit of added leisure (to spend the fruits of work – wages) becomes much more important. I think we have definitely passed the turning point in workers' concern for leisure versus wages in the package of the wages and time.

The following article from the front page of the *Wall Street Journal* (May 9, 1972) illustrates the point. It shows that two thirds of the members of a union are *already satisfied with their wages,* and have shifted their concern to *other* areas of their lives:

243

4 Days, 40 Hours

NOT BY BREAD ALONE: A psychological study of Teamster union members in Detroit and Pontiac finds 67% are "completely" or "well" satisfied with their present wages. But 74% would like greater health care, 65% express concern over work safety.

I think workers' concerns have changed and will change more over time; non-work hours will receive increasing priority; and union policies will eventually reflect the changed concerns of members.

And if union leadership is not responsive to memberships' changed and changing priorities, it will have to bend – or break.

Here is an example even now of a local union *withdrawing* from the international over the issue of the 4-day week. This is an article from the *Fargo, North Dakota, Forum and Moorhead News* (April 29, 1972):

Knight Printers Discard Union for 4-day Week

A National Labor Relations Board election held Thursday in the composing room of Knight Printing Co., Fargo, resulted in de-certification of Fargo Typographical Union local No. 186.

The action means that the Knight plant has dropped its union shop status and it leaves only two Fargo-Moorhead printing establishments with Typographical union contracts – The Forum and the Pierce Co.

The election was held after employees had petitioned to de-certify, and it came as an aftermath of a 4-day workweek of 10 hours per day, instituted by management on a trial basis last summer and continued through the winter.

Steve Gorman Jr., of Knight, said that production will now be geared to the 4-day workweek on a permanent basis.

The International Typographical Union would not approve a contract offered Knight compositors by the company which called for the 10-hour straight-time day. Union regulations require overtime compensation after eight hours daily.

Originally, office and union production employees at Knight had voted, 26-3, to stay on the 10-hour, 4-day week at the end of last summer's experimental period. Pressmen and bindery workers who had different union affiliation were given permission by their unions to make their own decisions.

This example ought to wake some people up – that this is what comes of being inflexible towards change.

A Note to Managers

The same principles apply to you.

A recent survey by 3 Boston University students (referred to later on) found 88% of workers they surveyed at 5 diverse Boston firms *want to try 4-day.*

Meanwhile, managers appear to be far less alert to the possibilities of change. The following is from *Poor's Workweek Letter:*

> *Nation's Business* (a publication of The National Chamber of Commerce, Washington) *just announced a poll of their readership. Here's how 12,703 respondents are reported as voting by U.S. News and World Report. To the following* (vague) *question . . . the readership response was 83% NO, and 14% YES:*
> "What do you think? Should the four-day week be widely adopted? Do you favour trying it at your firm?"

The most important thing to note about this survey is that most people, including managers, know very little about 4-day, in spite of the over 4,000 newspaper and magazine articles published about it in the past 2 years. Continuing with *Poor's Workweek Letter:*

> *People who know a lot about 4-day have different, more positive attitudes towards the innovation. For example, here's the response to the SAME questionnaire from an audience of businessmen in California* (in this case, mostly personnel directors) *AFTER they had had the opportunity to question me about it:*
>
>   (26 – unqualified yes
>   45 { 14 – yes, but it depends on firm's circumstances . . .
>   (5 – yes and no, it depends on firm's circumstances . . .
>   3 – uncertain
>   5 – no, because it depends on firm's circumstances . . .
>   8 – unqualified no
>   ―
>   61

And please note that the workers who abandoned their union for 4-day (previous section) had prior experience of 4-day.

Real experience with it leads to positive attitudes towards 4-day, because it works well for both managers and workers. The fear of change itself, which holds many back, is partly a product of simple ignorance of the workings of the innovation; this can easily be cured by learning about it.

Considering the yearnings of most workers for more leisure (not to mention the reports of companies increasing their productivity), managers as well as union leaders would be wise to investigate 4-day thoroughly, instead of rejecting it out of hand.

Why do you say that the attitude of people who have experience with 4-day is more positive than that of people who do not have experience with 4-day?

Because that's what the figures show, from whatever angle you look at them, and whether we discuss workers, or managers or union leaders.

Almost every 4-day company that has conducted a poll of employees' willingness to try 4-day *before* introducing it shows approximately 75% voting that they are willing to try the plan. (These figures are 6 months to a year old; more recent reports show higher percentages desiring to make a 4-day trial.) But *after* trying 4-day, when the company again surveys employees as to whether they want to retain it, the figures usually jump to the 90% level, and higher. These before-and-after results lead directly to the conclusion that experience with 4-day leaves workers feeling even more positive towards it than they felt beforehand.

The same goes for managers who try 4-day. Very few firms that try 4-day abandon it. This leads to the conclusion that managers who try it, like it. For obvious reasons, we are unlikely to get a chance to survey what experience does for a manager who does *not* like the idea of 4-day and yet institutes it; presumably, when a manager doesn't like the idea, he does *not* institute it. It is probable that only managers who are initially favourably predisposed towards 4-day institute it.

One has to note an exception here. Managers who feel that 4-day was installed over their dead bodies, so to speak, continue to dislike it even after experience with it – a reaction that most of us might share under similar circumstances. From time to time I hear of 4-day conversions made where management is split on the issue. Some people have reported to me that they feel their 4-day experiments were sabotaged by managers who were forced, whether by superiors or by subordinates, to try 4-day.

In cases like this, it is impossible for us to judge whether 4-day operated badly or whether the problem was the way it was instituted, although we suspect that *the way* 4-day is instituted is the operating

246

factor. (And, if true, persons researching *how* to adopt 4-day will want to be wary of this kind of situation.)

Again, on the whole, people who try it clearly like it more than people who have not tried it. This is also why we suspect that much of the resistance to 4-day is a product of ignorance about it (or of resistance to change itself), rather than a reaction to anything inherent to 4-day operations. This is not to belittle *real* objections to 4-day operations – it is merely to note that an important source of objections to it has nothing to do with 4-day operation itself.

What is the attitude of the general public towards 4-day?

The public's attitude towards 4-day has been growing increasingly positive. The attitude of workers who have *no* experience with 4-day is illustrated by several independent surveys. In March, 1971, the Gallup polls announced that 38% of the American public was for 4-40 – a result I considered extremely high at the time, because the concept had only recently been introduced to the public. (Very few of those sampled could have had an experience with 4-day, and some of them were *not* even members of the work force.)

At about the same time, *The Machinist*, a publication of the International Association of Machinists and Aerospace Workers (Washington, D.C.) invited its members to write in their opinions about 4-40. Editor Gordon Cole says member response ran about 50-50 pro and con, and he published a good sampling of the letters that came in.

About a year later, on February 16, 1972, the *Federal Times* (Washington), a weekly newspaper for civilians in government employ, announced a poll of their readership. Of 23,979 workers responding to the poll, 21,683 said they favour the 4-40 idea – slightly over 90%. A wide range of government workers, at all grades and levels, responded, showing an overwhelming preference for 4-40 over 5-40. (The one exception was that United States Postal Service workers grade 9 and above voted only 3 to 1 for 4-40.)

In April, 1972, three Boston University students surveyed 264 workers at 5 firms in the Boston area reporting that 88% of these workers want to try 4-day at their firms and that 69% had had discussions about 4-day with other workers at the firm. The students who did the study were mature people: Ottavio Forte, a member of the staff of Massachusetts Institute of Technology, holding a Masters degree in Engineering, along with Barbara Brady and Barbara

247

Fulton, nurses who work at hospitals in the Boston area. The 5 firms surveyed were: 2 hospitals, an engineering firm, a research laboratory, and a supermarket. The 88% finding was consistent within just a few percentage points over all 5 firms surveyed.

There have been many other polls, by newspaper reporters and so on, reporting very similar results, showing that at this point in time, receptivity towards trying 4-day has grown to a markedly high level among U.S. workers.

Among managers the results are somewhat different: they have also grown more positive in their attitudes towards 4-day, but not so markedly positive as workers have done. As mentioned in our introduction, the decision is much more complicated for managers than it is for workers – more information and more study is required for a manager to come to a decision on 4-day.

Dun's Review in July, 1971, reported surveying the nation's top business leaders and finding that these leaders, while conceding that some kind of shortened workweek lies ahead, felt cautious about any abrupt changeover to 4-40 and warned against possible harmful economic effect. Many of their comments indicated that these leaders were discussing a *shortened* workweek, rather than the rearranged workweek – indicating their level of knowledge about 4-40 was low at the time.

In a study issued in October, 1971, Lifson, Wilson, Fergusson, Winick of Dallas reported that of 285 businessmen responding to 1,000 questionnaires they mailed out, 10% were for 4-40, 20% were "neutral", and 52% were against it. (LWFW reported that 18% checked "other", probably indicating that they felt that it depended on the individual company's circumstances.)

This study, which was probably researched at about the same time as *Dun's*, reported a significant finding. While the respondents' concensus was that 18% of companies in the U.S.A. would be on 4-day in 1971, 33% in 1975, and 58% in 1990, at the same time 79% of the respondents said that they were *unaware* of their employees' feelings about converting to 4-day.

A Bureau of National Affairs (Washington) "Bulletin to Management" dated January 6, 1972, reports a survey by BNA of members of the American Society for Personnel Administration. Of 265 ASPA members queried, 181 responded. Twelve were already on 4-day at the time – almost 7%. And 17% reported they were seriously considering 4-day (13% of the *small* firms and 20% of the *large* firms – no numbers given).

The American Management Association (New York City) conducted a study in the summer of 1971 and released its results in February of 1972. Of 811 AMA members responding to 2,400 questionnaires sent out at "random" to the membership, AMA reports 43 of these members already on 4-day – over 5%; and 142 members seriously considering it (18%). (Both the AMA and BNA studies included extra focus on the companies practising 4-day, which we will discuss later.)

There have been numerous similar polls. For example, a poll of members of a Long Island business association (reported by the *Long Island Commercial Review* on April 28, 1972) showed of 125 returns, that 10% of these businesses were already on 4-day for some or part of their payroll; 14% had a "desire" for the 4-day week (but no current plans for adopting it); and 76% did not presently have or want a 4-day week.

The polls tend to show managers' increasing acceptance of and utilization of 4-day.

Results of Polls in Other Countries. Some Countries Seem to Show Managers Displaying a More Open Mind to 4-Day than in the U.S.A.: The Montreal firm Samson, Belair, Riddell, Stead, Inc., polled firms employing over 10% of the Canadian work force of 6 million people: 152 Canadian firms. In the study released in October, 1972, they report finding 17 firms already on 4-day – a little over 11%.

Of the 135 firms *not* on the 4-day week, they report that over three-quarters of the managers expressed definitely positive attitudes towards the rearranged workweek: 53% felt it to be a practical, viable arrangement that will gain general acceptance; 15% felt that it will be adopted, but that it will unfortunately take many years to implement; and 9% felt that it will be adopted generally within a very few years. Only 3.8% (6 firms) expressed completely negative attitudes towards 4-day, saying it is unwieldy and impractical and will be abandoned – 1 firm's manager held that 4-day is a "passing fad". (Twenty per cent expressed neutral attitudes towards 4-day.)

The study also reports that a Gallup poll of Canadians (probably taken at the same time the U.S.A. Gallup poll was taken) showed 34% of Canadian adults favour 4-40.

As for New Zealand, Mr. Paul F. McKimmey of the Auckland Regional Authority wrote me in August, 1971, that 3 N.Z. firms were already on 4-day, and that since a number of companies had expressed interest in 4-day, the Authority was beginning a field study of it. (We have not yet received a copy of the study.)

In Australia, final year students at the School of Management at Sydney Technical College issued a detailed 74-page report called "4-Day, 40-Hour Working Week for Australia?", in September, 1971, finding a receptivity to the idea that amazed me at the time, being far ahead of current U.S.A. reaction at the time.

Signs that managers in additional countries are interested in 4-day are numerous. The publication of this book in the Netherlands and in Japan shows the publishers' judgement that there is sufficient interest in the topic in these countries to enable them successfully to market a book. Four-day conferences are already being held in Switzerland and Germany. And subscribers to *Poor's Workweek Letter* reside in numerous countries. In June, 1972, a gentleman from West Germany (Heiner Kubler of Erzberger) sent me a short report on 4-day that he prepared, containing 5 German firms now on 4-day.

There is no doubt in my mind that interest in 4-day is growing throughout the world – as people open their minds to the evidence that some new attention to scheduling can pay off.

What *independent* confirmation have you (in addition to your *own* studies) that 4-day managers consider their 4-day operations successful?

In this section we are talking about managers with *actual* experience of 4-day, as distinct from the previous section in which we discussed managers who are only *considering* 4-day without having experienced it.

The Bureau of National Affairs study, mentioned above, found 12 of the American Society for Personnel Administration members polled already on 4-day, and added to its survey another 59 4-day companies whose names had been gleaned from press coverage. Of the total 71 4-day companies surveyed, BNA reports the following percentages (usually, the actual number of firms were not given):

Percentages	BNA findings at 71 4-day companies
32	report shortening their workweek while rearranging it.
76	report using some version of the 4-day week (as opposed to 3-day or perhaps something else not described by BNA).
48	use 4-40 for their 4-day schedule (whether something

250

Percentages	BNA findings at 71 4-day companies
	like 4-38 is included in the definition of 4-40 is not specified).
9	use 4-day for 500 to 1,000 workers at the firm.
3	use 4-day for 1,000 or more workers at the firm.
18	report their 4-day employees are union members.
73	said the idea originated at some point in the management hierarchy, as opposed to coming from workers.
17	said unions played some role in making the change (the role is not specified).
64	adopted 4-day after 1970.
73	said 4-day is permanent (no longer on trial).
51	instituted group meetings at some point in the change-over.
48	experienced no major problem in making the change.
89	said the change had accomplished the goals management had in mind when implementing the new workweek.
4	said the change had not accomplished these goals or said it was "too soon to tell", or did not answer the question).
1	report not being satisfied by the changed workweek.
79	report being satisfied (the rest are 14%, "too soon to tell"; 3%, "yes and no"; and 3%, no response).
35	cited "improved production" as their reason for satisfaction.
54	cited improved employee morale or lower absenteeism and/or turnover as their reasons.
11	cited "preferred hiring practices".

In the American Management Association study referred to previously, the researchers added a survey of 245 companies "thought to have a definite interest in the 4-day week" to the 811 AMA member firms studied. The 245 were gleaned, I believe, from a list of persons who had purchased cassette tape recordings through my publishing firm; and of these, 100 were found to have started 4-day. With the 43 AMA members on 4-day, the 100 non-member 4-day companies brought the total AMA surveyed to 143.

While the AMA questions are not strictly comparable to the BNA questions, where they *can* be compared, the results look remarkably similar to BNA results; and both the AMA and BNA results are

251

remarkably similar to the results I obtained in the original study reported in this book.

The AMA results are as follows – the AMA reported numbers for most items, and in these cases we added the percentages to make it easier for readers to compare AMA and BNA results:

Percentages	Numbers	AMA findings at 143 4-day companies
51	72	have single-shift operations; 41 have 2 shifts, and 14 have 3 shifts.
88	123 (of 140)	report using some version of the 4-day week – only 4 firms actually had 4-40 while others went as low as 4-32 and as high as 4-48.
7	10 (of 140)	report using a 4½-day week.
5	7 (of 140)	report using a 3-day week.
—	"few"	report being open only 4 days a week.
15	21 (of 139)	report their 4-day employees are union members.
92	127 (of 138)	report management introduced the innovation (but in 3 cases, unions initiated 4-day, while in the rest, presumably employees did so).
—	"few"	had experience with 4-day over 12 months' duration and these firms averaged 55 months' experience. Excluding the long-termers, average experience with 4-day was 5½ months.
64	92 (of 143)	adopted 4-day on a trial basis (83 provided formally for a return to 5-day if needed – I infer from this that 51 changed over to 4-day without calling it an experiment in the beginning).
65	*	instituted group meetings during the changeover.
7	*	used outside management consultants to help them make the changeover.
69	*	adopted 4-day to meet objectives centred upon business results.
31	*	adopted 4-day to meet strictly employee-oriented objectives (something like re-

*Numbers not given.

Percentages	Numbers	AMA findings at 143 4-day companies
		ducing absenteeism was interpreted and listed as *business*-oriented).
8	*	discontinued using 4-day.
51	73 (of 143)	answered a question asking them to cite the "principal disadvantage" of 4-day: 16 answers involved greater scheduling difficulties; 9, problems with working mothers; 8 (only 8!) cited fatigue; 7, employees disliked working overtime; 5, resentment from employees not on 4-day; 3, inadequate supervision; and only 1 to 3 responses on other problems.
—	1	cited increased moonlighting as the principal disadvantage.
100	145 (of 143)	(I am not at all sure how they obtained this result! But we'll count it as 100% for ease of computation) answered the query to cite the "principal advantage" of 4-day – their answers comprise the 5 items immediately below.
42	61 (of 145)	said "increased employee morale" or "additional employee benefit" (54); 4 cited increased management morale; 1, employees happy to get the chance to moonlight; and 2, increased leisure time.
13	19 (of 145)	cited lower absenteeism.
3	4 (of 145)	cited decreased turnover.
7	10 (of 145)	cited easier recruitment.
35	51 (of 145)	cited increased productivity of one sort or another: 9, "increased productivity"; 8, "better equipment utilization"; 6, better customer service; 5, increased production; 4, increased employee efficiency; 4, greater production scheduling flexibility; 4, "decreased costs"; 4, decreased overtime requirements; 3, fewer start-ups and shut-downs; 2, "increased profits"; and 1 each

*Numbers, not given.

4 Days, 40 Hours

Percentages	Numbers	AMA findings at 143 4-day companies
		of improved employee discipline and better competitive posture.
51	*	report costs remained about the same; 38% said costs decreased; and 11% said costs increased.
62	*	report production increased; 35% said it remained the same; and 3% said it decreased.
66	*	report productivity increased; 31% said it remained the same; and 3% said it decreased.
51	*	report higher profits; 45% said profits are the same; and 4% said profits decreased.
64	*	said ease of personnel administration was about the same; 20% said it was improved; and 16% said it deteriorated
49	*	said ease of production related scheduling remained the same; 26% said it was more difficult; and 25% said it was improved.
94	*	said vendor relationships remained the same; 5% said relations improved; and 1% said they deteriorated.
79	*	said customer relations remained the same; 18% said they improved; and 3% said they deteriorated.
59	*	said they received public relations benefits; 25% were uncertain; and 16% said they did not receive benefits.
69	*	said overall employee relations improved; 31% cited no change; and *no one* said relations deteriorated.
25	*	reported that executives also get an extra day off (how frequently, is not mentioned).
47	61 (of 130)	agree that 4-day employees moonlight more.
28	39 (of 136)	agree that employee fatigue increases on the longer workday.

*Numbers not given.

254

Percentages	Numbers	AMA findings at 143 4-day companies
93	129 (of 137)	disagree that the 4-day plan is inflationary.
88	115 (of 130)	disagree that 4-day is not adaptable to large companies.
72	98 (of 136)	disagree that employees are unprepared for additional leisure time.
65	87 (of 134)	agree that working mothers will have an easier time.

The attitudes of 4-day managers displayed in the last 6 items contrast sharply with the attitudes of managers who are not considering 4-day. Managers who are considering it, but have not yet decided, display attitudes that fall somewhere in the middle–neither so positive as the attitudes of 4-day managers nor so negative as managers not considering 4-day.

Neither study names the companies surveyed; so there is no way to judge how much overlap there is between the universes they studied, nor between the universes that they studied and the one I studied for Chapter 1.

However, whether they are partly going over ground that has been ploughed before, or not, these independently performed studies show that a high proportion of 4-day companies are highly satisfied with it, confirming the pioneering research in this volume. Although, I do find it worth noting that although both the BNA and AMA procured copies of *4 Days, 40 Hours* from my office, neither gives even one mention of the book – while both quote liberally from it.*

These are not the only studies that have been done. There have been many additional independent studies performed by business trade associations that have polled their own members, and so on. We cannot take the space even to mention all of them, let alone to quote from them: and it is not necessary to do so, since their results closely duplicate each other and the ones already reported here. It is worth mentioning, however, as a sign of the widespread nature of the interest in 4-day, that literally hundreds of student term

*These are not the only problems with literary theft that we have met. The prestigious *Wall Street Journal* used the galleys of the book, without credit, as the basis for a front page article that wowed the American public; a *New York Times Magazine* article by Gertrude Samuels quoted our authors for sentences on end without attribution to this book; *Newsday* published 2 articles using our material without crediting us; and so on.

papers and also masters degree theses were conducted in the past year – almost none included any field research.

A notable exception is a doctoral dissertation by Thomas J. Swierczewski, which is an in-depth study over time of one company's experiences with 4-day, and which includes several employee surveys taken over time. The company's results closely duplicate the average reported by the other studies. (The dissertation is referred to more fully in several places below.)

An interesting point to note about the BNA and AMA studies is that while they obtained very similar results, they interpret their results quite differently. As was widely quoted by a press thirsty for any negative information, BNA reports: "on the basis of numbers, the firms involved in changing the week are too few to predict a trend towards this change." Meanwhile, AMA agrees with us that 4-day is a growing movement, and predicts that "large U.S. corporations will begin to make the switch during 1972 and 1973, at least on a trial basis in selected operating and staff groups." This had already begun in 1971, and has continued in 1972.

What About Other Countries

The Canadian study by Samson, Belair, Riddell, Stead, Inc., referred to in a previous section, found 17 Canadian firms on 4-day. SBRS reports that the experiences of both labour and management are, on the whole, positive ones, stating: "the list of advantages closely parallels the American experience as outlined by Mrs. Poor in her book". Quoting our SBRS summary from a *Poor's Workweek Letter:*

The major difference between the Canadian sample and Poor's sample is that over 82% of the 4-day Canadians are unionized and all but 42 are males. Size of 4-day firms ranged from 15 to 9,600 employees, with 1,555 workers on 4-day. Number of employees on 4-day at each firm ranges from 3 to 375 (percentage ranges from 1% to 100%). The average is 92 at a firm, or 31% of its work force. Firms are mostly in manufacturing, computers, or trucking.

The major difference in results is that theirs appear somewhat more positive – for example, none of their sample has (so far) discontinued 4-day.

One firm that had discontinued 4-day (which they did discover) did not participate in the study.

In sum, there is ample independent confirmation that companies have continued to convert to 4-day in rather remarkable numbers and that they appear to be delighted, for the most part, with the changeover. And there has been no evidence whatsoever reported to the contrary.

What about studies of the attitudes of employees who have experienced 4-day?

Aside from innumerable newspaper and magazine articles on this subject, and the references to employee satisfaction given in the reports about 4-day managers (previously discussed), there are only 2 important independent sources of field work on this subject that have come to our attention.

About the first source, we quote from 2 *Poor's Workweek Letters:*

A SURVEY OF U.S.A. WORKERS. James A. Wilson, Associate Professor of Business Administration (Sociopsychology), University of Pittsburgh, released (10/71) some *preliminary* statistics from his on-going study of workers at 4-day firms. The following is from his four-page statistical summary of *questionnaires returned by 588 respondents at 51 4-day companies* – out of 2,500 questionnaires sent out to 100 companies across the U.S.A. (A Conference Report is available from the University.)

Respondents' Characteristics:
Average Age: 35.3 years.   *Marital Status:* 74% married.
Sex: 65% male.   *Average Income:* $7,000/year.
Percentage Having a Working Spouse: 41%.
Average Length of Employment with Company: 3.5 years.
Types of Jobs Held: 39% unskilled, 20% skilled, 13% managers or supervisors, 12% clerical or secretarial, 16% "other".

Since Your Company Has Changed its Schedule, How Do You Feel about the Following?

Questions Answered by 588 Respondents At 51 U.S.A. 4-day Firms	Answers – in Percents[a]			
	Agree[b]	Neutral	Disagree[c]	N.A.[d]
1. I like my work more now.[e]	70.6	20.7	6.1	2.6
2. My wife (husband) likes the new schedule more.	53.8	15.3	7.8	23.1
3. Most of the people I work with like it more.	84.2	7.1	4.0	4.8
4. My Union supports the new schedule.	9.2	14.5	5.8	70.6

Questions Answered by 588 Respondents At 51 U.S.A. 4-day Firms	Answers in Percents[a]			
	Agree[b]	Neutral	Disagree[c]	N.A.[d]
5. Absenteeism has decreased.	58.3	24.0	10.6	7.1
6. Overtime (over regular time) has increased.	20.2	25.2	55.4	9.2
7. I am now thinking about moving further away from work.	6.7	17.2	69.2	7.0
8. Few problems have been created in our department.	60.3	17.3	16.2	6.1
9. Immediately after work, I am tired.	46.5	19.2	29.5	4.9
10. My total monthly pay has increased.	20.8	27.7	45.1	6.5
11. With a longer work day and an extra day off, I am more tired now than before.	15.0	14.8	66.2	4.1
12. I know a great deal about the FOUR DAY WORKWEEK.	51.4	35.0	9.4	4.3
13. If I were to change jobs now, I would *not* look for a company with the same schedule I have now.	14.3	15.8	65.2	4.8
14. I am spending more money on my leisure time now.[f]	28.9	24.3	42.7	4.1
15. I can be at home for most of my children's meals and bedtimes if I wish.	44.9	18.2	12.1	24.8
16. I think the new schedule is a good idea.	85.0	6.1	6.5	2.4

PWL notes: a. Percents do not always total 100.0, probably due to rounding.
b. We collapsed "strongly agree" and "agree" into one column, for ease of reading.
c. We collapsed "disagree" and strongly "disagree' into one column.
d. The large non-responses probably indicate non-applicability of the questions, not lack of cooperation; e.g., in questions 2 and 15, the non-response percentage nearly matches the percentage not married; question 4 probably shows the non-unionized.
e. Compares with "I like the *company* more now than I did when we were on 5 days," Chapter 4: 5% say they like the *company* less now But only 46% said they like the *company* more. If these sets are comparable, there appears to be more increase in positive response to *work* than to *company*. Also see Chapter 4 for discussion of distinction between *work* and *job*.
f. Compares with Chapter 4: 31.6% said "yes" to "Do you find that you are spending more money for free-time activities since you began the 4-day week?"

Readers will note that the 85% agree response to the statement "I think the new schedule is a good idea" is a reasonably close parallel to the 92% that we report as saying they are "pleased" or "very pleased" with the 4-day week in Chapter 4.

In a later *Poor's Workweek Letter* we continued our report of Professor Wilson's study, as follows:

DR. JAMES WILSON asked *4-day workers* what would be the *maximum* number of *hours* they would be willing to work at a stretch on a regular basis, while still working the same number of hours in a month. The answers:

4-5	6-7	8-9	10-11	12-13	14-15	16-17	more than 18	N.A.
1%	1%	14%	52%	21%	3%	1%	4%	4%

The results are provocative. Only 2% say they would like a less than 8-hour day. Only 14% consider 8-9 hrs. optimal. A full 52% say they prefer 10-11 hrs.; and 29% say they would be willing to work 12 or more – with 4% willing to work over 18.

> *About a third of these workers who are experienced with 4-day show preference for trading even longer workdays for even larger blocks of leisure time.*

(*Caution.* These results are suggestive only: speculative preferences may not be identical to actual preference made in response to a real situation.)

Aside from Dr. Wilson's study, the only other important source of field work known to us is a doctoral dissertation by Thomas J. Swierczewski, Associate Professor of Business Administration at Bucks County Community College, Pennsylvania. Dr. Swierczewski did an in-depth study, completed in May, 1972, of one manufacturing firm that adopted 4-day. He studied both management and employees, conducting interviews before, during, and after the changeover, for a period of about 15 months.

While the study is too long and intensive to report here in detail, one aspect of it, concerning worker attitudes on 4-day, should be mentioned here. (Dr. Swierczewski's checklist for converting is included later on.)*

Over the period of time between October, 1970 (just before 4-day was introduced) and January, 1972 (after employees had had extensive experience with it) employee attitude towards 4-day developed from 52% in favour of it to 78% in favour. The percentage of employees disliking 4-day declined from 28% in October, 1970, to

*The dissertation, "A Study of One Firm's Installation and Utilization of a 4-day Workweek", comprises 250 pages, and includes 42 tables, 2 figures, a 13-page checklist, and an extensive bibliography. The purpose was to investigate the influence of the rearranged workweek on one firm's organizational effectiveness. (In the process, the author debunks a number of myths about 4-day, describes 4-day history, and so on.) Dr. Swierczewski makes the study available only through Bursk and Poor Publishing, Inc., Cambridge, Massachusetts, in xerox form, at $45 (prepaid in U.S. funds) including postage.

20% in January, 1972. (The "no opinion" category declined from 20% in the beginning to 2% at the final survey.

TABLE 1. LIST OF SOME FREQUENTLY CITED ADVANTAGES AND DISADVANTAGES OF 4-DAY FROM THE POINT OF VIEW OF EMPLOYEES. (Presented in no particular sequence.)

Advantages	Disadvantages
long weekends for travel, hobbies, building projects, visiting, and so on	little leisure time during workweek, long work hours interfere with evening courses, and other night-time activities
less time commuting	changes in regular car pools, meal times, wake-up times, conflict with spouse's work schedules, or children's school schedules, etc.
less cost for commuting	
easier, less aggravating commuting	
fewer work hours (constituting an increase in pay rate)	interface with 5-day institutions, such as schools
time for real relaxation	fatigue on the longer workday
time to conduct personal business during the workweek without missing work and losing pay	loss of overtime work
	public transportation less frequent during new commuting hours
time for family, children, marriage, and so on	interference with extra-curricular operations at work
facilities less crowded during the worker's weekend	spending too much money on leisure
easier to get babysitters	
less money spent on babysitters	fear of the dark when leaving work later than accustomed
pride in being a pioneer (pride in the firm, too)	workload is higher on the first day back to work (for white collar people only)
opportunity to use wages on leisure	
opportunity for more overtime and/or moonlighting	some supervisors on 4-day temporarily feel useless when they find the firm operates just fine when they are away (later, they realize that that's the result good managers are supposed to obtain)
spend less money on lunches, work clothes, and so on	
some supervisors have more of an opportunity to gain responsibility (when their supervisors take time off)	

Table 1 – *contd.*

Advantages	Disadvantages
time for creative thinking and creative meetings	husband complains about new dinner hour
	occasional overburdening of supervisors
	too much contact with grouchy spouse
	the "honey-do weekend" (explained later)

If 4-day is so wonderful, why do so many firms discontinue it?

Very few firms discontinue 4-day.

About 25% of the firms that do discontinue 4-day, later go back to 4-day again after modifying their schedules to overcome whatever obstacles the first new schedule had created.

So it is not correct to say that many firms have discontinued 4-day; on the contrary, very, very few have done so. My files show only 70 of 1,500 4-day firms have discontinued, and many of these have later readopted new, improved 4-day schedules. (There are probably many more firms that have discontinued, but that we do not know about; just as there are probably many more firms that have adopted 4-day than we know about.) Four-day discontinuations run only 4%; 96% of firms trying 4-day retain it.

Still, it is very important to inquire why *any* firm discontinues 4-day – why any firm discontinues a schedule that is supposed to be optimal.

In reviewing the experiences of firms that have discontinued it, I find *almost* no cases where 4-day itself failed to operate properly; instead, I find that managers failed to operate 4-day properly or that outside circumstances beyond the firm's control interfered. If we look at companies which have totally abandoned 4-day and gone back to 5-day, I find in almost every case that the problem lies in the manner of implementation or in something that has nothing to do with 4-day itself. Here are some examples (not listed in any particular order) – some are almost unbelievable, but are nonetheless true:

1. At one firm, where employees were given the choice of working 4-day or 5-day, side by side, the manager cut the wages of the 4-day employees and raised the wages of the 5-day employees. It surprised no one (except the manager) that most of the employees eventually opted for 5-day. The rule he broke is: unless a company is losing so much money that all jobs are seriously threatened, employees simply will not countenance a pay cut – 4-day schedule or not – especially, if they can obtain a rise by staying on 5-day.

2. One firm, after employees were on 4-day for just one week, had the husbands of its female workers literally march on the firm *en masse* demanding a return to 5-day. Their complaint: late suppers! Clearly, the firm had failed to anticipate its breaking of local norms, and had failed to do its proper homework.

3. At a few firms with union representation, 4-day was started without the international's approval; and the international put a stop to it. In one case, previously described, the local members withdrew from the international in order to retain the 4-day week – without overtime pay for the longer workdays. (In the other cases, 4-day was discontinued.)

4. At a few firms with union representation, the international refused to permit 4-day to continue even where the firm was paying for the longer workday at overtime rates!

5. A few *new* retail stores which failed to put sufficient funds into advertising their existence, failed to get enough customers to stay open 4 days a week, and discontinued 4-day. (The managers insist that 4-day was not at fault, but that their budgets defeated it.)

6. A few firms, accustomed to getting casual overtime from workers without paying for it, found that 4-day unleashed employees' desires for leisure, lessening both casual overtime and output.

7. Some firms institute 4-day without achieving prior consensus for the trial – and suffer sabotage from disgruntled factions as a consequence. The source of sabotage is almost always management, not workers! In some cases, middle managers have not been brought into the decision; in other cases, top managers only grudgingly permitted the trial at middle managers' instigation; in both cases, lack of initial consensus is the problem.

8. At some government organizations, 4-day is discontinued when

a new political administration takes over. The old guard maintain that 4-day achieved results; but the new guard say 4-day did not. Neither release data, so, who knows?

9. Some firms find that their employees are just too tired out by the longer workday, particularly when they must spend the workday on their feet. IN ALMOST EVERY CASE, we have discovered that days off were split during the week, instead of given all at once to form a long weekend. We judge, therefore, that the lack of the long weekend which *normally* accompanies 4-day is the problem. For example, out of over 50 hospitals currently using 4-day, at only 2 of them have the nurses found 4-day too tiring: neither of these hospitals, unlike their successful counterparts, gave nurses a long weekend. (Where work is not inherently strenuous, giving the third day off during the workweek instead of on the weekend has created no problems.)

10. Some firms that have discontinued 4-day are firms that instituted it illegally – that is, without regard to some law or regulation that forbids the particular schedule or pay terms that they adopted. When these firms got caught out, they were forced to discontinue 4-day. In some cases, the firms later obtained waivers permitting their particular schedule; in other cases, the firms followed whatever practice was required of them in order to retain 4-day. Almost none discontinued 4-day permanently.

11. A very few firms experienced lower productivity or output. The reasons for this tend to be inexplicable, because other firms in the same business, using similar schedules, got better results. One manager said he felt his problem was in his pay formula. He said he was going to introduce an incentive scheme, similar to a 4-day competitor's, and then try 4-day again.

12. Some firms choose a schedule that is not particularly good for them – and soon improve on it. Some firms that discontinued 4-day changed to 3-day.

13. At a few firms the employees simply do not value the leisure package sufficiently to want to put up with the inconveniences of the longer workdays. One company manager says he did not put sufficient effort into explaining 4-day to his workers, although I am not sure that would have made a difference, since people do have different tastes that must be taken into account.

14. Some firms experienced lower sales demand due to recession, and cut back on numbers of employees, on work hours, and/or

on workdays at the same time, abandoning 4-day as no longer appropriate for their new mode of operation.

15. In one case the predominantly female workers felt the leisure was not worth the extra effort that they had to put in during the workdays: hand processes, not machine processes, were involved in this case; and with *shorter* hours, the women did indeed have to work harder in order to keep up weekly production. (The matter might have been different if a full 40-hour week had been retained.)

The reader should note in reading through this list that in almost no case does a 4-day discontinuation involve the same basic disadvantages cited by 4-day companies which continue using it. Nor do they involve problems that the general public, unfamiliar with 4-day, are primarily worried about.

Firms that discontinue their 4-day experiments have used trial periods ranging from one week to one year. Usually, they know where they stand after a few months' trial.

Almost no firm that discontinues 4-day expresses bitterness about the experience. On the contrary, they usually feel proud of having tried the experiment, and frequently state that they plan to try 4-day again after making some adjustments. Frequently, they do.

Most negative information about 4-day has nothing to do with 4-day experience – and everything to do with myths about it and the normal fear of something new that one has not yet experienced.

Some of the myths and fears are exacerbated, if not entirely produced by persons who actively encourage negative attitudes towards 4-day, in order to further some personal advantage – as in the case of some consultants seeking publicity, some government officials caught without information, a few newspaper columnists seeking to create controversy to increase their readership, and so on. Honest investigation of 4-day experience shows very little negative outcome from these attempts at optimization – which should amaze no one, since that's what optimization means.

Isn't one of the biggest problems with the 4-day week the so-called "honey-do" weekend?

For those who don't know what the honey-do weekend is, men report that it's the wife saying: "honey, do this . . . honey, do that."

While it is indeed true that some husbands object to being set to work by their wives, it is just as important to note that their wives enjoy setting them to work.

Who are we to take sides?

More seriously though, long weekends do give a married couple more opportunity to fight. But fighting is very good for marriage. It clears the air. And I suspect that many marriages suffer from lack of opportunity to fight issues out to a full understanding. Four-day is beneficial in providing a long weekend for a good fight – and long weekends provide more time for making-up afterwards.

What about the effect of 4-day on people's sex lives?

The following is reprinted in its entirety from *Poor's Workweek Letter*. This essay was widely quoted by major U.S.A. media when it appeared in the early spring of 1972.

ANOTHER ESSAY ON THE CONSERVATION OF HUMAN BEINGS:

Sex and the Rearranged Workweek

It's just occurred to me that I (and all the other researchers and commentators) have missed a critically important aspect of the rearranged workweek: namely, that it provides the opportunity to stay in bed another morning each week.

How could researchers of our calibre have missed something so important for so long? And why didn't the respondents tell us in our interviews – or make notes in the margins of their questionnaires?

Well, that's the nature of a taboo. Nowhere in any reputable research on leisure I've read is there any mention at all of sex.

Yet sex is possibly the single most popular leisure activity, in whatever terms you want to define it – in numbers of afficionados, time spent in its pursuit, and cost/benefit ratio.

Why are people on the 10-hour day – and the 12- and 13-hour days – telling us that the long weekend more than makes up for these longer workdays? Why do they say the long weekend more than makes up for any added fatigue and tension on the job? Is it only due to devotion to travelling, visiting relatives, and cleaning house?

I feel I am making here an enormous contribution to the academic study of leisure: i.e., adding something known by every man in the street. As with other major discoveries, this one too was the product of accident. If I hadn't been working so hard on my research, I might have noticed it sooner; but I've only just had my first 3-day weekend in four years.

4 Days, 40 Hours

Now that I have discovered sex as a leisure activity, it would not amaze me to discover that the extra morning in bed is the single most important reason for the popularity of the rearranged workweek.

This discovery may explain why people who have experience with 4-day report much more favourable attitudes towards 4-day than those who have not tried it.

It may explain why people say 4-day is good for marriage, morale, and so on. It certainly explains why not one 4-day couple with children on a 5-day school schedule complains about the disparity in schedules.

Now, I wonder: could it also be the single most important reason for opposition to 4-day?

Our research shows 92% of workers on 4-day favour it, and only 8% are opposed. We may have here for the first time an index to the state of sexual relations in this country.

In any case, if the added morning in bed is a basic reason for the popularity of the rearranged workweek, then those who fear that union or government opposition might destroy the movement have nothing to worry about. It's simple common sense that mere institutions cannot win out over Mother Nature.

Do you have any tips on planning and implementing 4-day?

Yes, interviews with hundreds and hundreds of 4-day firms have created quite a list.

First, anyone considering implementing it should review the section on firms that discontinued 4-day, noting the problems that caused other firms to discontinue, and turning these into a list of practices to watch out for in your own case. (Review the other lists as well.)

Secondly, here is a list of *general* principles to keep in mind while you are in the consideration and planning stage.

1. Change itself is a problem, regardless of what kind of change is introduced. Don't expect smooth sailing.
2. Planning anything costs money. Planning 4-day is not free of costs. (It is *not* just *un*successful 4-day experiments that cost money.)
3. You are undertaking a risk when you introduce 4-day that it will not work for you – for whatever reason. Count that risk as a cost.
4. Research on 4-day, although it is quite consistent among all the independent researchers, is still in its infancy: your own judgement must be the final arbiter, not someone else's.

5. Nonetheless, it probably pays to arm yourself as fully as possible with the information that is extant. Read what you can locate, and talk to other 4-day companies. But pay attention to the worth of the source of your information; all sources are not equally reliable.

6. Your firm, however similar to another firm, is still unique. Don't carry analogy too far – but do look beyond the superficial to find unlikely analogies.

7. Plan thoroughly if you want to *optimize*, rather than just to improve things.

8. Since, if you do convert to 4-day, you will be going through the effort of introducing a major change, it becomes worthwhile to consider what other things should be changed at the same time.

Here is a list of specific considerations for the planning stage. Some of these are just plain common sense suggestions. (There's a tendency to suspend common sense while playing with a new idea.)

1. Plan, but don't plan forever, and do expect to have transition-period problems. No matter how thorough your planning, you probably cannot hope to anticipate everything. So, prepare to be flexible once you see how things are going. (At one firm, the top management had to man the shipping department for a week, until the schedule got ironed out. That's pretty expensive shipping. But they worked things out.)

2. Don't start your plan by picking out a schedule and then trying to fit your work into it. Start with your work, and build your schedule around it.

Now that 4-day has become somewhat popular, a number of managers approach the problem by asking themselves: how can we fit our work into a 4-day schedule? This approach is just as inappropriate as leaving your work on a 5-day schedule if 5-day is not optimal for you. The concept you are exploring, when you explore 4-day, is the concept of optimizing. So start with the work, and then ask: is there some schedule that would enable us to accomplish our work in a better way than the one we are now using?

There may be *no* schedule better than the one you are using right now; and, if so, that is a valid and useful thing to discover; and it is something that you may not discover if you merely

267

ask yourself how to fit your work into 4-day, since there is undoubtedly *some* means by which you can fit your work into 4-day, however unsatisfactory.

3. Four-day is not a panacea. If you have problems unrelated to scheduling, don't expect 4-day to solve them for you. Sort out what problems are amenable to scheduling changes and what problems are not. You may have to tackle unrelated problems with some *other* solutions. (The time at which you introduce 4-day may or may not be a good time for introducing other changes to tackle other problems. You will have to look deeply into this issue.)

4. Question your assumptions. This cannot be stressed too fully. So very much of what we do rests on assumptions that we do not even recognize as such, because we are so accustomed to them. Question, question, question. Many managers find, when they examine their assumptions, that factors which they considered immutable facts of life are no more than variables than can be manipulated and which it is advantageous to manipulate. Write out your assumptions, and label them as such, so you and others can examine them.

5. Do look at your entire system and not just a small segment of it. Every segment is part of the larger whole, and your results may turn out quite differently if you consider only a part and not the whole. Remember, you are trying to optimize an entire system.

6. Don't change a winning strategy. If you already have an optimal schedule, by all means don't change it. Some people change just to be fashionable – but obviously, the results will not be as good as the original schedule's results. Only change a winning game if you are willing to pay the price of getting results that are not so good.

7. Should you call in an outside consultant? Most firms will *not* require outside help in order to improve their schedules. Four-day is a simple change, and after all, who knows your firm better than you do? On the other hand, there are 3 cases in which a firm should consider calling in outside help. (*a*) If yours is a very small firm that does not have staff time available to amass data, and to consider and devise a schedule, it may be worth your calling in outside help to save yourself from taking staff off critical day-to-day operations. (*b*) If you are having severe problems unrelated to scheduling, or if you don't know whether your problems are related to scheduling, it may pay to

call someone in for help with problem analysis. And (*c*) if you are a very large company, with an enormous payroll, whose very size discourages innovative thinking, an outside consultant may be able to introduce more innovative, creative thinking than your staff could initiate.

I have seen too many large companies put junior personnel on the changeover problem; and the junior personnel do little more than collect newspaper articles.

Don't put junior personnel on the problem *unless* these juniors have already demonstrated that they are go-getters. If you have a large payroll, you ought to have very senior personnel on a task that is going to affect your profits substantially; and if you cannot release senior personnel, by all means call in outsiders. At the very least, call in an outsider if only to look at the assumptions and plans that your staff creates.

8. Review the lists of advantages and disadvantages cited elsewhere, as a source of ideas that may help you to formulate objectives and/or methods of achieving objectives.

9. Sort red herrings, or myths, from real information. This is not a case of "where there's smoke, there's fire". There has been enough research on 4-day to show that myths are no more than myths. You have enough to worry about – so forget myths.

10. One myth is that continuous process firms cannot use 4-day schedules. That's ridiculous: they already use all sorts of non-standard schedules in order to operate 6 and 7 days a week. If yours is such a firm, look at the section on continuous process companies, and also explore methods of scheduling notation explained below.

11. Since you are planning to *improve* your company's operations by changing your schedule, you will probably want to be able to *judge* whether the schedule does improve things for you. Therefore, before you change over, (*a*) spell out your objectives – preferably, in writing so that you and others can examine them thoroughly. (*b*) Articulate your criteria and/or constraints, for the same reason. (Some people consider objectives, criteria, and constraints as the same things. That's okay: the point is to spell these things out.) (*c*) Put all these items into as measurable terms as possible; so you will be able to measure results. (d) Plan to measure results periodically: monitoring activities is extremely important. (*e*) Set specific standards beforehand – numerical ones if possible; so you will be able to evaluate your

269

test. (It is perfectly legitimate to change these standards later on, when you see how things are going; but do begin with some standards in mind, however provisional you regard them.)

12. Work out your specific 4-day plan ahead of time. If it sounds ridiculous to have me say a thing like this to a businessman, please recall that quite a few businessmen have actually converted to 4-day without making a detailed plan beforehand. These people frequently succeed, but often they do *not* do as well as they could have done. Why take the risk?

13. It is a very good idea not only to plan your 4-day plan beforehand, but also to plan *how you are going to introduce the new plan* and also, *exactly how you are going to implement it.*

14. Plan a path of retreat, in the event that you don't like your 4-day results. Announcing that 4-day is under test is one good method – and it has the positive fallout that you are reminding employees of the rational thought pattern that businessmen find desirable.

   If you don't like the results, it may be very useful to you to analyse *why* the results were negative. (Also, I would appreciate hearing from you, because negative information about 4-day is so scarce.)

15. If you plan to measure results over time, don't be shocked if you note *some* deterioration of gains over time.

   Some of your gains will probably be due to the newness of the change, and you must expect newness to wear off after a while. For purposes of estimating results, try to sort out beforehand how much of your results will be due to hard scheduling changes and how much due to change itself.

16. Don't expect heaven: optimizing means that you are making the best trade-offs among conflicting objectives – but you are still making trade-offs. You *cannot* maximize all factors simultaneously: you can only aim to achieve the best balance of trade-offs available to your situation.

17. Consider all parties affected by the change. This does not mean that you must *consult* all parties, although it may be highly desirable to do so. But do *communicate* with all parties. In fact, plan your communications so that they will be clear and thorough, and *not* a source of additional headaches.

18. Consider whether to keep the fact that you are speculating about 4-day secret or not. If your employees have come to you with the idea, there's probably no advantage to be gained

by keeping secret your consideration of their idea, and every advantage to be gained by showing them that you are paying attention to it. If it's *your* idea, then your past history of relationships with your workers is the important consideration; but also consider what you want future relations to be like. (A firm instituting 4-day in a new start-up situation will find it easier, because there is no tradition to deal with.)

19. Don't try to create complex schedules in your head, or you run the risk of being defeated by simple lack of paper and pencil. Scheduling arithmetic is usually much too complex to work out in one's head. On top of this, accustomed as we are to 5-day scheduling, most of us have no familiarity whatsoever with other arithmetics. So, the use of a clear, simple written scheduling notation is essential.

Here is a format for notation that you may find useful (another format is displayed in Chapter 10):

EXHIBIT 1. A CONVENIENT FORMAT FOR USE IN DEVISING COMPLEX SCHEDULES.

The Plant's Calendar

All the Hours of the Day	All the Days of the Week						
	Monday	Tuesday	Wednes-day	Thurs-day	Friday	Satur-day	Sunday
AM PM			[This section shows how the plant's production hours are covered and by what specific group of workers. Use letters of the alphabet to denote these specific groups.]				

The Workers' Calendar

Workers' Groups	All the Days of the Week						
	Monday	Tuesday	Wednes-day	Thurs-day	Friday	Satur-day	Sunday
A B C etc.			[This section shows what days specific groups of workers are at the plant and what days they are off from work. (Try W for Work and O for Off.)]				

T–K

4 Days, 40 Hours

The following are examples of the format in use. The first example shows a schedule that is easy to format. (Note that we dropped some of the formality in the labelling, just as you would do if you were generating a number of alternative schedules.) The second example is much more complex, and provides several things to note about the flexibility this format permits.

EXHIBIT 2. TWO EXAMPLES OF THE FORMAT IN USE.

1. A Lipton Tea Company Type Schedule: a 3-Day Week for 6 Days of Plant Operation

	Monday	Tuesday	Wednes-day	Thurs-day	Friday	Satur-day	Sunday
7 AM to 7 PM	A	A	A	C	C	C	—
7 PM to 7 AM	B	B	B	D	D	D	—
A	W	W	W	O	O	O	O
B	W	W	W	O	O	O	O
C	O	O	O	W	W	W	O
D	O	O	O	W	W	W	O

2. A Hospital Schedule: a 4-Day Week for 7 Days of Operation

The Hospital's Calendar

	Monday	Tuesday	Wednes-day	Thurs-day	Friday	Satur-day	Sunday
7 AM	A	A	A	A	D	D	D
4 PM	B	B	B	B	B	E	E
5 PM							
9 PM	C	C	C	C	F	F	F
10 PM							
7 AM							

The Workers' Calendar*

Workers' Groups	Monday	Tuesday	Wednes-day	Thurs-day	Friday	Satur-day	Sunday
A	W	W	W	W	O	O	O
B	W	W	W	W	W	O	O
C	W	W	W	W	O	O	O
D	O	O	O	O	W	W	W
E	O	O	O	O	O	W	W
F	O	O	O	O	W	W	W

*Next week, A's switch with D's and work 3 days.
B's are part-time workers who may or may not switch with E's.
Next week, C's switch with F's and work 3 days.
Next week, D's switch with A's and work 4 days.
E's are part-time, like B's.
Next week, F's switch with C's and work 4 days.

This format accommodates a number of complications to scheduling that frequently crop up. As you can see from the exhibit, if you have a situation in which shifts overlap each other, you can indicate the overlap by extending lines from a group's entry hour to the hour at which it leaves. You may, in very complex cases, need to list all the hours of the day, even in half-hour increments. Further, if you have many workers coming in on a staggered basis during the day, you may need to use wide columns permitting you to chart the appearances of various groups, and you may even need to chart each worker separately. I have seen a hospital schedule so complex that each day has to be charted separately. (They are very pleased with the way the charts work for them.)

Secondly, if the cycle required by your firm takes more than 7 days to repeat itself, you will probably want to extend the worksheet horizontally, so you can map out all of the days of the cycle.

Some schedules are more complex than the illustrations we provide, using more workers, more complex on-off patterns, longer cycles, and so on. The more complex the schedule, the more essential are pencil, paper, and clear format. But I recommend pencil and paper even with the simplest schedule.

4 Days, 40 Hours

The following is a checklist to apply to the schedules that you devise and consider – *before* implementing them:

1. Generate alternative schedules – *around* your work.
2. Apply the principle of Occam's Razor to your schedules. Some firms create unnecessarily complex schedules. If the ones you create use most of the letters of the alphabet, think again: there may be a simpler way to accomplish what you want to do.
3. If your schedule calls for swing shifts, find out how your workers feel about this beforehand. Workers *sometimes* prefer keeping the night shift permanently, instead of swinging from day to night shift. If you inquire you will be able to take their preferences into account.
4. If your schedule calls for giving added days off during the week instead of bunching them all on a long weekend, poll your workers. You can usually arrange the schedule to give long weekends, if that's what your employees want. Be particularly wary of splitting the days off if the work is intrinsically fatiguing. A graduate thesis by James Marshall Maxfield, who researched the relationship between 4-40 and absenteeism, found no greater incidence of absenteeism on 4-day than on the previous schedule; in fact, he found a statistically insignificant decrease in incidence, studying a 4-day hospital. However, I noted from his figures that the total number of hours of absence appeared to increase; and I hypothesize that the increase was due to the particular type of 4-day schedule that was used: a schedule involving both 8-hour and 12-hour workdays and a schedule that did *not* give consecutive days off to form a long weekend. In other words, sometimes these female employees had to stand on their feet for 12 hours at a stretch (something that they were not accustomed to doing) and yet they did not get long weekends to rest up with. Hardly worth the change, from the employees' point of view.
5. In comparing alternative schedules, cost them out to help you make the comparison. But don't only cost direct labour; instead, take all systems into account including overhead factors; and also compare the cost of alternative schedules with expected revenue under these alternatives.
6. In order to create *any* schedule, you must forecast demand. Further, in order to compare costs of alternative schedules, you must forecast desired production levels. The need to select a (target) expected output level is often overlooked, but the

forecasted operating level is critical to selecting among alternative schedules; because different schedules are at least cost at *different* levels of output, and can be at maximum cost at other output levels.

7. In setting up criteria for developing your alternatives (and you should probably write out your criteria, so you can examine them carefully), you may want to include *flexibility* – particularly, if yours is a firm with frequently changing levels of output, or if you have a great deal of uncertainty about the predictions behind your choice of expected output level. You may want to trade off selecting one least-cost schedule for selecting a schedule that easily permits you to add or subtract production hours as your demand changes.

8. The following scheduling parameters should each receive some attention: rest breaks, turns, shifts, part versus full-time work, number of days of operation, which days, production hours/day, production hours/week, compensation (including holiday pay, sick leave pay, etc.), consecutive versus intermittent days off, different department on the same versus different schedules, informal traditions at work, attendance bonuses and/or penalties, and employees' concepts of fair play.

9. Once you have targeted a production level, ask yourself the very important question: if I could make more, could I sell more? Just as I suggested that you examine all your assumptions (above), don't forget really critical assumptions like sales levels! In other words: question, question, question!

The following are items to think about once you have devised a new schedule (or alternative schedules), and are thinking about implementation:

1. You probably should plan to consult with your employees before instituting a change. Now, many managers react to this suggestion by saying: "Management's *my* job, not *theirs*." While that point of view is correct, you must not overlook that a change in scheduling is actually a change in the *contract* that you established with your employees before they accepted the jobs you offered them. If you have a written contract, it is more likely to be obvious that you do indeed have a contract with your employees, and that their consent is required before you can make a change. But where you do *not* have a written contract with employees, don't make the mistake of thinking

you don't have a contract. The people who work for you came to work with a specific set of expectations about your company's behaviours – one of which was the 5-day week.

Leaving contractual ethics aside for the moment, it is plain common sense that if you want something to succeed, you had better get people's consensus behind it. Inviting employees' opinion is one means for encouraging consensus. And not inviting opinions is one way to discourage it.

That's why so many firms poll their employees before instituting a change. It is not a matter of relinquishing management responsibility: it's a matter of being really responsible and courteous towards workers. And it shows proper respect.

Furthermore, polling employees will give you the opportunity to invite suggestions which may be very valuable to you. For example, suppose you are trying to decide whether to split days off or not, and you're trying to anticipate employee feeling about this. Think of the value of asking *them* about it: *they* know the answer.

2. And don't overlook the value of polling your employees both *during* and *after* the trial. As one employee said: "Management said that they were putting 4-day in, partly for us. I didn't believe management really cared what we thought about the 4-day week or anything else until after they polled us a second time – and risked our turning 4-day down. Then I knew they really did care, just like they said."

There is a certain amount of unreasoning fear of talking with employees, a fear that deserves to be examined. Besides, you *do* want to know what they are thinking, don't you?

3. The more your plan calls for countervening important mores, standards, or values held by your employees, the more time and effort you should put into introducing the change to them. If your plan calls for asking employees to take their weekends during the workweek, employees may need time to adjust to what will be for them a novel idea. Explain everything thoroughly. Give people the chance to ask their questions.

4. Many employers point out *both* the pros and the cons of the change to employees; and this appears to be a very good practice. Don't get the idea that I am suggesting that you list the negatives out of proportion to their weight: a few employers, in their effort to be fair with employees, have bent over backwards explaining negatives, and instead of being helpful, have

induced a good deal of anxiety about the change. Take a balanced approach. Since you are proposing a change in the work contract, and since you are eliciting employees' reactions to the proposal, show yourself to your employees as being as open-minded as you really are. Show your awareness that 4-day is not a panacea, that it has its good and bad points which you are about to test; and, since you have put a good deal of study into the matter, show you are SHARING your information with employees in order to HELP them make the test. Employees who are approached in this straightforward manner put a good deal more effort into making the test a fair one, and also gain a high opinion of their employers' integrity.

5. Make it clear to employees that the company, too, must benefit from 4-day. Contrary to some managers' thinking, it is *not* out of place for you to point out what you hope will be the benefits to the company. Your employees are fully aware (often, *more* aware than managers) that half of the unwritten contract involves the company's benefits. Besides, if you don't make it clear that the company must also benefit by 4-day, you could find yourself in a situation later on where your employees are delighted with 4-day, but your company is suffering from it. Don't court this situation. Specify what you hope to attain for the company – and specify it in measurable terms, so you and your employees can see whether the objectives are attained on 4-day; and so, if they are not gained, you can retreat gracefully from the experiment.

6. Make the rules of the game very clear to yourself as well as to employees. Hand out schedules. Hand out written memoranda of all changes (new work hours, new break times, forms of compensation, holidays, and so on), in order to minimize confusion. If needed, go over the changes in person, in group meetings, or whatever; so everyone understands what is expected of them. Spell out your standards, and keep them high.

7. Being human, you cannot anticipate beforehand all the crises that may develop during the trial; therefore, provide some mechanism for dealing with whatever crises may occur. Provide a way for employees to bring to your attention whatever points disturb them, as these things crop up; and hopefully, solve some of these things fairly immediately. If you don't provide some mechanism for on-the-spot problem-solving, you will be

courting frustration that may later defeat a plan that would have been good for all of you. For instance, you may force a valued employee to quit when you might instead have helped solve his problem.

8. Even if you do not consult with your employees before instituting 4-day, don't introduce it in such a way as to make employees feel that you are forcing it down their throats. Even honey doesn't taste good that way. Several firms have deprived their employees of the real thrill they could have had, because management introduced 4-day in a high-handed manner. (Just think of the bridegroom who bought a house for his bride-to-be without consulting her: how pleased he was with himself! How surprised to find her angry! And how sorry he didn't let her come along on the shopping!)

9. Should you use a formal questionnaire for polling employees? So much depends on your size, your state of communications, the complexity of objectives you have developed, and so on, that we cannot answer this.

   But if you do use a questionnaire, be careful of the wording. Since you can hardly hope to create a completely neutral wording, at least be sure you do not create negative wording.

Here is an example of a questionnaire developed and used by Home Savings Bank, Boston, which is still happily on 4-day. Note that the questionnaire not only *polls* employees, but *teaches* them something. In fact, the bank itself was happily surprised to learn their employees' attitudes about enforcement of work rules. The employees clearly indicated that they expect and want management to enforce work rules. The implication here (and overly-permissive managers should take note) is that employees' principles of fair play require enforcement of work rules, and non-enforcement *violates* employees' principles.

EXHIBIT 3. AN EXAMPLE OF AN EMPLOYEE QUESTIONNAIRE (CREATED BY HOME SAVINGS BANK, BOSTON).
[Reproduced by permission]

I.   *Q:* If you were scheduled to work approximately the same number of hours per week, but worked them in four longer days and had the fifth day off from work, what would be your reaction?

     A: —— Terrific – 100% in favour
        —— OK – enthusiastic
        —— Not sure – would like to try it
        —— No opinion
        —— Against – would not like to try it

II. *Q:* If you were permitted to have an additional day off from work each week (except for weeks which contain legal holidays), which day would you prefer to choose?
   A: Please rank from 1–5 using 1 as your first choice.
   1st   2nd   3rd   4th   5th

III. *Q:* Realizing that everyone can not have the same day off, Monday or Friday for example, and also realizing that some days are busier than other days, Monday for example, how would you allocate the non-work days?
   A: —— Basis of seniority
   —— Random Selection
   —— Assignment by Department Head
   —— Rotating Basis
   —— Basis of attendance record
   —— Other ....

IV. *Q:* How would you suggest the bank deal with an employee who repeatedly abused the hours scheduled for a four day work week, which in turn causes more work for employees who come to work regularly and usually are on time?
   A: —— Fire or dismiss them
   —— Deduct money from week's pay
   —— Require abusers to work a five day week
   —— Other ....

V. *Q:* How would you suggest the bank deal with an employee who is frequently absent, but who has not been seriously ill?
   A: —— Fire or dismiss them
   —— Deduct money from week's pay
   —— Require abusers to work a five day week
   —— Reward those with excellent attendance records
   —— Other ....

The following is a different sort of checklist that you may want to review. It was prepared by Dr. Thomas J. Swierczewski, as part of the dissertation which we mentioned above, and is reproduced with his permission. (See a previous footnote for availability of the dissertation.)

A CHECKLIST FOR CONVERTING

These are items that should be included in any contemplated conversion to a rearranged workweek. Many of the items are interrelated, and cannot be considered independently from each other. Each manager should consider his situation as unique, and relate the items to each other in an appropriate fashion.

4 Days, 40 Hours

I. PRELIMINARY STEPS

1. **Who will do the feasibility study?**
   (*a*) Company personnel?
   (*b*) Outside consultants?
   (*c*) Both?

2. **Has all the relevant information been obtained?**
   (*a*) Which company personnel should attend meetings on the subject.
   (*b*) Has general source material been obtained – for example, *Poor's Workweek Letter*?
   (*c*) Have contacts been made with similarly situated 4-day companies?

II. PLANNING PROCESS

Are all segments of the management team represented in the planning process?
   (*a*) Specifically, have first-line supervisors' opinions been solicited?
   (*b*) Will brainstorming and/or buzz sessions be used?

III. EVALUATION CRITERIA

What objective criteria will be used for evaluation purposes?
   (*a*) Records of employee behaviour:
      (1) Absenteeism?
      (2) Tardiness?
      (3) Turnover?
      (4) Actual versus planned use of break time?
      (5) Early arrivals at punch-out stations?
      (6) Applications for job openings?
      (7) Number of grievances?
      (8) Vote for unionization?
      (9) Exploitation of sick leaves?
   (*b*) Financial effect of 4-day week on:
      (1) Profits?
      (2) Return-on-investment?
      (3) Costs?
         (*a*) Payroll?
         (*b*) Fringe Benefits?
         (*c*) Utilities?
      (4) Will maintenance be improved and influence asset life?
      (5) Are changes in depreciation policy warranted?
      (6) What are the cash flow implications?

   (c) Production and the 4-day week:
     (1) Will maintenance be improved?
     (2) How will productivity be affected?
     (3) Is it possible to minimize the number of change-overs?
     (4) Will improved tooling be required due to extended usage?
     (5) How will quality be affected?
       (a) Scrap rates?
       (b) Sales returns and allowances?
       (c) Customer service complaints?
       (d) Rework?
       (e) Rejection rate of inspectors?
   (d) Safety.

IV. LEGAL PROBLEMS

What are the legal implications?
   (a) Do laws restrict maximum hours that women may work?
   (b) Does the union contract require premium wage payments for all daily hours in excess of 8?

V. UNION IMPLICATIONS

Are unions involved?
   (a) Have union representatives been contacted?
   (b) What is the union position?
   (c) Can union objections, if any, be overcome?
   (d) If the union agrees to the concept will it demand a further reduction in the workweek or hours of work?
   (e) If the concept is adopted, what are the ramifications in regard to all provisions of the contract?
   (f) Is the restructured workweek acceptable to the local union, but unacceptable to the national union? If so, what new strategies must be undertaken?

VI. BASIC DECISIONS

1. Which workweek is best?
   (a) Compressed workweek?
   (b) Reduced workweek?
   (c) Staggered workweek?
   (d) Flexible workweek?
   (e) Any combination?

2. Will the workweek selected present significant administrative problems? Will the scheduling of meetings and training sessions become difficult?

3. **Who will be included in the programme?**
   (*a*) Production employees?
   (*b*) Management?
   (*c*) Office workers?
   (*d*) Salesmen?
   (*e*) Shipping and receiving personnel?
   (*f*) Maintenance workers?
   (*g*) Staff personnel?

4. **If all personnel are not to be affected immediately, but gradually, has the tentative schedule been determined?**

5. **Will manning requirements change?**
   (*a*) Will the schedule mandate additional supervisory and non-supervisory personnel?
   (*b*) Will the turnover rate be favourably influenced?
   (*c*) If so, will supervision become more effective so that more responsibility may be absorbed?
   (*d*) Does management intend to use overtime on the days off, or schedule meetings on these days?
      (1) If so, has consideration been given to the first-line supervisors' use of leisure time?

6. **Will overtime costs be prohibitive?**
   (*a*) Will increased productivity offset increases in overtime, and to what extent?
   (*b*) Will overtime rates be paid at the start of the workday (to provide incentive for early arrival) or at the end?
   (*c*) Will regular workers reject overtime in favour of block leisure time?
   (*d*) If so, have provisions been made to hire temporary workers?
      (1) Has the employment cost of temporary help been included in the financial implications?
      (2) Have the production inefficiencies of temporary workers been comprehended in production planning?

7. **Will a 3-shift operation hamper conversion?**
   (*a*) Can two, 10-hour shifts and one, 4-hour shift be used?
   (*b*) Is a labour force difficult to obtain?
   (*c*) If so, has the possibility of using part-time workers been considered for a 4-hour shift?

8. **Will overlapping shifts solve any peaking problems?**
   (*a*) Who will be in charge during the overlap period?
   (*b*) Are facilities sufficient to warrant overlap?

9. **Have changes in break time been considered? Is total break time going to remain the same and spread over a reduced number of days? Or is break time going to be reduced proportionally?**

10. **Has planning considered Problems with national holidays?**
    (a) Number of days?
    (b) Daily and yearly compensation?
    (c) Should the workweek be set as Tuesday through Friday to minimize the effect of national holidays on Mondays?
    (d) Holidays that fall on a non-working weekday?
    (e) Holidays that fall on a workday?

11. **Will vacation time and compensation be affected?**

12. **Will there be any changes in personal time off, sick days, jury duty, disability, retirement, and related calculations?**

13. **Has consideration been given to how employee complaints will be handled? Will interviews be used to determine if complaints can be alleviated?**

14. **Is phasing-in included in the plan?**
    (*a*) Have unique problems been identified?
    (*b*) If not, has consideration been given to gradual conversion which would minimize future errors?

15. **Is a sufficient adjustment period included in the plan?**

16. **Has a sufficient trial period been contemplated for evaluation purposes?**

17. **Has management considered recognizing increased block leisure time as a fringe benefit which could be used as a basis for obtaining some changes in operations that would be beneficial?**

VII. COMMUNICATION ASPECTS

1. **Have various means of communication been considered?**
   (*a*) How and who will make the announcement?
   (*b*) Have meetings or informal discussions with employees been scheduled?
   (*c*) Have booklets been prepared?

      (*d*) Have provisions been made to communicate the plan so that *all* employees understand its content?

         (1) Do all employees read and understand English?

         (2) If not, have provisions been made to bridge the language barrier?

         (3) Is a booklet printed in other languages feasible?

      (*e*) Have employees been told that a possibility exists for a return to the old schedule?

      (*f*) Has current information, positive and negative, been given to the employees?

2. If all personnel are not to be included has the fact been communicated?

      (*a*) If not, will a morale problem develop?

3. Has employee convenience been considered?

      (*a*) Have scheduled starting and quitting times taken into consideration travel during off-peak hours?

      (*b*) Have employees been told that commuting time and related cost are favourably affected?

      (*c*) Do employees realize that savings occur in conjunction with babysitting and lunch expenditures?

      (*d*) Have employees been informed of the results of attitudes of workers elsewhere?

VIII. PUBLICITY CONSIDERATIONS

Has proper publicity been planned?

      (*a*) Has a press release been prepared?

      (*b*) Have all personnel been encouraged to speak about the concept?

IX. EMPLOYEE ATTITUDES

1. Will questionnaires, interviews, or voting be utilized to determine employee attitudes?

2. If so, what standard will be used as a basis for determining action? Majority of those voting? Majority in each department? Two-thirds?

3. What action will be taken if all departments do not favour a change?

4. Will any employees quit?

      (*a*) If so, are their jobs critical?

      (*b*) Have plans been initiated to replace them?

5. **Does the new schedule interfere with the moonlighting that is presently taking place?**
   (*a*) If so, will these individuals quit?
   (*b*) Have replacements been contemplated?

6. **Will installation of the new schedule increase moonlighting and adversely affect the company?**

X. STORAGE SPACE IMPLICATIONS

Will additional storage space be required?
   (*a*) Must warehouse space be expanded?
   (*b*) Must storage space for work in process be increased?
   (*c*) Is loading and unloading dock space sufficient?
   (*d*) Will additional material handling equipment be required?
   (*e*) Will insurance rates change?
   (*f*) Will additional security measures be required?

XI. SUPPLY ASPECTS

How will relations with suppliers be affected?
   (*a*) Has advance notice been given?
   (*b*) Is the lead time sufficient?
   (*c*) Has a buffer stock been considered as a safety factor?
   (*d*) Have suppliers been contacted for opinions that could identify unique problems?

XII. CUSTOMER AWARENESS

1. **Have customers been considered?**
2. **Have customers been informed in order to prevent any confusion?**

How can you adapt the 4-day week at a continuous process company or at a company that has to stay open 24 hours a day?

Although a cursory glance will convince most people that 4-day cannot work in these situations, it is perfectly adaptable to 24-hours-a-day, 7-days-a-week operations.

The problem is a conceptual one. We can easily conceptualize the old schemes in our heads. But the new workweeks involve unfamiliar arithmetic and unfamiliar scheduling notation demands. (There are sample scheduling formats in previous sections.)

4 Days, 40 Hours

How do the companies arrange their schedules? That depends on the goals they are trying to achieve. The simplest concept for scheduling on a 7-day basis involves ignoring the 7 days in the standard calendar week. As explained in a previous section, companies frequently use things like 4 days on, 4 days off.

An important factor is whether there is a need to overlap manpower during certain periods of the day. Police departments find overlapping is very important, providing more police on duty during high crime periods of the day. A similar situation holds for hospitals. In these cases, 4-day has obvious applications.

Twenty-four-hour-a-day companies also find no problem with 4-day if there is something about their process that requires 2 different types of workers who depend on each other for their timing. This is the case with truck drivers and truck repairmen (oil delivery companies, dairy companies, and so on). Here, companies can use 10-hour shifts with ease. They use 4-hour shifts, or sometimes two 2-hour shifts to complete the 24 hours. (Almost always, at least some of the staff are on 8-hour shifts.)

The big difficulty comes where there are no part-time functions required or where there is no requirement for overlap. Then, how do companies work out 4-day?

The most frequent form is the 3 days on, 4 days off type of thing, usually involving 12-hour shifts that total 36 hours a week. This is by no means the only alternative, but it is an easy one to develop. One British company uses 12-hour shifts in a 3 days on, 3 days off pattern, getting an average workweek of 42 hours. But many other schemes are available; some get very complex, depending on the firm's requirements.

But we have not mentioned how continuous process or 24-hour-a-day companies can use 4-day in order to solve the question: how can I fit our work into the 4-day week? We firmly advocate starting with the work and building the schedule around the work. These examples are provided only to show that it would not be a fruitless task for a continuous process firm to investigate 4-day. For best results, the reader should devise a schedule tailored to the needs of his own firm and his own set of employees.

Since our institutions are geared to a 5-day workweek, how can 4-day workers manage? How can they deal with 5-day schools, 5-day offices, and so on?

Some of the advantages of 4-day come precisely from the fact that everyone else is still on 5-day – for example, some commuting advantages. But leaving these aside, there is a definite problem of coping with institutions geared to 5-day. The fact is, though, that people do cope, and relatively few people cite interface with 5-day as a big disadvantage, let alone as an insurmountable one.

On the other hand, we can expect friction with 5-day institutions to ameliorate over time. Just as these institutions developed their 5-day schedules in order to interact favourably with the 5-day work-week that developed, these institutions will change again, as new work patterns develop and take hold.

In fact, they are already beginning to change; in part, as a response to 4-day patterns; in part, because businesses, whether they are 4-day or not, are moving increasingly towards 7-day operation and towards the 24-hour day.

But, the prelude to change is, of course, increased public awareness of, interest in, and demand for change. We have mentioned elsewhere in this volume each of the following indications that public interest, awareness, and demand are on the increase: legislative changes; thousands of newspaper and magazine articles, TV and radio programmes, management seminars and workshops; research studies by trade groups, professors, and university students; the publication of this volume in numerous countries outside the U.S.A.; workers' clothing emblazoned with 4-day slogans, and so on. We will add now that there is widespread use of TGIT (Thank God It's Thursday) buttons.

TABLE 2. THERE ARE MORE FACTORS ENCOURAGING THE GROWTH OF 4-DAY THAN DISCOURAGING IT.

Discouraging Growth	Encouraging Growth
ignorance of the innovation	increasing public awareness of the innovation's performance
misconceptions, red herrings, myths	increasing availability of this guidebook and other good information
structural barriers – institutions quite naturally still geared to a	

Table 2 – *contd.*

Discouraging Growth	Encouraging Growth
5-day week institutional barriers to change legislation, past work contracts, and so on opposing interests – or persons who judge that their interests are opposing – some unions normal resistance to change	institutions already beginning to change some find, with more information, that their interests are not opposing (e.g., some unions permitting 4-day) normal desire to improve things profit squeeze – makes businessmen more willing to try something new public's desire for leisure – due to increasing affluence, and increasing concern with "the good life" an era in which people are more interested in trying new and better things than ever before

What has been the pattern of growth of 4-day and why do you call it a movement?

When I put the first edition of this book to bed, in October, 1970, I had located 36 4-day firms. Almost two years later, I am able to discover that just under 60 firms had actually been on 4-day at the time. Checks have confirmed that my files (which are the best available) tend to run approximately 100% behind the real data.

But, how likely is it that the 100% rule of thumb continues to be valid over time? I think it is unlikely; in fact, I strongly suspect that the gap between my files and the number of 4-day firms extant *widens* over time; because, as 4-day becomes more widespread and accepted, each 4-day conversion becomes less newsworthy and it grows less likely that 4-day firms come to my attention. (They come to my attention through: letters from 4-day companies; newspaper and magazine articles; word-of-mouth as I travel; trading of information with newspaper reporters who call seeking my list for their geographical area, or field of industry, and so on.)

Therefore, I feel certain that an estimate of 3,000 companies on

4-day at this time is an extremely conservative one. For instance, I would judge that it is much more likely that there are over 6,000 4-day companies right now than that there are only 2,500. I feel certain that there are at least 3,000 of them – and probably a great many more.

What about rate of growth? The rate of growth of 4-day companies is not consistent, even if one discounts the irregularities introduced by my patterns of travel and communications. Apparently, certain periods of the year are more auspicious for a change, such as, at the New Year time or right before summer holidays, and right around the beginning of autumn – but much less so, right at or on a holiday.

Using just the figures in my files, and not using my estimates at all, in the last several months, the average growth appears to be holding steady at about 100 conversions a month. (For a year prior to this, the growth rate was steadily growing.) If one credits my estimates and allowing for a growing information gap, the rate of conversions is probably still continuing to grow, rather than holding steady.

Reversions to 5-day have remained at a pretty consistent proportion – approximately 4%. (One should note that reversions are extremely newsworthy from the point of view of reporters, and unnewsworthy from the point of view of companies that revert; and these factors probably balance out.) If reversions are indeed as consistent as they appear, and if the estimates are correct, that would mean that reversions are declining as more people gain more knowledge of 4-day prior to converting to it, and permit such knowledge to affect their plans.

In terms of numbers of employees involved, the average size of 4-day firms still appears to be about 200 employees per firm (always discounting the few largest installations, which otherwise would throw off the average). If there are 5,000 firms on 4-day at present (which I would not consider an outrageous estimation), that means that there are about 1 million workers already on 4-day today – which may explain why we keep hearing so very much about it. This is a small proportion of the 86 million work force in America, but it is a great deal more than were on 4-day when we first published this book – which was some 7,000.

Of course, not all workers at all firms are on 4-day (the proportion runs about 70% on); but on the other hand, there has been a tendency for the larger firms to start 4-day lately, so that the 200-employee average is probably out of date by now and quite below the actual present average.

289

As to geographical concentrations in the U.S.A. the movement started initially on the east coast, moved to the west coast, and thence to the south. At this point in time, incidence of 4-day appears to follow incidence of population more than anything else, and all states have 4-day companies.

In terms of numbers of firms – even using the higher estimate, rather than my file counts – the number of 4-day companies is small; but it is a rapidly growing number, a consistently growing number and in my opinion, a number that spells out a trend, or a movement to be reckoned with.

It has spread around the world, as already mentioned. It has spawned additional innovations (mentioned below). And none of this is surprising, because 4-day helps people to solve problems that they want to solve; and there is little negative experience reported by people who have experience with it.

How can I get my company to go on the 4-day week?

See to it that decision-makers in your company get the facts about 4-day. When managers can see advantages to 4-day, they are more likely to be willing to try it. One method of getting the facts to decision-makers in your company is to give them a copy of this book. But read it yourself first, so you will be prepared to explain the pros and cons *verbally* – since I notice that most managers do *not* like to read long reports.

Where can I get a 4-day job? or how can I find more 4-day companies?

There are no employment agencies at present that specialize in locating 4-day jobs. Eventually, I suppose existing employment agencies will accommodate 4-day job-seekers. The only things one can do at present are to watch for newspaper and magazine articles about 4-day companies and to comb the want-ads – 4-day companies usually advertise the idea of 4 days' work for 5 days' pay, rather prominently.

Those who want the names of 4-day companies for research purposes can obtain them from my office in Cambridge, Massachusetts – for a fee.

Aren't there a lot of work innovations, other than 4 days, 40 hours, that are going on today?

There are a great many experiments going on today – and I would only take exception to the phrase "other than". The revolutionary concept that we are talking about and that is spreading around the world today is the concept of rearranging work in an attempt to optimize the way we conduct it – to increase profits and at the same time to improve people's lives. Using this concept, one can create all sorts of variations suitable for solving all sorts of problems.

Here is a list of some of the most promising experiments in rearranging work that people are trying today. Reading through this baker's dozen may give you an idea of the tremendous vistas open to someone who approaches the arrangement of work as a problem in and of itself, and as a *tool* for solving other problems. I hope you find this list stimulating to review; it may assist you in creating new variations to help you achieve your goals.

Each of the following is an innovation reported to achieve good results. All of these variations have in common the characteristic that they are win-win situations – good for both company and employees. (The variations can be used alone or together, as desired.)

1. *Out with Time Clock:* Companies are experimenting with removing clocks and replacing them with honour systems.
2. *Salary versus Hourly Pay:* Companies are putting hourly workers, both factory and clerical, on salaries, treating them as they do professionals, with the same benefits – and the same respect.
3. *Job Posting for Salaried Positions:* When companies were small, promotion usually came from within, and news of job openings spread easily by word-of-mouth. In today's large corporations, word-of-mouth is rarely sufficient for communication, and promotion frequently comes only through transfer to another firm.

    Such current practices are rarely functional for the firm – they damp motivation, lead to loss of talented employees, and cost the company extra for outside talent search and for orientation of new members obtained from the outside.

    Today, to source talent within the firm and to encourage upward mobility and "cross-fertilization" among departments, a number of large firms (Polaroid, among them) are revamping the old "from-within" policy by adapting the traditional union-hall and factory job-posting technique to salaried positions. The idea is to post all job openings (short of officer level) publicly within the organization. Anyone who feels qualified may apply. In exchange, everyone who applies must be seriously considered; and, if rejected, must by told WHY. (If the organizational climate is not open and supportive, the system may backfire on the employee and on the firm. For example, if management "punishes" an employee for his bid, the word will soon spread, and employees will not volunteer bids.)

4. *Permanent Part-Time Jobs:* Companies are removing the concept of *temporary* from the concept of *part-time*, hiring *permanent* workers for *part-time* slots. Occasionally, 2 part-time workers work back-to-back to fill one job slot. By this means, companies can recruit qualified workers who previously were unable or unwilling (money isn't that important to some people) to work full time. The concept is applied to professionals, such as lawyers, as well as to other jobs.

5. *Gliding Hours:* Called gliding hours, staggered hours, flexible hours, or whatever, this concept is becoming popular wherever traffic congestion is a major problem – and where isn't it? It is also applied to provide workers with individual flexibility. For example, some people are night birds, some early birds. Most companies enforce a range for entry and exit hours; some leave hours totally flexible.

6. *A Variation on Gliding Hours for Groups of Companies:* In New York City, about 250 large companies have banded together to stagger hours of arrival and departure for their respective work forces, in order to reduce traffic congestion in their area.

7. *Making People's Jobs More Complex:* Companies are responding to people's needs to feel responsible and productive by giving them more, rather than less complex jobs to do. Variations on this theme include: (*a*) training employees for more than one function at the firm, and having them interchange functions. In addition to making things more interesting for employees, the company is making its work force more flexible to its changing work needs, since people can fill in for each other as needed. (*b*) Companies are permitting workers to make full assemblies of a product, rather than one part of it, building entire automobiles, entire pieces of furniture, and so on.

8. *Interest-Free Loans to Non-Executive Personnel:* Companies are lending no-interest monies to all levels of workers who have

an important use for the money, where formerly this practice was confined to top personnel, and only for such things as a down-payment on a home. One company owner financed all his employees' purchasing of 10-speed bicycles, so they could have a healthful bike ride to work, instead of an aggravating auto ride – and a parking problem. (These employees save *money*, too, by saving wear and tear on their automobiles.)

9. *The Quiet Hour:* A few service firms are introducing the concept that the first hour or so of the day be reserved for totally silent work – no phones, and in one case, no talking and no circulating. Employees start an hour earlier than formerly, before phones traditionally begin to ring. They say that almost an entire day's work gets accomplished *before* the normal day starts.

10. *Telephone Lectures and Telephone Consulting:* One of the big headaches and one of the big expenses of importing expert advice to a company, trade association meeting, or to a group of college students, is transportation time and expense. I have been imported to companies on a telephone basis this year, giving the company the 2-way communication it requires while saving wear and tear on both the company and myself – and saving money for both of us.

11. *Write Your Own Paycheck:* I hear there is one company experimenting with permitting employees to specify the amounts of their own paycheck for the month, based on the employee's own evaluation of his contribution to the company for that period. They say the employees are, if anything, *conservative* in quantifying the value of their contributions.

12. *Company "Social Work":* Companies have long had such things as alcoholism programmes to help workers over problem periods, rather than losing employees who represent a large investment in training and experience. One company is now running a comprehensive social service for its workers. At his discretion (or by recommendation), the employee contacts the company's 24-hour-a-day hot line for whatever mental or physical health-related problems he or his family is experiencing. Full anonymity is guaranteed if desired. No adverse steps are taken against the employees who choose to use the service. The service refers them to experts, and underwrites the cost of treatment.

13. *Social Accounting Systems:* The employee has often been called

"the company's most important asset", but while there is a fairly satisfactory means of accounting for investment in and profits on assets such as equipment and real estate, people are only now beginning to develop systems which document the employee's value to the company. Variously called "social audits" and "human accounting", social accounting systems promise eventually to provide a means for making decisions about educating an employee, retaining someone who wants to leave, raising a salary, firing a worker, and so on. Companies will be able to create better human management policies once they are able to assign values to the results of policies.

What are some of the implications for society if these rearranged workweeks continue to spread?

There are quite a number of implications, both long- and short-range. Here is a partial list. (I am sure you can and will add your own.)

1. *Full-Time Cities:* We may well see the disappearance of the weekend as we now know it – as a few days a week during which just about everyone abandons work facilities and descends upon leisure facilities. Since the traditional workweek-weekend pattern creates peaks and valleys in our use of these facilities, the traditional pattern makes for uneconomic use of them. The disappearance of the weekend as we now know it (which appears to be in the cards), should mean less costly construction and operation of various systems. All sorts of systems – not just road systems or recreational systems, but telephone systems, educational systems and things that most of us rarely stop to regard as systems. Consequently, we can expect, if not a reduction in taxes, at least a brake on the rate at which they climb.

The same reasoning applies to the 24-hour workday. The currently standard attenuated workday creates daily peaks and valleys on our systems, adding extra cost to the creation and operation of these systems. The 24-hour company workday which we may be progressing towards should mean increased efficiency in the use of our resources, and decreased costs. More uniform usage of systems both on a daily and on a weekly basis should add to our comfort in the use of these systems as well as subtracting from our monetary costs. Just think of fewer busy signals in the phone system, for instance.

2. *Quality of Life:* The increases in productivity achieved by these innovations in work arrangement provide a practical solution to deliver us more useful leisure time and additional leisure time – now, when we want it, in our own lifetimes. There open before us vistas of possibilities for our developing and learning to lead "the good life". For spending more time with our loved ones, for learning to live with loved ones – and others, for developing ourselves as human beings in a variety of ways.

3. *Economic Underpinnings of Democracy:* The declining rate in the growth of productivity in some of our major industrial countries in the free world is, although almost unrecognized as such, one of the greatest threats to democracy in the world today. Unlike the drama of nuclear threats, the threat of economic decline is little understood.

   As rearranged workweeks and other innovations spread, they hold the promise of increasing the productivity that underpins our social systems and permits us to progress as a people.

   Enhancing our opportunity for leisure and our emphasis on it also opens new markets to business that can stimulate the growth of our economies – with the same beneficent results.

   These rearrangements also provide workers with increasing choice in *how* to make their wages and *when* to purchase the goods and services that they consume with their wages.

4. *Win-Win Examples:* The win-win nature of these innovations in work not only enhances the relationship between management and labour, but sets us goals to aspire towards in the other relationships that we pursue. The world has a long history of win-lose relationships, based on scarcity and on the consequent competition for obtaining the benefits of scarce resources – all leading to a multiplicity of examples of win-lose strategies, and very very little win-win.

   Win-win is an important style to learn more about and to cultivate. Win-win means sharing. It means peace. We need all the examples we can get if we are to break out of our history of win-lose and develop the win-win strategies and structures whose lack separates heaven from earth.

5. *Innovate, Innovate, Innovate:* People frequently ask of 4-day, "why now?" General recession conditions and the stress created

by them have created sufficient discontent with what we have so that people are increasingly overcoming their natural antipathy to change, and are more willing to try out innovations.

As 4-day and other innovations are adopted, and as they result in improvements, innovation loses some of the onus normally attached to it. People can become more receptive to the idea of innovating.

People can look on 4-day and ask themselves: if breaking out of a scheduling mould can create so many positive results, what *other* moulds would it be constructive for me to break? What other habits of thought, if broken, might achieve the results I seek?

We are stuck with change. Whether we like it or not, ours is a changing world. Why not take an otherwise dreadfully uncomfortable situation, and turn it to our advantage? Why not welcome change – and innovation – as an opportunity to create progress?

SELECTED BIBLIOGRAPHY
ON THE WORKWEEK

BOOKS
C. E. Dankert, F. C. Mann, and H. R. Northrup, eds.
  Hours of Work
  New York: Harper & Row, 1965
Millard C. Faught
  More Timewealth For You
  New York: Pyramid Books, 1970
William Goldner
  Hours of Work
  Institute of Industrial Relations
  Berkeley: University of California, 1952
Daniel H. Gray
  Manpower Planning: An Approach to the Problem
  London: Institute of Personnel Management, 1966
National Industrial Conference Board
  The Five-Day Week in Manufacturing Industries
  New York, 1929
Paul and Faith Pigors
  Human Aspects of Multiple Shift Operations
  Series 2, No. 13, Department of Economics and Social Science
  Cambridge, Massachusetts: M.I.T., 1944
Erwin O. Smigel, Ed.
  Work and Leisure: A Contemporary Social Problem
  New Haven: College and University Press, 1963

PAPERS AND PAMPHLETS
American Federation of Labor and Congress of Industrial Organizations
  The Shorter Work Week
  Papers Delivered at the Conference on Shorter Hours of Work
  Sponsored by the AFL & CIO
  Washington: Public Affairs Press, 1957
Chamber of Commerce of the United States
  A Shorter Workweek? An Information Manual on Key Questions
  Washington, 1962

Selected Bibliography

Victor R. Fuchs
  The Growing Importance of the Service Industries
  Occasional Paper #96, National Bureau of Economic Research
  New York, 1965
Marcia L. Greenbaum
  The Shorter Workweek
  Bulletin 50, New York State School of Industrial and Labor Relations at
  Cornell University
  Ithaca, New York, June, 1963
Joseph M. Viau
  Hours and Wages in American Organized Labor
  New York: G. P. Putnam & Sons, 1939

ARTICLES
"Four Days On, Four Off"
  Business Week
  February 23, 1963
Edward T. Chase
  "Four Days Shalt Thou Labor?"
  New York Times Magazine
  Sept. 20, 1964, p. 28
Howard Coughlin,
  "The Four-Day Office Week"
  Personnel
  May-June, 1966, p. 46–50
"Will the Five-Day Week Become Universal? It Will Not!"
  National Association of Manufacturers Pocket Bulletin
  Washington, 1926
"Shorter Hours, Same Pay – It's an Old Refrain"
  Newsweek
  January 26, 1962, p. 70
"If We Had a Twenty-Hour Week"
  New York Times Magazine
  February 4, 1962, p. 15
A. H. Raskin, "No 25-Hour Week for Him"
  New York Times Magazine
  March 18, 1962, p. 57
Riva Poor
  "4 Days, 40 Hours: Reporting a Revolution in Work Scheduling"
  New England Business
  July-August, 1970, p. 12–13
Sumner Slichter
  "How the Four-Day Week Would Affect U.S. Marketing"
  Printers' Ink
  October 9, 1959, p. 68–69
Kenneth E. Wheeler
  "Small Business Eyes the Four-Day Workweek"
  Harvard Business Review
  May–June, 1970, p. 142–147

Management Series

MANAGEMENT SERIES (cont.)

James J. Lynch
**A MANPOWER
DEVELOPMENT SYSTEM** 45p
Part 2 of *Making Manpower Effective*. Shows
the need to integrate manpower forecasting,
compensation planning and career development into a manpower development system.

CAREERS IN MARKETING 30p
An Institute of Marketing Review. A guide to
those seeking a job in the exciting field of marketing.

R. G. Magnus-Hannaford
SELLING AND SALESMANSHIP 30p
A clear, concise and forward-looking exposi-
tion of practical principles and their application.

Colin McIver
MARKETING 40p
Includes chapters by Gordon Wilson on the
Years of Revolution and Industrial Marketing.

Robin Neillands and Henry Deschampsneufs
**EXPORTING: A Basic Guide to Selling
Abroad** 37½p
Shows how smaller and medium-sized com-
panies can effectively obtain and develop
overseas markets.

Harold Norcross
**DYNAMIC BUSINESS
MANAGEMENT** 30p
A simple guide to the rudiments of successful
business management.

R. E. Palmer & A. H. Taylor
**FINANCIAL PLANNING
AND CONTROL** 40p
Explains the nature of the assistance which
levels of accounting can provide in the plan-
ning and control of a modern business.

GUIDE TO SAVING AND
INVESTMENT   50p
James Rowlatt and David Davenport

This lively, comprehensive and up-to-date
survey interprets the investment revolution,
explains what the Stock Exchange is and does,
shows how to assess the securities quoted on
the Exchange and how to work out the most
suitable investment policy to suit your personal requirements.

'Admirable ... recommended to intelligent
beginners as well as experienced investors.'
THE OBSERVER

General Titles and World Affairs